# a conspiracy of love

# a conspiracy of love

FOLLOWING JESUS IN A POSTMODERN WORLD

Kurt Struckmeyer

RESOURCE *Publications* • Eugene, Oregon

A CONSPIRACY OF LOVE
Following Jesus in a Postmodern World

Resource Publications
An Imprint of Wipf and Stock Publishers
199 W. 8th Ave., Suite 3
Eugene, OR 97401

www.wipfandstock.com

PAPERBACK ISBN: 978-1-4982-3449-8
HARDCOVER ISBN: 978-1-4982-3451-1

Manufactured in the U.S.A.

To my grandchildren
Henry, Eleanor, Wyatt, and Phoebe

May you work toward a better world
where children no longer weep from poverty and hunger,
where they no longer live in fear from violence,
and where they are taught kindness, compassion, and love.

Love freely.
Act compassionately.
Live justly.
Seek peace.

# contents

preface: losing my religion · ix
introduction: not just for Christians · xvii

PART 1: the way of Jesus

CHAPTER 1: following Jesus · 3
CHAPTER 2: the two gospels · 11
CHAPTER 3: the kingdom of God · 31
CHAPTER 4: a conspiracy of love · 51

PART 2: Jesus and the Christ

CHAPTER 5: the prophetic Jesus · 71
CHAPTER 6: the apocalyptic Christ · 91

PART 3: the path of transformation

CHAPTER 7: the postmodern world · 111
CHAPTER 8: the spiritual journey · 125
CHAPTER 9: cultural nonconformity · 144

PART 4: a conspiracy of love

CHAPTER 10: Bonhoeffer's vision · 173
CHAPTER 11: contemplation and action · 185
CHAPTER 12: the ethics of love · 200
CHAPTER 13: agents of love · 218

bibliography · 225

# losing my religion

*Each of us must develop a wholly personal religion, though this involves questioning, forsaking and honest searching. One's growth is often from unquestioning acceptance to questioning non-acceptance, to experiences of mystery and growth into certainty and a more personal relationship to God.*[1]

—M. Scott Peck (1936–2005)

IN THE EARLY 1990S, I was a big fan of the CBS television show "Northern Exposure," a funny and touching look at the lives of the eccentric inhabitants of the fictional town of Cicely, Alaska. Among other things, the show presented a weekly lesson in community, diversity, and acceptance.

One of my favorite characters was Chris Stevens (played by actor John Corbett), who was the "Chris in the Morning" disc jockey at KBHR, the town's radio station. An ex-felon, Chris was the town's only member of the clergy, having been ordained through an advertisement in Rolling Stone magazine. He took his spiritual calling seriously and often interspersed his morning show music with musings on the nature of life. One of those commentaries reflected on the words of Russian novelist Ivan Sergeyevich Turgenev (1818–1883) who proposed that truth is ever changing and elusive. I found myself agreeing with Chris Stevens' comments:

> *Like every human being, I've tried to make sense of things. I'm not sure I succeeded. I'm not sure anyone can.*

1. Howard and Howard. *Exploring the Road Less Traveled*, 173.

ix

*Isaac Newton thought the universe functioned like clockwork, a well-oiled machine. That's a comforting vision—neat, orderly, predictable. Unfortunately, it's a vision that's pretty much been shot to pieces by relativity, quantum mechanics, and the other bugaboos of twentieth century physics.*

*The universe is weird! We break our teeth developing theories, equations, systems. And where does it all leave us? "A system is like the tail of truth, but truth is like a lizard. It leaves its tail in your fingers and runs away, knowing full well that it will grow a new one in a twinkling."*[2]

I was born in 1947 in St. Louis in the aftermath of global war. I grew up in the center of the American heartland during the conformist 1950s and the contentious 1960s. In my youth, I became a passionate truth-seeker. Early on, I found remarkable insight into life's meaning and purpose in the stories, parables, and teachings of Jesus as recorded in the gospel accounts of the New Testament. My subsequent journey has often been an awkward and inadequate attempt to be faithful to the revolutionary message that I discovered there—the compassionate ethic and radical vision for living that Jesus proclaimed among the peasants and outcasts of first-century Galilee.

In my teens, I was introduced to the writings of German theologian Dietrich Bonhoeffer (1906–1945) who helped nourish a budding commitment to peace and nonviolence. A seminary student working with our church's youth group handed me a copy of Bonhoeffer's book *The Cost of Discipleship*. His writings struck a chord and initiated a decision to become a conscientious objector to military service during the war in Vietnam about five years later.

At my confirmation in the Lutheran church, my pastor selected a verse that he intuitively felt defined my adolescent religious journey. He chose a text from Paul's letter to the Romans.

*Do not be conformed to this world, but be transformed by the renewing of your minds, so that you may discern what is the will of God—what is good and acceptable and perfect.*[3]

Nonconformity and transformation would become the substance of my religious quest. Throughout my college years, my emerging religious convictions were put to the test by the reality of the war in Viet Nam. I scoured the university library for books that would help inform and support the stance of nonviolence and unconditional love that I believed Jesus

2. Chunovic, *Chris-In-The-Morning*, 61–62.
3. Romans 12:2

taught. I found very little. In addition to Dietrich Bonhoeffer, a few writings by Leo Tolstoy, Mohandas Gandhi, and Martin Luther King, Jr. were all I could discover. On Valentine's Day 1969, I registered as a conscientious objector to war with my local draft board. I composed a statement that explained my understanding of Jesus' call to love neighbors and enemies. The senior pastor of my congregation told me that although he could not agree with my position to refuse military service (the requirement to obey government as found in the 13th chapter of Paul's letter to the Romans was too important to his theology),[4] he still respected my conscientious stance (how could a Lutheran not?),[5] and he wrote a letter of support to my draft board, as did the associate pastor and a handful of theology students at the Missouri Synod's Concordia Seminary in St. Louis. When my college deferment ended in June, my local draft board called me to appear before them and within five minutes summarily denied my application as a conscientious objector. As I stood there, it became obvious that they had read nothing of what I had written nor had they read the supporting letters from the pastors and seminarians. In their minds, if I was not a member of a historic peace church like the Mennonites or Quakers, and had not been specifically taught peacemaking and nonviolence by my pastor, I did not qualify for CO status.

In July of 1969, I went to work for the General Motors Design Center in suburban Detroit. At the same time, I appealed my status to Selective Service officials in Michigan. While waiting for a decision, I was required to take a physical examination for military service. Because of a history of childhood asthma, I was declared 4-F. At nearly the same time, the Michigan appeal board had decided in my favor and granted me CO status. But in the end, 4-F trumped 1-O and I was deemed not qualified to serve my country in any capacity.

As the war in Vietnam raged over the next four years, I became convinced that most American churches, afraid of making a controversial stand in the midst of a war, were being unfaithful to Jesus by tacitly supporting their government's military objectives with little objection. By doing so, I believed that these churches were complicit in the evils of that war. I could not understand how they could so willingly send young parishioners off

4. Romans 13:1–7. This passage in Paul's letter to the churches of Rome states that everyone must submit themselves to the governing authorities and that those who rebel against authority are rebelling against God.

5. In 1520, Pope Leo X issued a bull of excommunication against Martin Luther for heretical writing. The following year, Luther was ordered by Holy Roman Emperor Charles V to appear before the Imperial Diet (assembly) at the city of Worms to recant or reaffirm the "errors" in his writings. Luther responded, "I cannot and will not recant anything, for to act against our conscience is neither safe for us, nor open to us. On this I take my stand. I can do no other. God help me."

to kill without any significant challenge regarding the war and its justification. And I reasoned, if the church was willing to support nearly any war
in history in contrast to the teachings of Jesus, what else had they missed,
ignored, or distorted about Jesus over the centuries?

Early in my working life, I continued to pursue an interest in nonviolence, biblical studies, and theology, with a particular emphasis on the
kingdom of God. It soon became my avocation. In the 1970s, I read books
by Harvey Cox, Hans Küng, William Stringfellow, and Clarence Jordan. Jordan's homespun commentaries on the Sermon on the Mount convinced me
that this ancient collection of Jesus' teachings defined what it means to be a
person of God and a follower of Jesus. I decided early on that if Christians
like Dietrich Bonhoeffer and Clarence Jordan were able to see and value
the costly demands of following Jesus, then surely others in the Christian
church should be able to expand my understanding of the radical nature of
the gospel, help me flesh out a contemporary life of faith, challenge me to
live it out daily, and engage me in changing the world.

Sadly, in the past forty years, that has rarely happened. Too often, I've
found the church to be a place of security and comfort for its members, not
a place of challenge and social engagement. Surely, there have been moments of prophetic witness by my pastors, but the vast majority of church
members and clergy are uncomfortable with changes to the status quo.
During this time, my relationship with the institutional church has waxed
and waned, but in the end, I have been deeply disappointed by the church's
passionless and feeble response to the dramatic social changes of the postmodern world and have been heartbroken to watch it slowly and steadily
decline into irrelevance.

A number of my closest friends are pastors and I have appreciated
their gifted insights over the years. Yet my own studies have brought me
a far greater understanding of the mission and message of Jesus than any
established church teaching I encountered along the way. Early on, I began
to form questions about Jesus' use of the term "the kingdom of God." As
I asked other Christians—both lay and clergy—about their understanding
of these words, I often got quizzical looks. It was obvious to me that the
kingdom of God was central to the message of Jesus. It formed the core of
his teachings and was the frequent subject of his parables. But for many in
the church, the reign of God was a peripheral concept not worthy of serious
attention, because they saw Jesus primarily as a source of personal salvation
and a pathway to heaven. It was the death of Jesus that mattered, not his life.
In the Lutheran Church of my experience, the kingdom of God was often
equated with the church itself—a comfortable interpretation, but not very
valid biblically.

In the mid-1980s, I began to read extensively about the historical Jesus, a field of study that blossomed among biblical scholars about that time. I began to integrate new discoveries about Jesus and the historical context in which he lived, into adult Bible study classes that I frequently led. Although usually sparsely attended, they were avidly supported by those who came, encouraging me that perhaps there was an unmet need among some for fresh new insights into Jesus and his message. In the late 1990s, I participated in a series of weekend retreats with scholars like Marcus Borg, John Dominic Crossan, and Walter Wink. In the fall of 1999, I attended the Jesus Seminar conference in Santa Rosa, California titled "The Once and Future Jesus." Speakers included John Shelby Spong, Marcus Borg, John Dominic Crossan, Robert Funk, Karen King, Lloyd Geering, Gerd Lüdemann, Thomas Sheehan, and Walter Wink. These and other brilliant scholars clearly understood the radical social, political, and religious nature of the historical Jesus. Although a close clergy friend was a partner in this journey of personal and theological growth, it seemed to both of us that the church at large was either uninterested or uncomfortable with what these exceptional people had found.

During Holy Week in 1998 and again in 1999, my wife and I participated in Habitat for Humanity's Easter Morning Build in Americus, Georgia. In each of these years, 1,000 volunteers came from all over the country to build 25 homes in a new neighborhood—the Easter Morning Community—with the goal of ending poverty housing in Sumter County, Georgia. The point that stuck with me most was that Christians of all kinds were working side-by-side as partners. Theology often divides people, but service to those in need can unite us. Our theological differences become unimportant when we work together to help a family in need build a house. I became aware that it is not what we believe but what we do to help the least of our brothers and sisters that really matters and it may be the only thing that truly connects us as followers of Jesus, the carpenter and builder.

In 2005, I was able to travel to El Salvador to commemorate the 25th anniversary of the assassination of Archbishop Óscar Romero with a group sponsored by the Center for Global Education. Teacher and author Jack Nelson-Pallmeyer was our group leader and the majority of the group were his university students in peace and justice studies. It was in El Salvador that I briefly met liberation theologian Jon Sobrino and learned from many others involved in the struggle for justice in Latin America about the relationship between liberation theology and the creation of base Christian communities among the poor. In the tiny rural community of Nueva Esperanza (New Hope), I heard the stories of local people who turned Bible study into political action to improve their communal lives. In the following year, a trip to Chiapas, Mexico with a group of seminary students introduced me to the lives of the indigenous people there and the Zapatista communities who were creating an alternative autonomous society in the midst of their world of poverty and oppression. These experiences led me to a further understanding of God's preferential option for the poor and convinced me that the reign of God will only emerge from the bottom or margins of society and will never arrive from on high. I became convinced that God works through human weakness, and not through power or authority.

After many years of participation in the life of the church, I can say with some confidence that following the radical teachings of Jesus is not central to religious life in most congregations in America. The institutional church often has other goals and objectives to pursue, and these keep church people very busy.

It seems to me that churches are too often like the blind men with the elephant. In my experience, many religious communities perceive only a fragment of the identity and mission of Jesus. I have rarely found a church that really grasped the radical gospel of Jesus and celebrated it in a meaningful way. Several years ago, Tony Campolo and Brian McLaren wrote a book about the church titled *Adventures in Missing the Point.* That pretty much sums up much of my experience with the church. Although my clergy friends remain committed to the church, I have gradually drifted away. In the end, I find my spiritual life in reading, reflection, and writing. My spiritual sustenance comes from family, friends, and a small group of progressive Christians who are willing to engage in spirited and candid study and dialog on a weekly basis.

Through the past half century, I have experienced the church in many settings—as part of a struggling inner city parish, a growing suburban congregation, and a tiny small-town church. I have been a part of churches with many ethnic roots: German, Slovak, Norwegian and African-American. Over the years, I have been a part of the church's engagement with social, political, and economic issues. As I came of age, I witnessed the church struggle with integration and civil rights, and then watched it segregate itself every Sunday morning for worship. I have seen it wrestle with the evils of war, and watched it feebly respond to U.S. military involvement in Vietnam, Central America, Afghanistan, and Iraq. I have seen the church grapple with women's social, political, and reproductive rights and their equal right to ordination—which far too many churches still deny. And most recently, I have watched the never-ending debate over the role of gay and lesbian people in the church and their frequent exclusion from equality in the body of Christ and its leadership.

On nearly every one of these issues, the larger church has found itself on the tail end of the struggle for peace and justice. It has rarely been a leader in these movements and all too often has been a distant follower. I have watched churches test the wind on nearly every social issue and adopt positions that will offend the fewest number of its members—often in the name of unity. I have observed that many churches rise to speak boldly and prophetically only after the matter has been resolved by society at large and the issue has been settled everywhere but in the church.

I wish the church was different. I wish it was more faithful in its calling. Yet I take heart that there are faithful people and communities who, though small, are engaged in the work of God on earth. Jesus often used images of a tiny minority who could accomplish great things—a bit of yeast in a large loaf of bread, a pinch of salt in a great kettle of soup, a tiny mustard seed scattered in a well-tended garden, a feeble lamp in a vast darkened house.

I am not a trained theologian. Nor do I consider myself a deep intellectual thinker. I am not a martyr or a prophet. I have not given up everything to follow the gospel. I have not been an activist for change. I have lived a fairly ordinary life. I simply believe that I am, like many of my readers, someone who wants to make a difference in the world, who wants to make the world a better place, a more humane place, a more compassionate place. I have always wanted to stand apart from my culture which often seems so shallow, superfluous, and irresponsible. I want my life to be a gesture of the kingdom of God, to be a sign of hope, to be a small example of light and life and change in a despairing world.

My faith, like that of many younger postmodern people, has grown out of my own experience. It has been shaped by my study, by living in the crucible of the American empire, by participation in counter-cultural political movements, by witnessing a society with a vast chasm between haves and have-nots, and by learning from poor people around the world who are engaged in Jesus' gospel of liberation and justice.

And so, I have been doing what Scott Peck recommended. I am developing a "wholly personal religion." As I've lost the religion of my childhood, I've found a new religion. And strangely, I believe that in the end, what I have found is not a religion *about* Jesus, but the religion *of* Jesus.

This book represents a lifelong journey to discover the way of Jesus. It is a book about discipleship—about being a student and follower of Jesus, about learning and doing. I'll be the first to admit that I'm a better learner than a doer. Although I try, I know I'm not a very good follower of Jesus. In the lifelong process of transformation, I am woefully unfinished. But I struggle daily to discern the path where Jesus has led and is still leading in our time and place.

If you care to join me in this journey of discovery, please read on.

## INTRODUCTION

# not just for Christians

---

*[Jesus] belongs not solely to Christianity, but to
the entire world.*

—Mahatma Gandhi (1869–1948)

FOLLOWING JESUS IS NOT just for Christians. The "way" taught by Jesus is not a particularly religious activity. Instead, it is a decisively human activity transcending all religions. It is not a way of believing; it is a way of living. It is centered in human love for one another and is focused on compassionate action toward those in need. It involves our ethics, politics, and economics. The way of Jesus calls us to radical generosity, service, and the pursuit of justice. Jesus offered a vision for humanity's future called the kingdom of God. It was not about a heavenly afterlife. It was and is about a better world for all people, especially the poor, the hungry, the sick, and the outcast.

The mission and message of Jesus is appealing to many people the world over—those of other religious traditions and those who do not identify with any formal religion. Gandhi reportedly said, "I like your Christ, I do not like your Christians. Your Christians are so unlike your Christ." Many postmodern people share that belief. The churches of the Global North are in decline and younger generations no longer seek meaning there. Yet, many of the people characterized as "nones" (no religious preference) and "dones" (those who have left the church) still find Jesus and his teachings compelling. Many of those who remain in the church struggle with how to remain faithful to Jesus while rejecting various aspects of orthodox creeds and dogma. Slowly, traditional "church Christianity" is giving way to some new path of living faithfully in the world. German pastor and theologian Dietrich Bonhoeffer (1906–1945) called it a "religionless" Christianity consisting of contemplative prayer and righteous action in the secular world.

*A Conspiracy of Love* offers many different people—those who remain in the church, those who dwell on its margins, those who have left, and those who have never ventured near—with a life of faith that is both intelligent and passionate. It invites people to let their lives be transformed by the radical love modeled by Jesus and to change the world through small conspiracies of resistance, compassion, justice, and peace. *A Conspiracy of Love* is a summons to rediscover and reclaim the transformative mission and message of Jesus for a postmodern world. It is an invitation to forsake a religion of comfort for a life of challenge, risk, and fulfilment. It is an appeal for all people of passion, zeal, and courage to embrace a life of service, justice, and nonviolence, and by doing so become followers of the "way" of Jesus.

# PART 1

---

# the way of Jesus

# CHAPTER 1

# following Jesus

---

*Lord, we do not know where you are going. How can we know the way?*[1]

—Thomas, the disciple

MILLIONS OF PEOPLE THROUGHOUT the world call themselves Christians. From Roman Catholics to Protestants, from fundamentalists to liberals, there are many different perspectives about what it means to be a Christian. One can become lost in the complexity of beliefs, dogmas, moral injunctions, and religious rites.

But in a larger context—that of daily life—it is often impossible to distinguish one Christian from another, or even a Christian from a non-Christian. Most Christians blend in with the values, lifestyles, economics, and politics of the predominant culture of their society.

But it wasn't always this way. Once upon a time, Christians stood out from the crowd.

Like many other great religious leaders, Jesus taught a way or path to his followers. His teachings point to an understanding of the religious life as a journey. He spoke about alternative paths encountered on the journey— the wide path and the narrow gate.[2]

He talked about seeking[3] and entering[4] the kingdom or reign of God. These are active words. They imply doing something, moving from where

1. John 14:5
2. Matthew 7:14–15
3. Matthew 6:33, Luke 12:31
4. Matthew 5:20, 7:21, 18:3, 19:23–24, 21:31, 23:13; Mark 9:47, 10:15, 23–25; Luke 18:17, 24–25; and John 3:5

we are to someplace new. These are not words of correct beliefs and doctrine, but words that call us to get up and get going.

Jesus called people to follow him in a way of living. As a result, the earliest members of the Jesus movement were known as followers of "the Way."[5]

## believing or following?

Lots of people believe in Jesus. They just love him to pieces. They worship and adore him. They praise his name. They invite him into their hearts and accept him as their Lord and Savior. But not many people are willing to follow him.

For the most part, believing *in* Jesus is really accepting a series of propositions *about* Jesus—that Jesus is divine, that he was perfect and sinless, that he died for our sins, that he will come again to judge humanity and to establish his kingdom. But this kind of belief does not necessarily take the teachings of Jesus seriously. One can conceivably believe that Jesus is the Son of God and yet still lead a self-centered life, ignore the cries of the poor, and demonstrate disdain and even hatred toward people of other races, cultures, or sexual orientations. In fact, this happens all the time among those who call themselves Christian.

All of this believing, loving, and worshipping Jesus is largely an internal experience, sometimes highly emotional in nature, and although it is frequently expressed in a corporate setting, it is often intensely personal and private. But following Jesus is not an internal state. It is an engagement with the outside world in a tangible way.

Some Christians are embarrassed to discuss their beliefs, while others are more than willing to profess their faith in public. Some may wear a cross as jewelry to symbolize devotion to Jesus. But publicly proclaiming Jesus as Lord is still not the same as following Jesus. "Why do you call me 'Lord, Lord,' and do not do what I tell you?" Jesus once asked.[6]

Following Jesus is about listening and doing. It is about putting into practice the things that Jesus taught. It is about a lifestyle of peace, justice, generosity, forgiveness, inclusion, and compassion that sets one apart from others.

---

5. See references to "the Way" in the Acts of the Apostles 9:2; 19:9, 23; 22:4; 24:14, 22

6. Luke 6:46

ING Jesus

## discipleship or church membership?

Churches often put a focus on discipleship. However, it has been said that some churches that claim to be teaching discipleship are just making "good church people." The call to increased worship, study, and stewardship often results in people who simply serve the institution of the church but do not make a significant difference in the larger world. Being a disciple should be radically different from not being a disciple. It involves much more than worship attendance, bible study, or service on a church committee. Admittedly, those can be important parts of a Christian's life. But they are merely food for the journey, not the journey itself. Hopefully, they provide nourishment, not a detour.

Discipleship should result in people who lead a radically different type of life, who are clearly counter-cultural, who are markedly different from the rest of the world—certainly different from the majority of Americans, including most American Christians.

Jesus calls us to transform the world. He calls us to spend our lives in the service of the least, the lost, and the lonely. That kind of life goes way beyond serving as an usher, a choir member, or a Sunday school teacher in a local congregation.

The content of true discipleship is found outside of the walls of a church in places where people are hurting, where people are hungry, where people are oppressed, where people are denied justice, where people are dying. This was where Jesus was engaged, and this is where he calls us to spend our lives, our resources, and our energy.

## cheap grace

In *The Cost of Discipleship*, German Lutheran pastor and theologian Dietrich Bonhoeffer (1906–1945) described the difference between what he called "cheap grace" and "costly grace." [7] Cheap grace, he proposed, is grace that is offered and accepted without a commitment and response from the believer. It is grace without transformation. It is grace without servanthood. Costly grace, said Bonhoeffer, moves us to respond to the call of Jesus, even to the point of giving our lives on behalf of others as Jesus did.

Danish philosopher Søren Kierkegaard (1813–1855) called the typical Christian response *admiring* Christ as opposed to *following* Christ.

---

7. Bonhoeffer, *Cost of Discipleship*. See chapter 1: "Costly Grace."

*What then, is the difference between an admirer and a follower? A follower is or strives to be what he admires. An admirer, however, keeps himself personally detached. He fails to see that what is admired involves a claim upon him, and thus he fails to be or strive to be what he admires.*[8]

The issue before us is whether we want to move from being admirers, and even worshippers, to being followers. If we want to take that step, then the question is "What does it really mean to be a follower of Jesus today?"

Is Christianity a set of beliefs, or is it a way of life? If it is a way of life, what kind of life does it involve? Is it delineated by following a clearly drawn moral code, or is it a more open and compassionate response to the situations that confront us daily? Does it involve our finances and our politics? What does a life of faith that is honest to Jesus look like? Even more precisely, how will this life of faith be expressed as we enter the postmodern world?

We live in a very different age than the pre-modern people to whom Jesus spoke in the first century. The early modern age began with the Renaissance and the invention of the printing press in the fifteenth century and reached a peak in the scientific revolution of the eighteenth-century Age of Enlightenment. The rise of capitalism and the industrial revolution in the nineteenth and twentieth centuries formed the late modern age, which is now rapidly transitioning to a postmodern age. In the pre-modern worldview, religion provided all the answers to the creation of life, human purpose, and ultimate meaning. In the modern age, science began to displace religion with answers based on reason and investigation. Today, postmodern people are rejecting both religion and science as a source of truth. They feel that these two approaches have equally failed us.

Postmodern people are witnessing a lack of coherence in American churches between orthopraxy (living rightly) and orthodoxy (believing rightly). To postmodern generations, the way a Christian lives speaks louder than any belief that Christians may profess. Christian behavior Monday through Saturday is more important to young people than what happens in worship on Sunday. People today simply are not asking pre-modern questions about whether Jesus physically rose from the dead, or whether he was born of a virgin. Instead, they ask about Christian behavior based on what they observe. "Why are Christians intolerant?" "Why do Christians suppress women?" "Why do Christians support warfare, torture, and the death penalty?" "Why do Christians persecute gay people?" "Why do Christians pursue a conservative political agenda which so often hurts the poor and rewards the rich?"

8. Kierkegaard and Moore, *Provocations*. See chapter 23: "Followers not Admirers."

## images of Jesus

One's theology is largely dependent on one's image of God. In addition—especially for Christians—it has to do with one's image of Jesus. Some people think of Jesus as a benign figure, sweet and gentle, meek and mild, holding cute little lambs in his arms and patting young children on the head. Others have come to see Jesus as a social critic, and even as a violent revolutionary. A great number of believers often find it difficult to think of Jesus as human at all. For them, he was God on earth, a divine being disguised in human flesh—all-seeing, all-knowing, and all-powerful. They see him as flawless, sinless, and sexless. They think of him as walking the earth without human feelings or failures. They imagine Jesus as a kind of supernatural superhero, able to perform miraculous deeds and read people's minds. The image of Superman from 1950s television comes to mind:

> *Strange visitor from another planet who came to earth with powers and abilities far beyond those of mortal men. Superman, who can change the course of mighty rivers, bend steel in his bare hands; and who, disguised as Clark Kent, mild-mannered reporter for a great metropolitan newspaper, fights a never-ending battle for truth, justice, and the American way.*[9]

Is this our image of Jesus—a supernatural visitor from beyond time and space with powers and abilities far beyond those of mortal men, and who secretly disguised as a mild-mannered carpenter from Nazareth was able to perform astounding miracles that defy the natural order? And do we believe that Jesus fights for or even supports the American way—our exceptionalism, our capitalism, our consumerism, our militarism? Many Christians would heartily agree with these propositions.

Such one-sided and exclusive concentration on Jesus as a divine manifestation renders him inhuman. It makes him someone we can worship and adore, but need not imitate—someone we can believe in, but need not follow. At the other end of the spectrum is the view of Jesus as a good man and a wise teacher. He has also been described as a religious genius, an expert psychologist, and the world's greatest salesman. Those pictures of Jesus focus on his humanity, but deny the incredible spiritual nature he embodied and ignore the radical social vision he espoused. Even if one denies the divinity of Jesus, one cannot ignore that he clearly embodied the spirit of God—a spirit of boundless love and compassion. Jesus was clearly a great ethical teacher, but even more, he espoused a powerful social vision that

9. Introduction to "The Adventures of Superman," a television series shown from 1952 to 1958.

continues to shape efforts to help the poor and create a better world through nonviolent social change.

As we approach the postmodern world, we must continually seek answers to the following three questions: 1) Who was Jesus? 2) What did he hope to accomplish? 3) What did he proclaim?[10]

After the death of Jesus, his followers began a process of re-evaluation and reinterpretation of his identity, message, and mission. Through this process, a number of widely different views of Jesus developed. For over three hundred years, competing images of Jesus circulated in the early church. In the fourth century, the Emperor Constantine convened church leaders to agree on a single orthodox view of Jesus and his relationship to God. The result was the image of Jesus we are most familiar with—the Jesus of the historic creeds of the Christian church—the Christ of traditional faith. The two most commonly used creeds have shaped the popular understanding of the nature of Jesus by creating a picture of Jesus that is extraordinary in the truest sense of that word.

The Nicene Creed includes these words:

> *We believe in one Lord, Jesus Christ, the only son of God, eternally begotten of the Father, God from God, Light from Light, true God from true God, begotten, not made, of one Being with the Father. Through him all things were made. For us and for our salvation he came down from heaven; by the power of the Holy Spirit he became incarnate from the Virgin Mary, and was made man. For our sake he was crucified under Pontius Pilate; he suffered death and was buried. On the third day he rose again in accordance with the Scriptures; he ascended into heaven and is seated at the right hand of the Father. He will come again in glory to judge the living and the dead, and his kingdom will have no end.*[11]

The Apostle's Creed, often used in baptisms, has this to say about Jesus:

> *I believe in Jesus Christ, [God's] only Son, our Lord. He was conceived by the power of the Holy Spirit and born of the Virgin Mary. He suffered under Pontius Pilate, was crucified, died, and was buried. He descended into hell. On the third day he rose again.*

---

10. Borg, *Jesus, a New Vision*, 8.

11. A preliminary form of the Nicene Creed was adopted in the city of Nicaea by the first ecumenical council hosted by Constantine in 325 CE. The final form of the creed is said to have been revised at the second ecumenical council held in Constantinople in 381. This took place about 350 years after the death of Jesus.

*He ascended into heaven, and is seated at the right hand of the*
*Father. He will come again to judge the living and the dead.*[12]

Biblical scholar Marcus Borg (1942–2015) has summarized the popular image of Jesus found in the creeds in terms of what they have to say about his identity, his message, and his mission. The creeds propose that Jesus was the divinely begotten Son of God, the risen Christ, true God and true man. The message of Jesus is entirely missing from these creeds, since they skip without pause from his miraculous birth to his death by crucifixion. But the implication is that Jesus was primarily focused on inviting his hearers to believe that what he reportedly said about himself and his role in salvation was true. His mission, again by implication, was to be sent into the world to die on a cross as a means of reconciliation between God and humankind. Borg concludes that the phrase "Jesus died for your sins" captures his purpose in a nutshell.[13] Theologians and bishops of the imperial church slowly shaped this image of Jesus over a period of many centuries. John's gospel provides the primary source for this understanding of Jesus:

*For God so loved the world that he gave his one and only Son, that*
*whoever believes in him shall not perish but have eternal life.*[14]

The Jesus of the creeds is not a Jesus one can easily follow. This is a Jesus demanding worship, reverence, and awe. However, what if the orthodox image of Jesus is wrong? What if Jewish and gentile apocalyptic authors, Hellenistic theologians, and imperial church councils created an image of a cosmic Christ who is vastly different from Jesus of Nazareth? What if the real Jesus—the Jewish teacher and healer who lived in the first century—had a very different mission and message? What if the farthest thing from Jesus' mind was a sense of his divinity and his role in our eternal salvation? What if, instead, the message and mission of Jesus was to ask us to join with him in an effort to transform our daily lives, our social relationships, and our civic life toward mutual love, compassion, justice, and peace to a radical degree? What if Jesus was more concerned about a new kind of life on this side of the grave, rather than a heavenly existence after death?

---

12 The Apostle's Creed was not authored by the disciples of Jesus, later called apostles (meaning *messengers*). The creed was most probably shaped about the same time as the Nicene Creed and originated as a statement of belief called the Old Roman Creed, first referred to in a letter dating from 390 CE. The current form of the creed was refined and finalized sometime after the death of Charlemagne (d. 814) in the early ninth century.

13. Borg, *Jesus: A New Vision*, 3.

14. John 3:16

Following Jesus in the postmodern world involves a radically different understanding of the identity, mission, and message of Jesus than the traditional understanding presented by the pre-modern paradigm of Christianity. For thinkers of the modern era, beginning with the scholars of the Enlightenment, another markedly different image of Jesus—a new paradigm—has emerged. For centuries, scholars have been trying to peel back the layers of the church's accumulated traditions to discover what Jesus authentically said and did. They have been looking for the man behind the myth. And since about 1980, the quest for the historical Jesus has begun to take shape in a remarkable way.

If we are able to rediscover the life and teachings of Jesus in a fresh way, to understand how Jesus confronted the social issues, politics, economics, and religion of his day, we may be able to bridge the gulf between the ancient world and the postmodern world.

# CHAPTER 2

# the two gospels

_The Spirit of the Lord is upon me, because he has
anointed me to bring good news to the poor._[1]

—Jesus of Nazareth, quoting the prophet Isaiah

IN THE TWENTY-FIRST CENTURY, a vast gulf separates devoted Christians in
America. Two competing streams of faith have shaped the churches in our
society. Both have their roots in the earliest days of the Christian church.
A theological battle has been waging for the past century between two opposing viewpoints about the Bible and two different gospel messages of the
New Testament. Moreover, these biblical viewpoints are just part of a larger
theological divide about the essence of the Christian faith and the content
of the Christian life.

In _The Heart of Christianity_, Marcus Borg described two very different
ways of seeing what the Christian life is all about—two different visions of
Christianity. Borg labeled these as an "earlier paradigm" and an "emerging
paradigm."[2] Others might call them conservative Christianity and liberal
Christianity, or traditional Christianity and progressive Christianity, although Borg did not prefer those terms.

The earlier paradigm is still the majority voice in American Christianity today, but according to Borg, it no longer speaks to millions of Christians
who are uncomfortable with its definition of the faithful life.

_This earlier way of being Christian views the Bible as the unique
revelation of God, emphasizes its literal meaning, and sees the
Christian life as centered in believing now for the sake of salvation_

1. Luke 4:18
2. Borg, _Heart of Christianity_, 6–20.

11

*later—believing in God, the Bible, and Jesus as the way to heaven.
Typically, it has also seen Christianity as the only true religion.*[3]

The dominance of the earlier paradigm causes many progressive Christians to wonder if they can still call themselves Christian if they do not buy into biblical literalism, religious exclusivity, and a heavenly afterlife as the goal of the Christian life. According to Borg, an emerging alternative paradigm has been developing steadily for the last century and has become a kind of grassroots movement within the mainline denominations.

> *The emerging paradigm sees the Christian life as a life of relationship and transformation. Being Christian is not about meeting requirements for a future reward in an afterlife, and not very much about believing. Rather, the Christian life is about a relationship with God that transforms life in the present.*[4]

Borg, in his characteristically compassionate pastoral manner, was careful to say that "the issue isn't that one of these paradigms is right and the other wrong. Rather, the issue is functionality, whether a paradigm 'works' or 'gets in the way.'"

> *The earlier paradigm has nourished and continues to nourish lives of deep devotion, faith, and love. The Spirit of God can and does work through it. It has for centuries and still does. When it leads to a strong sense of the reality and grace of God, to following Jesus, and to lives filled with compassion and a passion for justice, as it sometimes does, all one can say is, "Praise the Lord."*
>
> *But for millions of others, the earlier paradigm no longer works. Unpersuasive to them, it has become a stumbling block. What is the Christian message, the Christian gospel, for people who can't be literalists or exclusivists? What do we have to say to them? In an important sense, this is an issue of evangelism. For these millions, the emerging paradigm provides a way of taking Christianity and the Christian life seriously.*[5]

## two different gospels

I believe that these alternate forms of Christianity are based on two very different gospel messages found in the pages of the New Testament. The term

3. Ibid., xii.
4. Ibid., 14.
5. Ibid., 18.

*gospel* derives from an Old English word meaning *good news* or *glad tidings*. In Greek, it is *euaggelion* (*yoo-ang-ghel'-ee-on*). From this Greek word, we derive the English terms *evangelical* and *evangelism*.

As one reads the four gospels and the letters of Paul, it becomes evident that there are two distinctly different messages of good news proclaimed in those ancient writings—two contrasting narratives at the heart of Christianity. The first message of good news that we encounter in the New Testament is presented in the gospels of Matthew, Mark and Luke: the good news announced by Jesus. The second gospel is the good news announced by Paul in his letters or epistles, and in the gospel of John. To clarify the difference, we might say that the first is the gospel *of* Jesus, while the second is a gospel *about* Jesus.

The gospel *of* Jesus is primarily a social gospel, announcing good news to the poor. It is the proclamation of the present and future kingdom of God—a just and peaceful human society. The most authentic message proclaimed by Jesus was never about himself or his role in the salvation of the world. Those ideas were later developed by his Hellenistic followers. Instead, the gospel *of* Jesus was about what he believed God desired in the world, about the radical transformation that God was seeking in human lives and social relationships. It was and is a gospel about redeeming our life together in the here and now. It seeks the common good by elevating the status of those at the bottom of the economic ladder. The gospel *of* Jesus is good news to the poor.

The gospel *about* Jesus changes all that. Paul is very clear about the gospel he is proclaiming. In a letter to the house churches of Rome, he declares that he has been:

> Set apart for the gospel of God . . . the gospel concerning his Son, who was . . . declared to be Son of God . . . by resurrection from the dead, Jesus Christ our Lord."[6]

In another letter to the house church at Corinth, he says:

> Now I should remind you, brothers and sisters, of the good news that I proclaimed to you . . . that Christ died for our sins in accordance with the scriptures, and that he was buried, and that he was raised on the third day in accordance with the scriptures.[7]

The good news proclaimed by Paul puts the emphasis on Jesus himself and the salvation from sin that Paul believed resulted from the death and

---

6. Romans 1:1–4

7. 1 Corinthians 15:1–4

resurrection of the Christ. Someone once said that as Jesus taught his disciples, he pointed their attention toward the centrality of the kingdom of God, but all the disciples could see was his pointed finger. It was the messenger and not the message that ultimately dominated and shaped the history of the church. The gospel *about* Jesus is a message of good news that the death and resurrection of Jesus has changed everything for humanity in relation to a wrathful God. It is a gospel aimed at individual lives and their eternal fate.

John's gospel enhances Paul's gospel *about* Jesus. In John's narrative, Jesus repeatedly speaks about himself and his close relationship to God, who he regarded as a metaphorical father. A series of "I am" statements in John's gospel are intentionally designed to recall the words of God to Moses in the book of Exodus. When Moses asks God's identity, *Elohim* (*el-o-heem'*)—a Hebrew word meaning *god* or *gods*—responds in this way:

> *Elohim said to Moses, "I AM WHO I AM." He said further, "Thus you shall say to the Israelites, 'I AM has sent me to you.'"*[8]

In John's gospel, Jesus declares:

> *I am the bread of life . . . I am the light of the world . . . I am the gate for the sheep . . . I am the good shepherd . . . I am the resurrection and the life . . . I am the way, and the truth, and the life . . . I am the true vine.*[9]

The most explicit reference is this verse where Jesus proclaims that he existed even before the patriarch Abraham, an ancient Sumerian figure whose exploits date about 2,000 years before Jesus:

> *Jesus said to them, "Very truly, I tell you, before Abraham was, I am."*[10]

What is missing from the gospel *about* Jesus is the kingdom of God. Paul and John rarely refer to it. Paul, in fact, says little about the wisdom tradition of Jesus. The life and teachings of Jesus are not central to Paul's message. John's gospel includes none of Jesus' parables but instead offers us lengthy discourses like those of ancient Greek philosophers. Together, Paul and John present us with a very different figure than the Jesus of Matthew, Mark, and Luke. Paul clearly states in his letters that the human Jesus is of no real concern to him.

8. Exodus 3:13
9. John 6:35, John 8:12, John 10:9, John 10:11, John 11:25, John 14:6, John 15:1
10. John 8:58

*Even though we once knew Christ from a human viewpoint and
as a man, that isn't how we know him now.*[11]

Marcus Borg differentiates between the Jesus of history—a real human being who lived and taught among us—and the cosmic Christ of the
Christian faith, a product of Paul and the Hellenistic Christian community
who were focused on an impending apocalyptic event: the future appearance of the Son of Man, the resurrection of the dead, and a final judgment of
humanity. Borg calls these contrasting images the pre-Easter Jesus and the
post-Easter Jesus. In other words, the pre-Easter Jesus was a human teacher
of love and compassion, while the post-Easter Jesus was an apocalyptic figure of judgment, reward, and punishment.

The distinction between these competing New Testament gospels and
their images of Jesus is extremely important, because which message one
hears and responds to will shape one's Christian faith and life. The gospel *of*
Jesus focuses on personal and social transformation while the gospel *about*
Jesus focuses almost exclusively on individual salvation from God's wrath.
The gospel *of* Jesus is primarily a social and public gospel; the gospel *about*
Jesus is an individual and private gospel.

## kingdom versus atonement

One could term this division as the *gospel of Jesus* versus the *gospel of Paul*.
Writer and activist Jim Wallis (b. 1948) uses a different terminology: the *gospel of the kingdom* as opposed to the *atonement-only gospel*. Wallis remarks:

> *There is the original New Testament message called the gospel
> of the kingdom, which was intended to transform both people's
> lives and their societies; and there is a more modern message that
> concentrates mostly on individuals, a narrowly focused message
> we'll call the atonement-only gospel. By focusing so much on what
> happens after we die, we have neglected the agenda of Jesus for
> how we live now.*[12]

In Christianity, *atonement* refers to a doctrine that describes how sinful
human beings can be reconciled to God by the pardoning of sin through the
death and resurrection of Jesus Christ. In the centuries after Paul, theologians developed many alternative theories about how this atonement works.
For example, one theory proposes that the death of Jesus was a *ransom* paid
to the Devil to release humanity from its captivity to sin. Another sees the

11. II Corinthians 5:16
12. Wallis, *On God's Side*, 14.

death of Jesus as a final *sacrificial offering* to God to obtain forgiveness for humanity's sin. A third claims that the death of Jesus becomes a *substitute* for our deserved punishment, with Jesus standing in for humanity as God metes out retributive justice for sin. In each of these theological schemes, Jesus becomes a central figure in in a cosmic game of sin and forgiveness that reconciles humanity to God. Whether atonement theology uses the image of an extortion payment, a bloody sacrifice, or a human scapegoat to make sense of Jesus' death, most conservative Christians see this as the central gospel message.

Wallis describes a friendly debate in 2011 with Albert Mohler (b. 1959), the president of the Southern Baptist Theological Seminary in Louisville, Kentucky. The topic was whether social justice was an integral part of the gospel. Wallis said "yes," but Mohler said "no." Mohler argued that social justice was important but *the* gospel—the *true* gospel—was the atonement brought about in Christ that saves us from our sins and secures our souls for a future in heaven.[13]

The Southern Baptist Convention is the largest Protestant denomination in America and its membership is second only to the Roman Catholic Church. Its theological stance has enormous influence. It is important to note that the SBC was created in 1845 when southern Baptists split from those in the north over the issue of slavery. In part, the theological distinction made by Mohler and many other Christian conservatives originally developed to justify slavery in the nineteenth century and to support racial segregation in the early- to mid-twentieth century.

> To reconcile racial apartheid with the Christian faith, white segregationists developed a theological defense system. If Christianity was about saving individual souls, they argued, then worrying about earthly injustice was an unspiritual distraction from the "gospel." If individual sin was the only thing that mattered, then white Christians needed only to live upright personal lives—even within a racial apartheid system. Pro-segregation Christians viewed the idea of systemic sin as unbiblical—or worse yet, as godless communism.[14]

Many Southern Baptists and other conservative denominations now recognize that social justice is called for in the Bible, but their theology is rooted firmly in the past.

The great divide between Christians is whether the *life* of Jesus or the *death* of Jesus is more important. The creeds of the church favor the latter.

13. Ibid., 53.
14. Ayers and Bean, "Reimagining the Bible Belt," *Sojourners*, 19.

None of Jesus' teachings about how to live in the present—the need for love, compassion, forgiveness, generosity, and justice—is considered important in the key confessions of the church.

One's orientation to the gospel *of* or *about* Jesus will determine one's central mission as a believer or a follower. The atonement gospel of Paul calls his adherents to a mission of evangelization and conversion so that others may experience a heavenly afterlife with God. The social gospel of Jesus calls his followers to transform both individual lives and social structures to deal with the pervasive issues of human suffering: poverty, hunger, shelter, education, and employment. One gospel is afterlife oriented; the other is centered in the present. It is all a question of whether one puts an emphasis on the teachings of Jesus or the teachings of Paul.

These two streams of Christianity have existed side by side since the beginning, often integrated by Jesus' followers in the early church. But today, these two competing gospels are dividing Christians around the world into irreconcilable camps. In the twentieth century, historian Martin Marty saw these expressed in the United States as what he termed as *Public Protestantism* and *Private Protestantism*. The Public Protestants responded to the social gospel in the Progressive Era from the 1890s to the 1920s and sought to remake American society as an expression of God's kingdom. They focused on eradicating poverty, ignorance, disease, and crime. Private Protestants sought to keep the church solidly within the individualistic sphere, focused on the condition of the human soul. One could easily extend Marty's terminology beyond the Protestant denominations to include Roman Catholics and others with the broader terms *Social Christianity* and *Private Christianity* in the current debate over the understanding of the gospel message.

## transformation versus salvation

Traditionally, Christian theology and practice has concentrated on issues of sin and salvation. Personal redemption from God's righteous wrath has become more important than the transformation of human behavior or the struggle for justice in human society. In orthodox theology, we are passive recipients of God's grace, not hands-on actors in the transformation of the world. The third chapter of Genesis introduces us to a mythological origin of human sin—the story of temptation and disobedience in paradise.

> *Now the serpent was more subtle and crafty than any other wild animal that Yahweh God had made. He said to the woman, "Did God really say, 'You shall not eat from any tree in the garden'?" The woman said to the serpent, "We may eat of the fruit of the trees in*

> *the garden; but God said, 'You shall not eat of the fruit of the tree that is in the middle of the garden, nor shall you touch it, or you shall die.'" But the serpent said to the woman, "You will not die; for God knows that when you eat of it your eyes will be opened, and you will be like gods, knowing good and evil." So when the woman saw that the tree was good for food, and that it was a delight to the eyes, and that the tree was to be desired to make one wise, she took of its fruit and ate; and she also gave some to her husband, who was with her, and he ate. Then the eyes of both were opened.*[15]

Clearly the story in Genesis is about humans becoming like the gods, creating their own sense of morality—knowing right from wrong, good from evil. But in the Apostle Paul's theology, this is a strategic story about how sin entered the world through the disobedience of one man—Adam (not Eve)—and how it required the sacrifice of one man—Jesus—to overcome its legacy among us.

> *Therefore just as one man's trespass led to condemnation for all, so one man's act of righteousness leads to justification and life for all. For just as by the one man's disobedience the many were made sinners, so by the one man's obedience the many will be made righteous.*[16]

For fundamentalists, the story of Adam and Eve is not a metaphorical tale of origins. They believe the story of our descent from one man and one woman must be literally true if Paul's theology is to be taken at its word. Therefore the theory of human evolution from earlier primates is seen as a theological threat. If sin did not enter the world through the first divinely-created human, the Pauline salvation story falls apart, at least in the conservative mind.

But, according to social gospel theologian and pastor Walter Rauschenbusch (1861–1916), until Paul developed this doctrine of sin and salvation, the temptation and fall of humanity in the Garden of Eden was not of theological importance in the Hebrew Bible. The idea of original sin and our need for redemption is simply not there.

> *There are scarcely any allusions to the story in the Old Testament. The prophets were deeply conscious of the sins of men, but they did not base their teachings on the doctrine of the fall . . . In the synoptic sayings of Jesus there is not even a reference to the fall*

---

15. Genesis 3:1–7. The fruit of the tree would make one "wise." Interestingly, the term *Homo sapiens* means *wise humans.*

16. Romans 5:18–19

*of Adam . . . Not until we come to Paul do we find any full and*
*serious use of the story of the fall in the Bible.*[17]

Although the church has built its entire doctrine of human redemption on the story of the fall, Jesus and the earlier Hebrew prophets paid little attention to it. Once again, we see the difference between the gospel *of* Jesus and the gospel *about* Jesus, which is immersed almost entirely in personal salvation from the inherited guilt of original sin—something Jesus said nothing about. Absolutely nothing.

As Rauschenbusch points out, in the gospel *about* Jesus:

> *The traditional doctrine of the fall has taught us to regard evil as a kind of unvarying racial endowment, which is active in every new life and which can be overcome only by the grace offered in the Gospel and ministered by the Church.*[18]

But, Rauschenbusch says, in the social gospel *of* Jesus, evil becomes "a variable factor in the life of humanity, which it is our duty to diminish for every young life and for every generation."

## the nature of sin

According to some theologians, sin is an act that violates God's will, intentionally or unintentionally. Sin is sometimes viewed as anything that disrupts the ideal relationship between an individual and God, and to a lesser extent between that individual and other human beings. It is a breakdown or separation in these relationships. In the New Testament, the English word *sin* is most commonly translated from the Greek *hamartia* (*ham-ar-tee'-ah*) that signifies missing the mark. It is a failure, a fault, or an error—human behavior that does not measure up to an ideal standard. Some have compared it to an archery contest, or perhaps a handgun shooting range, where the target is widely missed. And when we miss, according to some theologians, it is our own damn fault, or in the case of original sin, the damn fault of our entire species. The traditional confession of sins in the Latin mass intoned, "*mea culpa, mea culpa, mea máxima culpa*" (translated as "my fault, my fault, my greatest fault"), while the penitent's right fist beats on the chest three times. The Lutheran confession of sins for Ash Wednesday puts it this way: "We have sinned by our fault, by our own fault, by our own

17. Rauschenbusch, *Social Gospel*, 40.
18. Ibid., 43.

most grievous fault in thought, word, and deed, by what we have done and by what we have left undone."

Today, another group of theologians has begun to see sin not as missing a target of ideal human behavior, or violating any number of select divine commandments, or even being in a state of rebellion against or separation from God, but rather as the fundamental state of ego-centrism that consumes our lives. This understanding of sin is consistent with the gospel *of* Jesus. At its core, sin in both the individual and the social context is rooted in human self-centeredness, self-obsession, and selfishness. It is found in the condition of living for oneself alone and a callous disregard for the needs of others. My desk dictionary lists 142 compound words that begin with the word *self*, including self-absorption, self-concern, self-centeredness, self-importance, self-indulgence, self-interest, self-righteousness, self-serving, and selfishness. This is the underlying nature of human sin—an overwhelmingly dominant focus on myself, my needs, and my desires.

## original sin

For the church, it is often not what we do as individuals but what we are as human beings that is the issue. Traditional Christian theology since the time of Augustine (354–430), a Bishop of the city of Hippo in North Africa, has focused on original sin, a kind of inherited human condition, first brought on by the transgression of Adam and Eve. This puts all the emphasis on an inherently sinful nature that is transmitted biologically (sex plays a key role in original sin), and that makes the theological claim that without the intervention of God we cannot possibly do anything good. That theology needs to be put to rest.

If one wants to think about children being born in a condition that leads to sin, human selfishness is it. Humans are profoundly selfish beings. We are all born that way. It is the natural state of every infant. A baby is only aware of his or her own needs and insists that those be met immediately. As we mature, we learn to balance our needs with those of others—family, friends, spouse, and children. Yet, we still feel a powerful pull to put our own needs first. This may be more culturally true for men than for women, but selfishness affects us all. Selfish egocentrism results in a preoccupation with one's own internal world. Egocentrics regard themselves and their own opinions or interests as being the most important or valid.

As humans, our hearts are filled with worry, insecurity, and self-concern. We are anxious about the future. Whether we admit it or not, we perceive the world as a cruel place, and realize that in a largely selfish world, others will surely be indifferent to our needs and welfare. We thus believe we must care for ourselves first and provide for our own future security at the expense of anyone else. The egoistic self thus pursues goals that attempt to insulate and protect it from a seemingly random and harmful universe. We search for a sense of security through wealth, possessions, pleasure, prestige, power, exclusive solidarity, and self-centered religion. In the process, our hearts become concentrated in our materialistic culture and the things that conventional wisdom deems to be of importance.

At its worst, callous unconcern for the feelings of others leads to all kinds of sociopathic behavior, including crime and violence. Egocentrism is the foundation of nearly every breakdown in human relationships. Self-centeredness is the root of infidelity and the sexual exploitation of women by men. When one's own interests are placed over the welfare of others, spouse and child abuse, even incest and pedophilia, can result.

Individuals will always be sinful. We will continually make bad choices and we will inevitably screw things up in our personal lives. But contrary to what some conservative preachers may claim, most humans are not totally depraved. Aside from some sociopaths, the majority of us may be frequently dishonest, sometimes immoral, occasionally unscrupulous, and now and then wicked, but few are totally and hopelessly evil. Says Rauschenbusch:

> We are equipped with powerful appetites. We are often placed in difficult situations, which constitute overwhelming temptations. We are all relatively ignorant, and while we experiment with life, we go astray. On the other hand, we are gifted with high ideals, with a wonderful range of possibilities, with aspirations and longing, and also weighted with inertia and moral incapacity to achieve. We are keenly alive to the call of the senses and the pleasures of the moment, and only dimly and occasionally conscious of our own higher destiny, of the mystic value of personality in others, and of God.[19]

## the ancient domination system

This focus on the self often leads to alienation, isolation, and separation from others. A life lived for one's self results in a hard and cold heart. It drives out compassion and concern for the needs of others. It often spawns a desire to dominate and control others in service to the self. Selfishness is at the root of those enduring political systems in which a few wealthy

19. Ibid., 45.

and powerful people control the economic life of the many, extracting their productivity to maintain luxurious lifestyles.

Throughout history, nearly every society has favored an elite group of individuals and families at the expense of the majority of less-fortunate inhabitants. For thousands of years, economic elites have rigged society in their favor by crafting systems that would benefit their prosperity and ensure their control over the nation's political and economic affairs. Historically, they have used unjust economic systems to extract wealth from the sweat of slaves, peasants, and laborers, while contributing little to the common welfare. Social control has been maintained with violence and military might, often supported by religious institutions. These societies have invariably been patriarchies where the authority and desires of men have dominated the lives of women and children. The system has frequently favored one race, tribe, or ethnic group over others.

Biblical scholar Walter Wink (1935–2012) has referred to these societies as manifestations of an enduring *domination system* that has been part of the human story since the rise of civilization in the ancient near east. Wink describes the domination system in this way:

> It is characterized by unjust economic relations, oppressive political relations, biased race relations, patriarchal gender relations, hierarchical power relations, and the use of violence to maintain them all. No matter what shape the dominating system of the moment might take (from the ancient Near Eastern states to the Pax Romana to feudal Europe to communist state capitalism to modern market capitalism), the basic structure has persisted now for at least five thousand years, since the rise of the great conquest states of Mesopotamia around 3000 BCE.[20]

We easily observe the domination system in the structure of kingdoms, empires, and dictatorships. It has been embodied in traditional customs and religious teachings throughout history. But when democratic systems in a largely secular culture are controlled by wealthy and powerful forces, the same results occur. Massive tax cuts for the wealthiest, bloated military budgets, welfare for giant corporations, vast prison systems, and cuts to social services for the poorest Americans are all signs of a domination system.

Walter Wink notes that the teachings of Jesus were a prescriptive remedy to the domination system of his time. The kingdom of God that he described is an antidote to the disease of the domination system. The vision of Jesus stands in direct opposition to the political and economic aims of these pervasively unjust social structures. It is a vision of the domination

20. Wink, *Powers That Be*, 39–40.

system turned upside-down. Therefore, every act of resistance to the domination system, every protest of its unjust laws and structures, every effort to transform it for the common good is a sign of the coming kingdom of God that Jesus proclaimed.

In the reign of God, all typical domination values are reversed. The first shall be last and the last shall be first. The greatest people in the kingdom shall be servants. The powerful shall be brought low and the lowly lifted up. The hungry shall be filled with good things and the rich sent away empty. The kingdom particularly belongs to the poor, the hungry, and the mourning because they will gladly welcome its coming. The rich will find it almost impossible to enter because they are too entrenched in the domination system and will resist the change it promises.

## the contemporary politics of selfishness

In the classic domination system, the self-interest of those at the top of a society leads to a politics of selfishness and greed. It is expressed in a stance of self-righteous self-sufficiency of the "haves" that ignores the needs of the "have nots" or judges their worthiness to receive help. It is summed up in the phrase "I got mine; you get yours."

Recently, in the United States, the politics of selfishness has been exemplified by the opinions and draconian budget proposals of Republican congressman Paul Ryan (b. 1970) who ran as a vice-presidential candidate in 2012 and became Speaker of the U.S. House of Representatives in 2015. Ryan has attributed the development of his political ideas to Russian émigré philosopher and writer Ayn (rhymes with *fine*) Rand (1905–1982). Born Alisa Rosenbaum, Rand is known for her two best-selling novels, *The Fountainhead* (1943) and *Atlas Shrugged* (1957) that express a libertarian philosophical system she called Objectivism. This view holds that laissez-faire capitalism—a completely free and unregulated market—is the ideal economic system. She called for a government and business separation similar to the church and state separation in the U.S. Constitution.

In the market system of capitalism, individuals pursue their exclusive self-interest. That is the basis of capitalist economic theory, but it has always posed a moral problem in relation to the contrasting idea of the common good held by many religions. Capitalist philosophers claim that when the self-interest of capitalists is pursued without restraint, everyone benefits— but that has rarely been the case. At its heart, Ayn Rand's philosophy proposes that the proper moral purpose of one's life is the pursuit of one's own happiness. This "ethical egoism" states that individuals ought to do what is in their own rational self-interest as opposed to "ethical altruism," which holds that individuals should dedicate themselves to helping and serving others. In 2005, Paul Ryan said, "The reason I got involved in public service, by and large, if I had to credit one thinker, one person, it would be Ayn Rand. And the fight we are in here, make no mistake about it, is a fight of individualism versus collectivism."[21] Ryan saw the objectivist morality of those who were "working toward their own free will to produce, to achieve, to succeed" as under attack. In a 2009 video posted to Facebook, Ryan said. "I think Ayn Rand did the best job of anybody to build a moral case of capitalism, and that morality of capitalism is under assault." The language of the objectivist debate describes society divided into "makers and takers" and "producers and moochers." This language reflects a self-righteous capitalism that imagines a class war pitting virtuous producers against lazy parasites, and against those who want to use the power of the state to redistribute the wealth of the producers.

The objectivist philosophy celebrates greed and selfishness. Ayn Rand personally rejected Christianity because it was concerned with altruism as an antidote to selfish egoism. Because Rand was an avowed atheist, Paul Ryan, who is Roman Catholic, ran afoul of the American bishops when he publically espoused her cause. More importantly, some of the bishops criticized Ryan for proposing a budget that would cut programs that serve the poorest and most vulnerable Americans in opposition to Catholic social teaching. Afterward, Ryan began to distance himself from Rand, but her philosophy continues to underlie his political and economic stance. And among Tea Party members and libertarians, this philosophy reigns supreme. It is the dominant philosophy of the Republican-controlled U.S. Congress and of many state governments controlled by conservative politicians. Economist John Kenneth Galbraith (1908–2006) once commented, "The modern conservative is engaged in one of man's oldest exercises in moral philosophy; that is, the search for a superior moral justification for selfishness."[22]

We cannot eliminate the dark side of our human condition, but we can summon the better angels of our nature to make us a more humane, kind, and decent people. Even if persistent social selfishness cannot be eliminated, it can be mitigated and minimized by people of good will. The hope of the reign of God is that a transformation of the politics of selfishness is possible through the efforts of transformed individuals who are committed to nonviolent social change motivated by love and compassion.

21. "Collectivism" is a favorite term of those who espouse the politics of selfishness. It is carefully chosen to suggest that working toward the common good is a movement toward a communist economic system where the rights of the individual are suppressed.

22. Galbraith, "Let us Begin," *Harpers*.

## giving up selfishness

Following Jesus involves a movement away from self-obsession and toward the needs of other people. We begin the journey of transformative discipleship by denying ourselves and emptying our hearts of self-centered devotion.

> *Then he said to them all, "If any want to become my followers, let them deny themselves and take up their cross daily and follow me."*[23]

The call to deny one's self often sounds like a Lenten discipline. It conjures up images of people renouncing chocolate, Cheetos, or cheeseburgers. But Jesus is talking about something more fundamental. It is a call to give our lives to love and compassion. And it is a call to put the needs of other people first. Jesus is our model. Dietrich Bonhoeffer called him "the man for others."[24]

Although most New Testament translations use the phrase "let them deny themselves," a few offer variations of "let them forget themselves" or "let them give up the things they want." The New Living Translation says, "You must turn from your selfish ways." Selfishness is the fundamental nature of individual sin and is the root cause of the social sin of the domination system that causes so many people around the world to be oppressed, disenfranchised, and forgotten. But Jesus calls us out from the lordship of selfishness to a new mode of life. He calls us to risk everything for that new mode of thinking and living.

## the way of Jesus

The first-century followers of the Way reflected a conspicuous stance within their culture based on the gospel *of* Jesus. Their love, compassion, and care for one another made them a distinctive community in their societies. Their small communities provided a social safety net for their members at a time when others were totally on their own.

A glimpse of the early Jesus movement is found in the New Testament book called the *Acts of the Apostles*, or more simply as *Acts*. It describes the community of Jesus' followers in the city of Jerusalem in the weeks and months after his death. Their life together reflected the contours of the ministry of Jesus among the peasants of Galilee: love one another, care for one another, support one another, and share generously with one another.

23. Luke 9:23
24. Bonhoeffer, *Letters and Papers*, 382.

The term *apostles* in this text, refers to the disciples of Jesus after the Resurrection. Before his death, they were *disciples*—students and followers of Jesus. Now they have become his apostles—messengers of his vision.

> *Awe came upon everyone, because many wonders and signs were being done by the apostles. All who believed were together and had all things in common; they would sell their possessions and goods and distribute the proceeds to all, as any had need. Day by day, as they spent much time together in the temple, they broke bread at home and ate their food with glad and generous hearts, praising God and having the goodwill of all the people. And day by day the Lord added to their number those who were being saved.*[25]
>
> *Now the whole group of those who believed were of one heart and soul, and no one claimed private ownership of any possessions, but everything they owned was held in common. With great power the apostles gave their testimony to the resurrection of the Lord Jesus, and great grace was upon them all. There was not a needy person among them, for as many as owned lands or houses sold them and brought the proceeds of what was sold. They laid it at the apostles' feet, and it was distributed to each as any had need. There was a Levite, a native of Cyprus, Joseph, to whom the apostles gave the name Barnabas (which means "son of encouragement"). He sold a field that belonged to him, then brought the money, and laid it at the apostles' feet.*[26]

For several hundred years after the death of Jesus, it was their distinctive behavior—the sharing of goods, the welfare of the destitute, a radical social equality, and a commitment to nonviolence—that set Christian communities apart from mainstream culture. From the first small peasant communities in rural Galilee and urban Jerusalem to the rapidly spreading house-churches of Paul in the trading towns of the Mediterranean and Aegean seas, the early Christian movement consisted of counter-cultural groups existing on the margins of society. In the beginning, they were composed of marginalized people—tenant farmers, fishermen, day laborers, slaves, and outcasts—although they soon attracted artisans, merchants, and a few wealthy elites to their ranks. They became communities of radical equality that cut across class differences, economic status, ethnic backgrounds, and gender roles. These communities developed a lifestyle outside of accepted Roman norms that offered their members security in an insecure world without social safety nets. Each tight-knit community of compassion provided its members with food, shelter, and material support when necessary.

25. Acts 2:43–47
26. Acts 4:32–37

## faith: living or believing

However, in the centuries after Jesus died, the central focus of his follow-ers gradually altered. As the center of Christianity moved away from Jew-ish Palestine and into the Hellenistic urban centers, a transformation took place. It had to do with a shift from faith as a way of living to faith as a way of believing. This was not a sudden change or a sharp demarcation in the life of the early church. The gospel *of* Jesus began to decline in significance as the gospel *about* Jesus ascended. By the fourth century, when Christianity became the official religion of the Roman Empire, the way of belief began to dominate in the church and the unique way of life evidenced in the Jesus movement began to fade. Theologian Harvey Cox (b. 1929) has recognized this distinct shift by calling the early stage of the church the Age of Faith, and the latter stage the Age of Belief.[27] The Roman Emperor Constantine (c. 272–337) represented the demarcation between the two periods.

Understanding the difference between faith and belief is vital. Faith is essentially an act of trust, a confidence and hope that allows one to risk everything, even putting one's life on the line. Faith is evidenced by one's lifestyle and ethical behavior. Belief, on the other hand, is principally an intellectual assent to certain ideas or propositions. Faith dwells in the gut, while belief resides in the head. Faith is about loving one's enemies, shar-ing one's goods, and speaking truth to power. Belief is about accepting the concept that Jesus was the son of God, that he performed miracles, and that he died for our salvation. Because following Jesus requires risk, the gospel *of* Jesus requires faith; it calls for a living trust. On the other hand, the gospel *about* Jesus demands unqualified belief. Unfortunately, many people today use *faith* and *belief* as synonymous terms. The more faith is seen as belief, the more we miss the point.

In the late Middle Ages, when Martin Luther (1483–1546) developed the Reformation doctrine of "justification by grace through faith," the idea of faith as *belief* became even stronger. Luther was reacting to the good news that he saw in Paul's letter to the Romans: "For we hold that a person is justi-fied by faith apart from works of the law [Torah]."[28] For Luther, justification by grace meant that sinful people are made right with God by God's gracious forgiveness through the sacrificial death of Jesus. The caveat, of course, is that God's grace, while freely given—now that the cosmic account has been set-tled—must be accepted through one's faith, or more accurately, one's belief.

Paul said,

27. Cox, *Future of Faith*, 4–5.

28. Romans 3:28

*But now . . . the justice of God has been disclosed . . . through faith in Jesus Christ for all who believe . . . Since all have sinned and fall short of the glory of God; they are now made just by his grace as a gift . . . effective through faith.*[29]

The key to receiving God's grace is two-fold according to Paul:

*If you confess with your lips that Jesus is Lord and believe in your heart that God raised him from the dead, you will be saved. For one believes with the heart and so is justified, and one confesses with the mouth and so is saved.*[30]

The gift of forgiveness in the gospel *about* Jesus rests squarely on the head of the believer. This creates a personal dilemma. How does one know if one's faith is sufficient to meet God's criteria for the acceptance of grace, especially in an Age of Belief? Exactly what does one have to believe to be saved? Is it just two things as Paul suggests—to confess that Jesus is Lord and to believe that God raised Jesus from the dead? Or does it also require belief that Jesus died for one's sins? Does it demand assent to everything in the creeds? Does it involve affirming key doctrines of the church? Does it involve confessing one's sins? Does it include baptism? Is it two things, ten things, twenty things? For centuries, theologians of various denominations have argued over the correct beliefs that would ensure one's salvation. Regardless of the details, in the Age of Belief the essential focus of Christianity was a way of believing certain truths about Jesus in order to get to heaven.

## James' minority opinion

An alternate voice in the early church to Paul and Luther was the New Testament letter of James. Luther reportedly said that he would give his doctor's beret to anyone who could reconcile James and Paul. James wrote, "You see that a person is justified by what he does and not by faith alone . . . Faith without works is dead."[31]

*What good is it, my brothers and sisters, if you say you have faith but do not have works? Can faith save you? If a brother or sister is naked and lacks daily food, and one of you says to them, "Go in peace; keep warm and eat your fill," and yet you do not supply*

29. Romans 3:21–25
30. Romans 10:9–10
31. James 2:24–26

*their bodily needs, what is the good of that? So faith by itself, if it*
*has no works, is dead.*[32]

James' epistle was like a minority report in response to Paul's theology. It held that faith without corresponding action was empty. James' concern was not about how one gets to heaven. He was describing a life of faith on earth. It was a response to the words of Jesus which said, "Why do you call me Lord, Lord, but do not do what I say?"[33] Paul had said that only two things were important: to confess that Jesus is Lord and to believe that God raised Jesus from the dead. Period. End of story. However, Paul was talking about the requirements for a personal salvation. Jesus, on the other hand, says that there is much more involved in being his follower. Beliefs leading to personal salvation do not necessarily lead to a life of faith that responds to the social gospel of Jesus. Luther eventually reconciled James and Paul when he wrote, "We are not saved by works; but if there be no works, there must be something amiss with faith."

The president of a large evangelical youth organization contacted me a few years ago. He wanted help with a web site that would attract young people, especially the Millennial generation (born between 1982 and 2000). Once they landed on the home page, he wanted them to be able to read a short prayer inviting Jesus into their lives and then make a decision by clicking an 'I accept Jesus' button to gain salvation. My question to him was "OK, if that means that they are now saved, so what? What's next?" I was essentially asking what difference it would make to the life of the world that someone had accepted Jesus into his or her heart. That is the issue raised by James' epistle. You say that you have faith? Then show it by how you live. Do good works. "Bear good fruit" is what Jesus would say. It is the gospel *about* Jesus in conflict with the gospel *of* Jesus.

## cheap grace

As we mentioned earlier, theologian Dietrich Bonhoeffer contrasted cheap grace and costly grace in a critique of "easy Christianity."

> *Cheap grace means grace sold on the market like [cheap merchan-*
> *dise]. The sacraments, the forgiveness of sin, and the consolations*
> *of religion are thrown away at cut prices. Grace is represented*
> *as the Church's inexhaustible treasury, from which she showers*
> *blessings with generous hands, without asking questions or fixing*

32. James 2:14–17
33. Luke 6:46

*limits. Grace without price; grace without cost! . . . Cheap grace is grace without discipleship, grace without the cross, grace without Jesus Christ, living and incarnate.*

*Costly grace is the treasure hidden in the field; for the sake of it a man will go and sell all that he has. It is the pearl of great price to buy which the merchant will sell all his goods. It is the kingly rule of Christ, for whose sake a man will pluck out the eye which causes him to stumble; it is the call of Jesus Christ at which the disciple leaves his nets and follows him. Costly grace is the gospel which must be sought again and again, the gift which must be asked for, the door at which a man must knock. Such grace is costly because it calls us to follow, and it is grace because it calls us to follow Jesus Christ. It is costly because it costs a man his life, and it is grace because it gives a man the only true life.*[34]

The church's proclamation of grace can be, and often is, passively received without changing how we live. Our souls may be redeemed but our lives are not necessarily transformed. We can continue to lead self-absorbed lives ignoring the cries of the poor, and many Christians do. We often find ourselves captive to a culture dominated by selfishness, greed, and violence.

Social activist and journalist Dorothy Day (1897–1980) said that our hearts must change in order to follow Jesus.

*The greatest challenge of the day is: how to bring about a revolution of the heart, a revolution which has to start with each one of us? When we begin to take the lowest place, to wash the feet of others, to love our brothers with that burning love, that passion, which led to the cross, then we can truly say, "Now I have begun."*[35]

The gospel of Jesus invites us to go beyond ourselves and live for others—feeding those in need, sheltering them, clothing them. Followers of Jesus do not undertake good works to get to heaven; they do so because charity, service, and a commitment to justice represent the faithful lifestyle that Jesus invites us to enter.

To fully understand the social gospel of Jesus and to follow the distinctly counter-cultural Way of Jesus, it is important to recover the message and mission of the kingdom of God that has been lost, hidden, or misrepresented in far too many Christian churches. The kingdom of God is not about personal redemption; it is about social transformation. It is about engaging in a conspiracy of love to change the world.

34. Bonhoeffer, *Cost of Discipleship*, 47.
35. Day, *Loaves and Fishes*, 215.

CHAPTER 3

# the kingdom of God

*Hope is not blind optimism. It's not ignoring the enormity of the task ahead or the roadblocks that stand in our path. It's not sitting on the sidelines or shirking from a fight. Hope is that thing inside us that insists, despite all evidence to the contrary, that something better awaits us if we have the courage to reach for it, and to work for it, and to fight for it. Hope is the belief that destiny will not be written for us, but by us, by the men and women who are not content to settle for the world as it is, who have the courage to remake the world as it should be.*[1]

—Barack Obama (b. 1961)

AT THE HEART OF the gospel of Jesus is the *kingdom of God*. This one phrase sums up the entire ministry of Jesus and his whole life's work. As we read the gospels of Matthew, Mark, and Luke, we see that every thought and saying of Jesus was directed and subordinated to one single thing: the realization of the reign of God's love, compassion, and peace within human society. Jesus spoke of the kingdom of God more than any other subject. His number two topic was the danger of personal wealth and a call to radical generosity with those in need.

Although Jesus spoke in Aramaic—a Semitic language similar to Hebrew—the New Testament gospels and letters were written in Greek. The Greek word which we have translated into English as *kingdom* is *basileia*

---

1. Barack Obama, presidential victory speech, November 7, 2012.

(*bas-il-eh'-ah*). Jesus would have used the Aramaic word *malkutha* (*mal-kooth'-ah*). Both *basileia* and *malkutha* share the same meaning: kingdom, realm, reign, or rule. The expression *kingdom of God—basileia tou theou* (*bas-il-eh'-ah too theh'-oo*) in Greek and *malkutha d'elaha* (*mal-kooth'-ah dehl-ah-hah'*) in Aramaic—points to the ruling activity of God over human social relationships. Herod the Great had the title of *basileus* (*bas-il-yooce'*) or king. So *basileia* has to do with *who* governs the common life and *what kind* of government they establish. When Jesus used the term *kingdom of God* it was a vision of the kind of government or social contract that God desired for humanity. And Jesus declared that this new form of compassionate interdependence was rapidly coming into being. He urgently announced to his contemporaries, "The kingdom of God is at hand!"[2]

But today—when we see that 20 percent of American children live in poverty (40 percent if they are black or Hispanic), when we recognize that 80 percent of the global population live on less than $10 a day and half on less than $2 a day, when we are confronted with constant violence at home and carnage abroad, and when we witness environmental degradation around the world—one begins to question the effectiveness of God's ruling activity. Just looking around at the sorry state of the world today, only a fool would claim that God is king, that God reigns supreme, or that God is in any way in charge of this mess. So just what was Jesus talking about, anyway?

The phrase *kingdom of God* occurs nearly eighty times in the canonical gospels. There are four references in Matthew (his distinctive variation *kingdom of heaven* is used another thirty-four times). Fourteen references are in Mark, twenty-two in Luke, and two in John. Outside of the four gospel accounts, the term *kingdom of God* is not very common in the New Testament. The expression is used six times in Acts, eight times in Paul's letters, and once in Revelation. In the Hebrew Bible, the specific phrase does not occur at all. The concept of God as the true king of Israel was widespread, but references to the *kingdom of Yahweh—malkut Yahweh* (*mal-koot' yah'-way*)—are rarely found.

Interestingly, although Jesus spoke frequently about the kingdom of God, he never referred to God as our king. His preferred anthropomorphic metaphor was *father*—a much more intimate term. Actually, the Aramaic term that Jesus used—*abba* (*ab-bah'*)—is even less formal than father. Many scholars suggest that a closer translation would be the intimate papa or daddy. In this regard, the Gospel of Thomas, which is a collection of 114 sayings attributed to Jesus, has seventeen references to the kingdom of God

---

2. Mark 1:15. English translations vary: "The kingdom of God has come near" or "The kingdom of God is at hand."

in four different forms. Six simply refer to *the kingdom* without a qualifier, two designate the *kingdom of God*, one reference is to the *kingdom of heaven*, but another six sayings refer to the *kingdom of the Father*.

## the kingdom in Israel

Unlike the other nations that surrounded them, the ancient Hebrew tribes at first had no hereditary king. They believed that Yahweh ruled directly over them. During times of crisis, a charismatic leader would inevitably rise up to temporarily lead a tribal coalition until the crisis was resolved. These leaders were called *judges*—*shophetim* (*sho-fet-eem′*) in Hebrew. The term *judge*—*shophet* (*sho-fet′*)—is used in the sense of a bringer of justice—one who accomplishes justice on behalf of Yahweh. In the Hebrew book of Judges, the term more distinctly means deliverers, liberators, rescuers, or emancipators. These leaders—men and women—served as both tribal war leaders and arbiters of intertribal justice on God's behalf.

The first book of Samuel in the Hebrew Bible tells the story of Samuel, a temple priest who became a *shophet* (*sho-fet′*), and of Saul, who became the first Hebrew king—*melek* (*meh′-lek*)—of Israel. The time period in which the story is set was sometime around 900 to 1,000 BCE. Samuel was one of those inspired leaders who believed he was called by Yahweh to lead during a period of political crisis. The Philistine tribes, who held the fertile land along the Mediterranean shoreline, began pushing inland from their fortified cities on the coast. They were better armed—having chariots—and better organized than the Israelites whom they twice defeated in battle according to the biblical story. Eventually, Samuel led the Israelites to victory against the invading Philistines at a decisive battle near the town of Mizpah, just north of Jerusalem.

As Samuel grew older, the Israelites began to worry when and where the next charismatic leader would arise. The tribes demanded that Samuel end the current system of ad hoc judges and select a king to rule over them like other nations, in order to establish a strong central government and a regular line of succession in leadership. In a sense, they were moving from a tribal federation with Yahweh as their spiritual king to a unified state with an earthly king.

Samuel warned the people that by establishing a kingdom, they would be creating a domination system in which they would be ruled by a rich oligarchy who would take the best of their land, crops, cattle, and flocks. The wealthy aristocracy would send their sons to war and enslave their sons and daughters as servants in palaces and on royal estates.

> *So Samuel reported all the words of Yahweh to the people who were asking him for a king. He [Yahweh] said, "These will be the ways of the king who will reign over you: he will take your sons and appoint them to his chariots and to be his horsemen, and to run before his chariots; and he will appoint for himself commanders of thousands and commanders of fifties, and some to plough his ground and to reap his harvest, and to make his implements of war and the equipment of his chariots. He will take your daughters to be perfumers and cooks and bakers. He will take the best of your fields and vineyards and olive orchards and give them to his courtiers. He will take one-tenth of your grain and of your vineyards and give it to his officers and his courtiers. He will take your male and female slaves, and the best of your cattle and donkeys, and put them to his work. He will take one-tenth of your flocks, and you shall be his slaves. And in that day you will cry out because of your king, whom you have chosen for yourselves; but Yahweh will not answer you in that day."*[3]

The writer recounts that as Samuel prayed, he heard Yahweh say to him, "Listen to all that the people are saying to you; it is not you they have rejected, but they have rejected me as their king . . . Listen to them and give them a king."[4] The story relates that Yahweh then selected Saul, a tall, handsome man from the tribe of Benjamin to be Israel's first king. Samuel, acting as Yahweh's agent, anointed Saul's head with oil as a symbol that he had been chosen for a divine purpose. God later rejected Saul because of his disobedience in battle, and Samuel was once again sent to anoint a new king. (Saul's crime was that when he attacked the tribe of Amalekites, he did *not* slaughter every living creature as Yahweh had demanded. He *did* kill all of the men, women, children, babies, and unhealthy animals, but spared the king and the best livestock.) Disappointed in Saul's poor performance, Yahweh deposed him and selected David as a new king. Samuel then dutifully anointed David for the role he was to play.

## the domination system in Israel

The establishment of a kingdom in Israel constituted a dramatic change. From the time of the exodus from the empire of Egypt under the leadership of Moses (c. 1300 BCE) until the establishment of the Hebrew monarchy under David (c. 1000 BCE), the Hebrew people had struggled to maintain a

3. 1 Samuel 8:10–18
4. 1 Samuel 8:7, 22

society that stood in contrast to the many domination systems of the Near East. It was intended to be an egalitarian state with a minimal gap in wealth between the richest and the poorest. With the rise of the monarchy, this was no longer to be. The Hebrew people officially established a domination system. They had escaped from the bondage of the Egyptian domination system, and now, as a forgetful people, they created one of their own. It is no coincidence that David and his son Solomon soon established a temple in Jerusalem to complement the palace of the king. The royal palace and the temple that gave it divine authority went hand-in-hand in ancient domination systems. The king, the high priesthood, and the aristocracy were joint agents of exploitation, extracting tithes and taxes from the peasant class, not to provide for the common good, but to increase their own wealth and luxury. Soon, the role of the social prophet would arise to call the ruling class to establish a more just society in the name of Yahweh.

## how would God govern?

Biblical scholars generally agree that the kingdom of God is not a reference to a geo-political area like the United Kingdom of Great Britain and Northern Ireland or the Kingdom of Bahrain. Instead, the biblical concept of *basileia tou theou* (*bas-il-eh'-ah too theh'-oo*) has to do with the activity of ruling and the people who are ruled, but not a specific territory ruled. In other words, Jesus was talking about what we might call God's kingship or lordship (to use Medieval terms) over a group of people or the ruling activity of God in their lives, rather than God's kingdom as a geographic area with a capital and borders. Thus, we often see the *rule of God* or the *reign of God* used as synonyms.

*Empire* has sometimes used as a substitution for *kingdom* in translating the words of Jesus for a contemporary audience. The Fellows of the Jesus Seminar have translated the kingdom of God as *God's imperial rule*, providing us with a verb. It nicely contrasts the idea of God's ruling style over against Caesar's imperial rule of the Roman Empire.

Still for many of us, the terms *empire* or *imperial rule* are as problematic as kingdom. On the one hand, empires seem a part of the past, as equally dated as kingdoms—just bigger. Empires have changed over thousands of years from a regional to a trans-global presence. The great empires of the past—Egyptian, Babylonian, Persian, Greek, Roman, Mongol, Holy Roman, Ottoman, Spanish, Dutch, French, British, German, and Russian—are now just history. Yet many observers suggest we are living in the midst of an American Empire in which not only its cultural dominance but its military presence is found in nearly every corner of the globe. So perhaps empire still carries significant meaning for us today. Yet, sometimes when you live in the heart of an empire it is hard to see the forest for the trees.

For Jesus and his followers, the terms *kingdom* and *empire* had great power. Beyond the domination system created by the local rulers of Jewish Palestine, they saw political, economic, and social power evident in the massive might of the Roman Empire. When the early church communities confessed "Jesus is Lord"[5]—*Iésous kurios (ee-ay-sooce' koo'-ree-os)*—it was a treasonable and blasphemous statement made to counter the required imperial oath "Caesar is Lord"—*kaisar kurios (kah'-ee-sar koo'-ree-os)*. It was a matter of shifting allegiance. The followers of Jesus were confronted by two competing ruling styles, demanding a moral and political choice that faced each person. When there is a Pharaoh, a Caesar, or a Führer on hand to epitomize the extreme examples of the pervasive domination system, the choice seems straightforward. But at other times, when empire is not nearly as obvious, when the ruling style is a democracy, when the powers and principalities are global banks and corporations, the choice is often less clearly defined or readily apparent.

When the terms *kingdom* and *God* are combined in a phrase, the realms of religion and politics inevitably come together. One's religion will often inform one's politics. That can be a good thing. For instance, in the establishment of the United States, the broad principles of religious humanism as held by the founders were woven into the founding documents. They separated church and state but not religion and politics. This protects religious groups from being controlled by the state, and vice versa. When an institutional religion and a national government are integrated, we can easily move toward the concept of a *theocracy*, a form of government in which a political state is understood to be governed by immediate divine guidance through a religious authority. A theocracy is something more than a government founded upon religious principles. It usually involves a state ruled by clergy, or by officials who are regarded as divinely guided, such as the Pope in Vatican City, the Grand Ayatollah in the Islamic Republic of Iran, or even that of the United States as envisioned by the Christian Right. In a theocracy, the official state religion—or the leader's favored religion—and a corresponding morality become the law of the land. But the ruling style of God as proclaimed by Jesus is far removed from the idea of a modern state ruled by *Sharia*, the sacred law of Islam, or by some rigid morality and social conservatism of Christian fundamentalism.

---

5. Referenced in three of Paul's letters: Romans 10:9; 1 Corinthians 12:3; and Philippians 2:11

Theologian John B Cobb (b. 1925) prefers the terms the *divine commonwealth* or the *commonwealth of God*. Commonwealth is a traditional English term for a political community founded for the common good. This has many advantages over the despotic connotations associated with kingdom and empire, but it is a somewhat unfamiliar term in the United States outside of the states of Kentucky, Massachusetts, Pennsylvania, and Virginia. They adopted the term to distinguish themselves as a region governed by the people rather than a monarchy. Commonwealth certainly captures the intent of Jesus' message by clarifying that God would always govern for the common good rather than for the benefit of a wealthy minority.

## noun versus verb

Rather than translate the kingdom of God as the *reign of God*, *empire of God*, or *commonwealth of God* (all nouns), it may be more accurate to refer to the *ruling of God* or the *governing of God*, or, as Harvey Cox (b. 1929) prefers, the *reigning of God* (all verbs focused on God's activity in the world). Cox says:

> In my own teaching, I prefer to use the phrase "Reigning of God."
> It implies something that is going on—not a place, but a "happening." This is the grammar Jesus used in speaking of it. To be a "follower" of Jesus means to discern and respond to the initial signs of this "happening" and to work to facilitate its coming in its fullness.[6]

John Dominic Crossan (b. 1934) concurs in a slightly different way—it "is not so much *where* God rules the world as *how* God rules the world." He combines the verb with a set of ruling values.

> When you read "kingdom of God," therefore, mentally rephrase it as the "ruling style of God." It imagines how the world would be if the biblical God actually sat on an imperial throne down here below.[7]

The *governing style of God* might have more meaning in our context. How would God govern our city, state, or nation? Of course, one's idea of God's governing style depends entirely on one's image of God—an angry tyrant, a loving parent, or a distant uncle. As followers of Jesus, we should

6. Cox, *Future of Faith*, 45.
7. Crossan, *Greatest Prayer*, 78.

always look to Jesus for help in clarifying God's essential character and ruling style.

Although the reign of God was at the center of Jesus' proclamation, his meaning of the term was never clearly defined. Jesus usually spoke of it in the form of parables, with imaginative pictures of seeds, pearls, and unemployed workers. For most Christians, however, the image of the kingdom is rather vague. There is still no consensus among scholars, much less the average parishioner, about what was in Jesus' mind when he spoke of God's kingdom.

Over the centuries, a variety of interpretations of what Jesus meant by the kingdom of God have been put forth. We will briefly examine six of the most common explanations: the reign of God as 1) heaven, 2) an inner spiritual experience, 3) the church, 4) a separate society, 5) a new state, and 6) a new world.

## heaven

Many Christians probably believe that *heaven* is the proper understanding of the kingdom of God. The term in Matthew's gospel, the *kingdom of heaven* often causes massive confusion and leads to this distorted misconception. The kingdom of heaven is not a term that was used by Jesus, but rather is a secondary form created by the author of Matthew's gospel as another way to proclaim the kingdom of God without specifically mentioning the word *God*. As God's dwelling place, heaven is a symbol that sometimes stands for God. The first-century author of Matthew's gospel (written circa 85 CE) wrote to a predominantly Jewish-Christian audience. He modified the term kingdom of God because of the Jewish aversion to speaking the name of God.[8] Pious Jews did this to avoid breaking the commandment that prohibits taking God's name in vain, even if unwittingly. So for Matthew's community the *kingdom of heaven* had the same meaning as the *kingdom of God*. Today, however, when clergy use the term *kingdom of heaven*, they only perpetuate misconceptions that the kingdom of God is a reference to a realm in the sky. "Your kingdom come, your will be done on earth as it is in heaven" was the prayer of Jesus' followers.[9] So in this sense, Jesus acknowledges God's presence in a heavenly kingdom, However God's rule

8. For instance, when the Hebrew Bible was translated into Greek, the name Yahweh was replaced by the Greek words *ho kyrios* (*ho koo'-ree-os*), translated in English as "the LORD," in order to avoid speaking God's name and inadvertently taking it in vain.

9. Matthew 6:9–13, Luke 11:2–4

over heaven's supernatural denizens is presumably in good shape; it's earth that needs help.

Of course, in the first century the term *heaven* did not have the same connotation that we give it today. Heaven—*ouranos (oo-ran-os')* in Greek—simply meant the visible sky. A more accurate translation of the term in Matthew's gospel would actually be the *kingdom of the heavens*, or the *kingdom of the sky*. The pre-modern Mediterranean worldview conceived of the sky as not just the dwelling place of Yahweh, but of all the gods. The concept of heaven as a place where the righteous go after death was not yet developed in Hebrew culture; that would happen only when Greek philosophy transformed Christian theology over a period of decades, if not centuries. First-century Jews—including Jesus and his followers—believed that when people died—both good and bad alike—they departed to the shadowy world of Sheol, until their memory was forgotten.

The popular interpretation that the kingdom of God is synonymous with a heavenly realm is at odds with the vision expressed by Jesus. He desired to see God's governing style prevail in this world. The kingdom of God according to Jesus is solidly in the here and now, in the midst of our everyday reality. Jesus was solely and passionately concerned about transformed lives, transformed communities, and transformed societies that would benefit all of humanity, especially the poor and excluded.

## an inner spiritual experience

Many Christians understand the kingdom of God to mean the rule of God in people's hearts. They believe the kingdom is present when individual lives are ruled by God—whenever women and men submit themselves to God's ruling style in their interrelationships.

This was Martin Luther's (1483–1546) viewpoint. He saw the kingdom of God as an inner spiritual reality in the midst of the world. He imagined two parallel realms in which God rules—two kingdoms—1) the political kingdoms of this world ruled by the sword and 2) an individual spiritual realm ruled by scripture, faith, and the Holy Spirit—reflecting the Greek philosophical dualism of body and soul or secular and spiritual. In Luther's mind, God was ultimately in control of both human spheres, ordaining the physical sphere to the control of secular civil governments and religious institutions and the spiritual sphere to the work of the Holy Spirit within the individual conscience. This meant, on the one hand, that secular authorities had no legitimate rule over the faith of a Christian. On the other hand, this left civil authorities to do pretty much as they pleased in their own realm, since they were answerable to God alone. The church generally stayed out of the secular ballpark as a critic as long as secular rulers stayed out of the spiritual arena of individual conscience. This spiritual view of the kingdom of God was focused on an inward experience of the head and the heart and it implied an individual rather than a corporate dimension. For Luther, this thinking reflected his own battle with religious and secular authorities over his conscientious stand to interpret scripture, speak, and write as he saw fit. But the kingdom of God is not found in just one of these realms; it is found in an integration of both spheres of life.

God's ruling style *is* present in the lives of men and women who have committed themselves to that vision. But it is wrong to place all the emphasis solely on an individual relationship with God. Kingdom by its very nature implies a collective order. A kingdom in a literal sense implies a monarch ruling over a group of subjects. It suggests that there are social standards and policies for the conduct of collective life in that kingdom. Mennonite professor Donald Kraybill states "The kingdom is not present through a series of hot lines from the King to each individual subject."[10]

In the past, Jesus' words in Luke 17:21 have been translated to read, "The kingdom of God is *within* you." More recently the Greek *entos* (*entos'*)—which can mean either *within* or *among*—has been translated to read, "the kingdom of God is *in your midst*" or "the kingdom of God is *among* you." *Within* implies an individualistic and private realm, while the newer translations reveal the corporate and public nature of the kingdom.

If the kingdom of God implies a conjunction of religion and politics, then it actually represents the congruence of Luther's two kingdoms. It is a vision of individuals, whose internal lives are being changed dramatically, resulting in a new way of living and relating to one another in the social, political, and economic sphere. Therefore, it involves both a personal transformation and a social transformation. The kingdom of God doesn't leave the physical realm to the civil authorities; it challenges the powers and principalities at their core.

## the church

Saint Augustine of Hippo (354–430) was one of many theologians through the ages who thought that the kingdom of God referred to the organized society we call the church. Even in our own day, Christian preachers often speak as if the kingdom is just another word for the church. This

---

10. Kraybill, *Upside-Down Kingdom*, 26.

interpretation at least has a corporate dimension—a *group* of people who recognize the rule of God in their hearts.

As much as we try to talk of the "one holy and apostolic church" and the "holy catholic church" as a universal body of believers, one cannot avoid the fact that the church is manifested in a wide variety of human social institutions with offices, hierarchies, a history, divisions, prescribed sets of beliefs, rituals, etc. Jesus was pretty clear that the kingdom of God has no place for hierarchies, titles, and exclusionary practices. Finally, the checkered history of the church, including religious warfare and crusades, approval of slavery, intolerance of other faiths, religious schisms, torture and burning of heretics, and many other acts of hatred and violence, suggests that this institution is not the kingdom that Jesus envisioned. In spite of creedal claims, it is not a very *holy* institution. If the kingdom of God is in any way like the church, it is in the context of a faithful community, but not as an institution.

## a separate society

Some people believe that the kingdom of God will be an earthly utopia created by men and women based on the ethical principles of Jesus. Throughout history, they have created social experiments based on the teachings of Jesus. This often leads to groups of people who withdraw from "evil" society and create alternative communities in which they legislate kingdom values as community laws. (The civic moral reforms led by John Calvin (1509–1564) in Geneva, Switzerland in the mid-1500s is an example of this viewpoint, as are numerous utopian societies that flourished in America in the eighteenth and nineteenth centuries.)

But the kingdom of God is not geographically or socially isolated from the center of society. The kingdom is not a demand for social avoidance or withdrawal. The kingdom of God is found squarely in the middle of social evil, injustice, domination, and exploitation. As Donald Kraybill points out,

> *Kingdom action does not take place outside of the societal ballpark. It's a different game played in the middle of the old ballpark. Kingdom players follow different rules and listen to a different coach.*[11]

11. Ibid., 24.

### a new state

Many of Jesus' contemporaries were looking to restore the ancient kingdom of Israel as an independent nation, free from Roman control. They wanted to return to the idealized glory of the kingdom under David and Solomon. They were waiting for God to act through an anointed king—a messiah.

But Jesus clearly rejected the messianic role of a military conqueror and king. The mission and message of Jesus does not validate any earthly state or nation, in spite of what Pat Robertson (b. 1930) and Jerry Falwell (1933–2007) have proclaimed regarding the role of America. God's kingdom and ruling style cut across all national boundaries. The governing style of God stands in opposition to the domination systems of nation states, especially to their unjust favoritism toward the wealthy and the use of violence to support the status quo.

John's gospel reports that Jesus said to the secular and religious authorities of his day:

> *My kingdom is not of this world [kosmos]. If my kingdom were of this world [kosmos], my followers would be fighting to keep me from being handed over to the Jews. But as it is, my kingdom is not of this realm [kosmos].*[12]

This statement should not be understood to mean that the kingdom of God is otherworldly or spiritual in nature. Biblical scholar Walter Wink argues that the Greek word *kosmos* (*kos'-mos*) which is often translated as *world* in this context really refers to an *ordered system*—specifically, it refers to the domination system as the normalized state of civilization in the world. The kingdom of the world is a governing style of domination, exploitation, oppression, and violence. Jesus' statement means that the kingdom of God is based on a different set of values than the present system of politics, economics, and social relationships. Furthermore, Jesus consistently rejects the use of political force, power, or coercion in the kingdom. According to Wink, Jesus is really saying, "My kingdom is not part of this or any domination system."

### a new world

There are some who believe that the kingdom of God is a reference to a new world based on the metaphoric imagery in the book of Revelation of a new heaven and a new earth. In this apocalyptic scenario, this world will

---

12. John 18:36

end, replaced by a new one. This interpretation is often associated with the earthly return of Jesus at some future date. Many Christians believe that at the second coming of Jesus, the kingdom of God will come in its fullness.

The church is woefully mired in apocalyptic imagery that forecasts the ultimate destiny of the world. Its roots are found in a body of literature that grew up during the three centuries preceding the life of Jesus. The Greek word *apokalupsis* (*ap-ok-al'-oop-sis*) means uncovering, unveiling, or disclosing. The writers of apocalyptic literature saw history as divided into two ages— *aiōn* (*ah-hee-ohn'*)—this present evil age and the righteous age that is to come. Apocalyptic writers offered imaginative visions of the coming age, often in vividly symbolic language. The two most obvious examples are the book of Daniel in the Hebrew Bible and the book of Revelation in the New Testament.

These writers believed that the present age was wholly evil and could not be reformed. There was therefore no solution for this present age other than total destruction and obliteration, followed by replacement of something totally new. The coming age would be wholly good and righteous. God's chosen people would at last be vindicated and would receive the place that was theirs by right. Apocalyptic writers believed this could never happen by human activity alone. Therefore, they looked for the direct intervention of God in human history. God would blast this present world out of existence and bring in God's new golden age. The event was called the *Day of the Lord*. It would be a time of terror, destruction, and judgment in which things as they are would be shattered out of existence, and the new age tempestuously born. The Day of the Lord would be the birth pangs of a coming new age.

In a period of persecution, apocalyptic thinking flourishes. Some members of the Jesus movement began to look for Jesus' imminent return to vindicate them within the Jewish community where they were increasingly seen not as another harmless sect, but as dangerous heretics who were a threat to the continuation of the traditional faith. They were told to conform or leave the synagogues. Those who had looked for a messiah to throw out the Romans and take back the throne of Israel needed Jesus to somehow play that role to justify his place in the future of Judaism. By clearly rejecting the role of conqueror, Jesus failed as the Jewish messiah, at least during his first time around. But some apocalyptic followers believed he would establish his messiahship at a future time in a spectacular way. Strangely, it is not the kingdom of *God* that the early Christian communities looked for, but the future kingdom of *Jesus*. Eventually apocalyptic concepts influenced the gospel writers to put words into the mouth of Jesus about the approaching destruction of the present order, embellished by images of Jesus returning as a conquering warrior, judge, and king.

But Jesus suggested something quite different—the kingdom is very near or already here in our midst.

*The time is fulfilled, the kingdom is at hand.*[13]

*The kingdom of God has come upon you.*[14]

*The kingdom of God is in the midst of you.*[15]

Any New Testament references to the coming of a *new world*, or a *new creation* may also be understood as the inauguration of a *new age* or *new order* within our contemporary world. God's new order as conceived by Jesus is a new age breaking into the present one. Change will come not from replacement but by transformation. Jesus' parables of the mustard seed and the leaven illustrate his vision. Tiny seeds of the mustard plant sown in a cultivated garden will transform it as this unruly and uncontrollable weed takes over. A small amount of yeast or leaven placed in a large amount of bread dough will transform the dough, causing it to rise and change from within. Once started, neither mustard seed nor leaven can be controlled.

## getting to the heart of the kingdom

If we read the gospels closely, none of the traditional interpretations—heaven, an inner spiritual experience, the church, a separate society, a new state, or a new world— fit with the visionary images in the proclamation of Jesus. In fact, most are an attempt to domesticate the vision of Jesus—to control it, to water it down, to render it harmless. But in spite of the best efforts of the church, the vision of Jesus for humanity's future refuses to be controlled.

Although the concept of Yahweh's reign over the people of Israel had a long history in the Hebrew Bible, it underwent a radical mutation on the lips of Jesus. The kingdom of God as preached by Jesus is a vision of a profound transformation of human beings and human institutions—social, political, economic, and religious—to a form that expresses the character and nature of a God of love. It combines elements of personal and social transformation in the spiritual and political realms.

According to Jesus, God's new order is something of great value, yet it is often hidden from view by the overwhelming presence of injustice and violence, and must be uncovered or recovered. It is something that has been lost and must be found again. It is something we have long believed

13. Mark 1:15
14. Luke 11:20
15. Luke 17:21

is impossible, but must now struggle and hope for again. The kingdom is something that cannot be seen in and of itself, yet its effects are plainly visible. To enter the kingdom, in fact to even *see* the kingdom, one must experience a dramatic change—a reorientation, a rebirth. So just what *is* the kingdom of God as preached by Jesus of Nazareth?

The kingdom of God that Jesus described in metaphors and stories was the action of a social-political movement led by the God of love to restore what Jesus believed to be God's intention for humanity from the very moment of creation. Rather than the Jewish dream for restoration of political and religious power through external divine action, Jesus painted a vision of God changing the world from within through the creation of a new community bonded together in new egalitarian social relationships. Jesus described what would happen when love finally broke through the hearts and minds of people to transform their actions and relationships into a society based on compassion, generosity, and equality. Jesus proclaimed that the kingdom had already arrived and could be clearly seen and entered into if a person underwent a radical transformation of the beliefs and values of power and success that conventional wisdom has implanted in their hearts.

## personal and social, spiritual and political

The reign of God must be understood as both personal and social transformation. Everything that Jesus says about the ruling style of God is true in both dimensions. Any attempt to see it as one or the other is an incomplete understanding of the kingdom. Personal transformation must lead to social transformation. And social transformation can only come about through the efforts of transformed people.

The governing style of God is also both spiritual and political. It cannot be seen as just a spiritual kingdom that has both individual and social dimensions like the church; it must also be seen as having political and economic implications for individuals and their communities. It is not just about good people offering personal service and charity to those in need, it is about a wholesale transformation of the social order that will eliminate human suffering and need among us.

The mission *of* Jesus was the implementation of the governing style of God on earth—to change the very nature of the world in order to prevent the living hell in which so many dwell today.

## your kingdom come

One of the major questions for theologians is how the kingdom of God will come about. Did Jesus announce the arrival of the kingdom in his lifetime? Did Jesus see the kingdom coming gradually within human history? Or did he see it coming at some future time, appearing suddenly and bringing about the end of history? Is the kingdom present, future, or both?

This topic is subject to as much disagreement as is the nature of the kingdom itself. In fact it is usually intertwined with the nature of the kingdom. If the kingdom is a future reality created by God through some dramatic event, such as Jesus' second coming, then we do not have to take the kingdom seriously today in our present lives. Preachers and theologians will often remind us that this is *God's* kingdom. God will bring it about in God's time with or without our assistance. If Jesus inaugurated the kingdom in his lifetime, but it is dependent upon his return to reach fruition, is there anything we can do other than wait? On the other hand, if the kingdom of God is a present reality that will transform the world within human history, then Jesus' call to work toward the kingdom has immediate importance to us.

What made Jesus so unique was his conviction that the reigning style of God had already started happening. It wasn't to be found in a new king who would ascend the throne of Israel with a trumpet blast, nor would it come about through a bloody military liberation which would overthrow oppressive rulers. The fundamental message of Jesus' proclamation was the day of God's reign has already dawned—it is here in our midst. The liberation from oppression that the prophets proclaimed and the poor had long desired to see is now present. Jesus' healing of outcasts, eating with the unacceptable, and announcement of good news to the poor were all signs that God's ruling style had arrived.

## apocalyptic versus prophetic

Jesus stood more in the tradition of a *social prophet* than an *apocalyptist*. The prophetic message is often a cry for social, economic, and political justice. It is always a summons for people and nations to obey God and to serve God within this present world. To the prophet, the present world needs to be transformed, not destroyed and recreated.

The prophet believes that in the events of history—within time and within the world—a faithful people can change the present order. In one sense a prophet is an optimist, for, however sternly he or she condemns things as they are, he or she nonetheless believes that they can be mended if people will accept the way of love, compassion, peace, and justice. But a prophet is also a realist, understanding that there will always be resistance to change and risk for the messenger.

Apocalyptists are pessimists, for they do not believe that things as they are can ever be cured. For them, the world is beyond mending. It is wholly given over to incurable evil. They look forward to the destruction of the current world and the creation of a brand new world. They see termination, not reformation, as the only viable path forward. Both the prophet and the apocalyptists look for a better age to come, but the apocalyptic mind requires a total reboot.

John the Baptist is presented as an apocalyptic preacher, while Jesus was a prophetic preacher. Both announced the coming of the kingdom of God. But Jesus preached a way out of the current situation without total destruction. Rather than the hand of God acting to change by replacement, Jesus painted a vision of God working to change the world from within by transformation. Unfortunately, Paul and the early church, including the gospel writers, were apocalyptists. In many ways, they misunderstood the mission and message of Jesus.

The question remains, will the future fulfillment of the kingdom of God require an apocalyptic act of God? A growing number of biblical scholars now agree that Jesus rejected the notion that God will act momentously on the Day of the Lord or that God intends to bring about the end of the world. But the kingdom of God as proclaimed by Jesus still has elements of both present and future. So when will it come fully? Or perhaps, the more fundamental question is will it ever be entirely fulfilled?

## the kingdom as a vision

The kingdom of God was the metaphor Jesus used to describe his vision of the way things were meant to be in human society—how things could be dramatically different within us and among us—and to understand Jesus you have to understand the nature of a vision. It is reminiscent of Bobby Kennedy's phrase, "Some men see things as they are and say why? I dream things that never were and say why not?"

Visions always deal with the future. Indeed, a vision is where tomorrow begins, for it expresses what those who share the vision are working hard to create. Since most people don't take the time to think systematically about the future, those who do, like Jesus, Gandhi, and King—and who base their strategies and actions on their visions—have inordinate power to shape the future. They each had a passion for an ideal which they expressed as a vision and inspired others to respond.

Dutch sociologist Frederick Polak describes how charismatic leaders influence the future through a vision.

> *Themselves under the influence of that which they envisioned, they transformed the nonexistent into the existent, and shattered the reality of their own time with their imaginary images of the future. Thus the open future already operates in the present, shaping itself in advance through these image makers and their images—and they, conversely, focus and enclose the future in advance, for good or ill.*[16]

If the governing style of God is understood as a vision for our corporate life together, then we can begin to understand how it can be both present and future, because that is how a vision operates. The power of a vision is that while it describes the future state to be achieved, it begins to immediately shape the present. One author has said that "the right vision is so energizing that it in effect jump starts the future by calling forth the skill, talents, and resources to make it happen."[17] A community or organization doesn't wait for a vision to magically happen, they work together to make it a reality. Jesus chose to take the long awaited dream of a just and compassionate society, and by articulating and acting on it, made it a vision that would lead to the transformation of the world.

When people embrace a vision of the future, they begin to live it out in the present. The main course may take a while to prepare, but we're eating the hors d'oeuvres right now and setting the table for the soup, salad, entrée, and dessert courses. In liturgical language, we are enjoying a foretaste of the feast to come. But the reality is that the final consummation of the vision may never come about completely in human history. And it may never come about, as many imagine, at the *end* of human history. We have no indication that the vision of Jesus will ever be fulfilled. But the dream is that it *could* be fulfilled through the power of transforming love, compassion, and nonviolence and it is worth struggling to achieve. The reality is that if no one acts upon a vision, it only remains a dream. The proclamation of the reign of God by Jesus is a call to action. The vision of God's new order is an invitation to a journey. The destination is hoped for, but not assured. If we choose to follow Jesus, and contribute to making the kingdom of God a reality, we are called to spend our lives in the pursuit of this vision.

16. Polak, *Image of the Future*, 124.

17. Nanus, *Visionary Leadership*, 8.

A vision is like a seed that is planted in the hearts and minds of people. When it takes root and is nourished it can grow to accomplish astounding results. Jesus used this imagery with the kingdom of God. It is like a mustard seed, about the size of a grain of sand. Like an invasive mustard plant thrown into a well-tended garden, the reigning style of God has been rooting itself in the domination systems of the world and continues to spread its subversive message, even to our day.

For most of us, the kingdom of God is an obscure concept. We don't know where to start looking for it. Let me offer my own biases about where the kingdom is most likely *not* found. The kingdom is *not* found in personal isolation. It is *not* found through spiritual disciplines. It is *not* found in ritual worship. It is *not* found in corridors of power or success. It is *not* found amid wealth and possessions. If we search for the kingdom in these places, we will not find it. It will only be found on a very narrow road—one less traveled.

Jesus gave us some clues where to find the God's new order in the way that he lived. The kingdom of God is found in community. It is found where people are hurting and suffering. It is found where people are engaged in healing, caring, and sharing. It is found where people are working for peace and justice. The kingdom of God is found in the world in simple everyday acts of kindness, compassion, and reconciliation. Look for it, seek it out, search for it. Like leaven in bread dough, we cannot observe it working, but we can see the results of the transformation it causes.

The reigning of God is about a radical shift in human life that stirs the political wind. It is the understanding that a new regime is about to change everything. This is not the old style of change in which one despot is replaced with another. This is about the end of despotic rule entirely, replaced by new social relationships based on equality, compassion, and liberation. This is an announcement that something dramatic is happening in the world. Ancient dreams are becoming reality. A movement is forming, and people are joining. Freedom is coming. Justice is arriving. It is chaotic, but it is exciting.

The leader of this movement is not visible, but the people are—seen here and there engaged in work for change. Some actions are small, under the radar. At other times the results of the individual and collective work for change becomes readily apparent. There isn't any central coordination, just a common vision guiding the work of many people. Occasionally, a prophetic voice is raised and the powerful take heed.

Yet the challenge is huge. The rule of the rich and mighty is the normal state of civilization, and the old systems refuse to change. Many people benefit from the current situation and the status quo. The purveyors of self-interest and greed are frightened that a different world may no longer favor them. And the economic powers who rule the world's nations are not about to give up their power and privilege and wealth without a fight. They have laws and police forces and armies at their disposal. They show little hesitation to use armed violence, imprisonment, torture, and capital punishment to maintain control. The powerful dominate our information through news media that are controlled by the government or by wealthy corporations. For the people of Jesus' revolutionary new movement in any time or place, it is always a season of challenge and danger and risk, which calls for great personal courage, sacrifice, and faith.

# CHAPTER 4

# a conspiracy of love

---

*I don't know your religion*
*But one day I heard you pray*
*For a world where everyone can work*
*And children they can play*
*And though you never got your share*
*Of the victories you have won*
*You sowed the seeds of equality*
*In your daughters and your sons*[1]

—Tommy Sands (b. 1945)

OVER THE CENTURIES, THE church has rarely understood the true nature of the kingdom of God as proclaimed by Jesus, and for many people in the church it is not even on their radar screen. In 1917, theologian and Baptist minister Walter Rauschenbusch (1861–1918), a proponent of the Social Gospel, wrote:

> *The doctrine of the Kingdom of God was left undeveloped by in-*
> *dividualistic theology and finally mislaid by it almost completely,*
> *because it did not support nor fit in with that scheme of doctrine.*
> *In the older handbooks of theology it is scarcely mentioned, except*
> *in the chapters on eschatology; in none of them does it dominate*
> *the table of contents. What a spectacle, that the original teaching*
> *of our Lord has become an incongruous element in so-called evan-*
> *gelical theology, like a stranger with whom the other doctrines*

---

1. Tommy Sands, "Your Daughters and Your Sons," 1985.

*would not associate, and who was finally ejected because he had*
*no wedding garment!*[2]

Mislaying Jesus' message is Rauschenbusch's polite way of saying what has happened throughout the history of the church. Actually, the church has done its best to hide and suppress the message of the kingdom of God because it is too political, too radical, and too threatening to the status quo. And in the alliance between church and state known as Christendom that flourished from the fourth to the eighteenth centuries, the church itself represented the status quo of the domination system. Many churches in our nation still represent and defend the status quo today.

As recently as 2006, Brian McLaren (b. 1956) titled his book on the kingdom of God *The Secret Message of Jesus: Uncovering the Truth That Could Change Everything.* The so-called secret message that McLaren introduces is Jesus' proclamation of the kingdom of God. Clearly, the evangelical world where McLaren had his roots has done its best to bury the kingdom of God in subservience to a theology of personal salvation. It is unsettling that Brian McLaren, one of the freshest and brightest voices on the evangelical scene, believes that the central message of Jesus in the gospels—the kingdom of God—was somehow hidden from view in the gospel texts he had read for many years. The kingdom of God isn't a hidden or secret message and never has been. It was clearly and forcefully expressed in the first words out of Jesus' mouth as he embarked on his ministry:

> *Jesus came to Galilee, proclaiming the good news of God, and say-*
> *ing, "The time is fulfilled, and the kingdom of God has come near;*
> *repent, and believe in the good news."*[3]

McLaren is simply expressing what has become a common perception in our churches. One can become blinded to the central message of Jesus by a centuries-old theology that focuses solely on individual salvation from personal sin. In the process, we've been handed a phony Jesus by the church—a domesticated Jesus, a spiritualized Jesus, a non-dangerous Jesus, a middle-of-the-road Jesus. But by any measure, Jesus was a societal radical. The word *radical* comes from the Latin *radix* (*ray'-dicks*) which means *root*. A radical gets down to the fundamental causes that lie at the root of a problem. Jesus dealt with human fundamentals—the root causes of poverty and suffering, of selfishness and greed, of violence and strife, of domination and oppression—and he offered radical responses. He wanted to create a dramatic change through profound personal, political, economic, and social

2. Rauschenbusch, *Social Gospel*, 25–26.

3. Mark 1:14–15

transformations. He called people to adopt a radically different kind of life. Jesus was essentially proclaiming a social revolution. Thankfully, McLaren now recognizes that Jesus proclaimed first and foremost "the radical revolutionary empire of God."

> *This revolutionary image of Jesus didn't come to me in Sunday school as a boy. There, Jesus was a nice, quiet, gentle, perhaps somewhat fragile guy on whose lap children liked to sit. Or he was a fellow in strange robes who held a small sheep in one arm and always seemed to have the other raised as if he were hailing a taxi. The revolutionary image of Jesus didn't come to me in adult church either. There, Jesus' main job was to die so my sins could be forgiven and I could go to heaven . . . Or else he was a teacher whose words could be quoted to condemn people our church or denomination didn't approve of. But Jesus wasn't presented as someone whose message would overturn our thinking as well.*[4]

## finding new metaphors

Sometimes the metaphor gets in the way of the vision. As a metaphor, the *kingdom of God* does not work very well in present circumstances, nor will it conceivably work any better in the future. Kingdoms are diminishing around the world. Democracies are rising. But no matter what form governments take, domination systems abound. So it would be helpful to find a new metaphor that people can better understand and connect with in the twenty-first century. We need a fresh language that will better describe the vision of Jesus and our role as his followers in a postmodern world.

Brian McLaren put it this way:

> *When Jesus spoke of the kingdom of God, his language was charged with urgent political, religious, and cultural electricity. But today, if we speak of the kingdom of God, the original electricity is largely gone, and in its place we often find a kind of tired familiarity that inspires not hope and excitement, but anxiety or boredom . . .*
>
> *For many people today, kingdom language evokes patriarchy, chauvinism, imperialism, domination, and a regime without freedom—the very opposite of the liberating, barrier-breaking, domination-shattering, reconciling movement the kingdom of God was intended to be! . . . If Jesus were here today, I'm quite certain he*

4. McLaren, *Secret Message of Jesus*, 33.

*wouldn't use the language of kingdom at all, which leaves us won-*
*dering how he would articulate his message.*[5]

McLaren proposes six alternative metaphors for the contemporary world: the *dream* of God, the *revolution* of God, the *mission* of God, the *party* of God, the *network* of God, and the *dance* of God. Each one captures a bit of the essence of what Jesus was talking about. Episcopal theologian Verna Dozier (1917–2006) developed the idea of the *dream of God* in her book of the same name.[6]

## the revolution of God

McLaren's suggested phrase *the revolution of God* implies the radical nature of the change that Jesus envisioned.

> *This metaphor claims that we human beings have created a to-*
> *talitarian regime—a regime of lust (where too many people are*
> *reduced to sex objects or hyped into sexual predators), a regime of*
> *pride and power (where some thrive at the expense or to the exclu-*
> *sion of others), a regime of racism, classism, ageism, and nation-*
> *alism (where people are identified as enemies or evil or inferior*
> *because of the color of their skin or the physical or social location*
> *of their birth), a regime of consumerism and greed (where life is*
> *commodified, where people become slaves to their jobs, where the*
> *environment is reduced to natural resources for human consump-*
> *tion, where time is money, which makes life become money). This*
> *regime is unacceptable, and God is recruiting people to join a*
> *revolutionary movement of change.*[7]

## the God movement

Farmer and New Testament Greek scholar Clarence Jordan (1912–1969) sometimes substituted the term *God Movement* for the kingdom of God, focusing on the people and their mission directed by God. He believed that the people who are engaged in living out the vision of Jesus are the only visible and tangible aspects of God's governing style. Jordan believed that Jesus saw his followers, the people who journeyed with him—as evidenced by their counter-cultural lives and actions—as proof that the ruling style of

5. Ibid., 138–139.

6. Dozier, *Dream of God*, 125.

7. McLaren, *Secret Message of Jesus*, 142–143.

God has broken into our world and is continually confronting, challenging, calling, and changing us.

Commenting on the story of Jesus' temptation in the wilderness[8] at the beginning of his ministry where the devil offers him three different paths to power and greatness, Jordan said:

> So Jesus rejected the three mightiest ideas that had bid for the mind of man—materialism, ecclesiasticism, and militarism. These three absolutely could not have been part of his movement. Having tested these big ideas, he turns to setting up his own platform on which to base his own movement.
>
> Now, before he could do that, he had to have a following. He had to have people who would lend themselves to this idea. You cannot have great ideas in the abstract. They have to take flesh. They have to take form. Jesus had to have back of him a body of people, however large or small, who would share his ideals, share his convictions, and lend themselves to his movement.[9]

## the network of God

Brian McLaren's term *network of God* works well in this context because it is not identified with a particular people or community but suggests a broad informal global social network like those created today through Internet connectivity. Jesus is reported to have said, "The kingdom of God is spread out upon the earth, and men do not see it."[10]

A modern parallel of this kind of network might be the extraordinary internet community that helped elect Barack Obama to the American presidency. Millions of people, often working in anonymous isolation yet united around a common mission, were able to create astonishing results. In the Arab world, political and social revolutions have been fueled by cell phone and internet connectivity which has produced mass demonstrations for regime change and reform in a matter of hours. The Occupy Wall Street movement in America used the same technological interconnectivity to organize their local and nationwide activities. In nearly every instance, it is difficult to pinpoint a movement leader, and often specific proposals for change are lacking. But these movements all reflect people united with a

---

8. Matthew 4:1–11

9. Jordan and Lee, *Substance of Faith*, 59.

10. Gospel of Thomas 113

vision of a different future. And they are actively working to make it happen, sometimes putting their lives on the line.

Walter Wink described the kingdom of God as *God's domination-free order*. It always stands in opposition to systems of inequality, exploitation, and oppression. Therefore, the people who engage in God's revolutionary activity for a domination-free order can be envisioned as an invisible and intangible global network engaged in small, individual, anonymous actions of compassion, generosity, and justice on a daily basis. But these small acts must be oriented toward fundamental change of the governing system, not just charitable activities toward victims of the status quo. Working toward the realization of the kingdom of God requires a dedicated resistance movement.

## the conspiracy of God

I am beginning to gravitate toward *the conspiracy of God* as a new metaphor for what Jesus was describing, especially in light of his parables of the mustard seed and the leaven. McLaren's metaphors of the *dream* of God (the vision), the *revolution* of God (the activity), and the *network* of God (the people) all come together for me in the *conspiracy* of God. I see the conspiracy of God as the subversive activity of a people focused on Jesus' vision of a better world—a world governed by love.

The word *conspiracy* derives from the same root as *spirit*. The Latin root *spirare* (*spee'-rah-reh*) means *to breathe*. For example, the word *respiration* is *to breathe again* and *inspiration* means *to breathe in*—to be filled with the spirit. To *conspire* normally connotes agreement or unity in an activity, but it literally means *to breathe together*. Those engaged in a conspiracy are so united around an idea or action that they are seen to breathe as one. I believe that Jesus called his followers to engage in a conspiracy of profound personal and social transformation that will undermine the global domination system in every family, town, and nation. And when two or three people engage in this conspiracy, they become co-conspirators in a conspiracy network inaugurated and led by Jesus. He said, "Where two or three are gathered in my name, I am there among them."[11] Jesus suggested that this kind of conspiracy would create a manifestation of his ongoing presence—a sign of resurrection, a sign of new life, a sign of dramatic change in the world.

11. Matthew 18:19

## parables of conspiracy

When Jesus began to teach the people about the kingdom of God, he spoke to them in parables. Two of these parables in particular—the parable of the mustard seed and the parable of the leaven—suggest that the kingdom of God is the radical change that happens when a catalyst acts covertly to transform and disrupt the status quo. In both cases, something small and seemingly insignificant achieves a remarkable end.

Listen first to the analogy of the subversive action of the tiny mustard seed scattered in a well-tended garden and then to the quiet conspiracy of a pinch of leaven as its transforms a large batch of bread dough. This is Luke's version of the first parable:

> *Then he would say, "What is the kingdom of God like? What does it remind me of? It is like a mustard seed that someone took and tossed in the garden. It grew and became a tree, and the birds of the sky roosted in its branches."*[12]

What did this mean to the listeners of Jesus? For centuries, Israel had been on a downhill slide, its kingdom conquered and divided several times over. The Jewish people looked forward to the day when God would act to reverse this trend. They longed for a glorious new age of power and triumph with God's chosen people at the head of the nations. Their poetic metaphor for greatness was the tall cedar of Lebanon, comparable to the huge redwood trees of California. In the popular imagination, Israel would one day be the greatest of all nations just as the great cedar of Lebanon was the greatest of all trees.

Instead, Jesus proposed this parable, "What is the kingdom of God really like? It is like a mustard seed"—proverbially the smallest and most insignificant of all seeds—"that someone took and sowed in his garden."

Some scholars tell us that in first-century Judaism, a mustard plant—which is really no more than a common weed— was forbidden in a household garden because it was fast spreading and would tend to invade a well-tended garden plot. In the Jewish view of the world, order was identified with holiness and disorder with uncleanness. Hence there were very strict rules about what could be planted in a household garden. The rabbinical law of diverse kinds ruled that one could not mix certain plants in the same garden patch. In stating that a man threw a mustard seed into his garden, the hearers are alerted to the fact that he was sowing disorder and subverting rule-based holiness. An image of impurity and disorder thus becomes the starting point for Jesus' vision of the kingdom of God.

12. Luke 13:18–19

In addition, botanically speaking, the mustard plant grows to only about four feet in height. It puts out a few branches. No self-respecting bird would build a nest in this puny shrub.

There are four versions of this parable in the gospels, three in the synoptic gospels (Matthew, Mark, and Luke) and one in the Gospel of Thomas, a sayings gospel discovered seventy years ago in the Egyptian town of Nag Hammadi. In the gospels of Luke and Matthew, contrary to all botanical good sense, the mustard seed turns into a large tree. In Mark's gospel, it turns into the greatest of shrubs. In Thomas's gospel, it turns into a great branch so that many birds can rest in its shade. All of these expectations are contrary to the facts. A mustard seed does not become a tree, nor the greatest of shrubs, nor does it put forth a great branch, however much one may want it to.

Most likely, Jesus described the shrub accurately. But, the gospel writers desired an image of something great. In other words, the myth-creation of the writers subverted the parable. The parable was meant to change one's idea about the nature of the kingdom of God, but what happened was that the old mindset of greatness began to reinterpret the parable to conform to cultural expectations.

According to Jesus, the kingdom of God is like a mustard seed, which some man improperly tossed into his vegetable patch. It soon became an invasive shrub, destroying the well-planned order of the kitchen garden. At best, a few birds found shade under its modest branches. That's all. The parable subverts all the grandiose ideas about what the kingdom of God is going to be like when it finally arrives. It will most likely develop through acts of sabotage and insurrection toward the domination system.

The kingdom of God, according to Jesus, will not fulfill the expectations of those who look for greatness. It is not something impressive and glorious. It is not great and mighty. It will not arrive with fanfare and trumpets. It will simply appear in the midst of ordinary life. And to most people it will be so insignificant that they will not even discern its presence, other than to note that something is messing up the status quo.

Luke's gospel has Jesus describe the imperceptible nature of the kingdom:

> You won't be able to observe the coming of the kingdom of God. People are not going to be able to say, "Look, here it is!" or "Over there!" On the contrary, the kingdom of God is right there in your presence.[13]

13. Luke 17:20–21

The gospel of Thomas has two related sayings:

*It will not come by watching for it. It will not be said, "Look here!"
or "Look there!" Rather the kingdom is spread out upon the earth,
and people don't see it.*[14]
*What you are looking forward to has come, but you don't
know it.*[15]

If we are looking for a great and powerful entity that dominates the earth, we are on the wrong track. This is not Jesus' idea of success. The kingdom of God manifests itself in the modest changes in our attitudes and in the little improvements in our behavior that no one may notice, including ourselves. Our small acts may go unnoticed, but they contribute to something much larger.

Jesus told another parable about the nature of the kingdom:

*The kingdom of God is like yeast that a woman took and concealed in fifty pounds of flour until all of it was all leavened.*[16]

Modern people often think of yeast or leaven in a positive sense—fermentation, new life, and growth. But for the people of Israel, leaven was a symbol of contamination. In ancient times, leaven was made by placing a small lump of dough in a damp, dark place for a few days. As microbes in the air begin a process of fermentation and decay, the dough acquires a sour taste and soon becomes inedible. It is now active leaven. If left longer, it will become rancid and rotten. However, if it is mixed into a new batch of dough, bubbles created by the microbes will cause the bread to rise.

For the Jewish people, both leaven and the process of leavening were symbols of corruption. Leavened bread was a symbol of the unholy, the profane—a sign of everyday life. Unleavened bread was the proper symbol of the holy, the sacred—used to celebrate Passover, the feast of unleavened bread.

In this parable, the leaven is kneaded into a large amount of dough and in time the whole batch becomes leavened. The amount of flour—three measures or fifty pounds—suggests that what is taking place is not just ordinary corruption but monumental corruption. The leaven itself is not visible in the dough, but the effect of its action is gradually noticeable, sometimes taking us by surprise. In this parable Jesus points out that God does not operate in the world by great signs and wonders. God's action in our lives is present in a very real but often hidden way, in ordinary, almost unnoticeable

14. Thomas 113
15. Thomas 51:2
16. Luke 13:20–21

aspects of human life. We are left with the hope of transformation without any noticeable experience of it happening.

The conspiracy of God is revealed in action—the activity of transformative change. It involves simple everyday acts of compassion, acceptance, forgiveness, and service. Every act that weakens the domination system, strengthens the kingdom of God. Through small actions by many people, the world can be transformed. But it is not just about isolated actions of unconnected individuals. It is also about doing things together—community organizing, political action, public demonstrations, and acts of resistance.

Perhaps the best metaphor I can come up with to describe this activity is a small movement at the margins of society prodding the powers and principalities of an unjust world toward transformation. It is a network of people in our communities and around the globe who are connected by a common vision and mission. It begins small, working from the bottom up, but the whole purpose is to effect great change over the lives of many people who are hurting and suffering under the way things are. The kingdom of God is an active conspiracy at the margins of power that intends to subvert and disturb the normalcy of the world by living out a radically transformed lifestyle in its midst. This is what Jesus described in his images of the mustard seed in a well-tended garden, the tiny bit of leaven in a large batch of bread, the pinch of salt which flavors a meal, and the small lamp that provides light in the midst of a great darkness. This is the conspiracy of God.

## the centrality of love

I want to take this conspiracy metaphor another step further. I don't believe that one has to be a Christian to be engaged in the work of the conspiracy of God. After all, the peasants Jesus spoke to in Galilee, Judea, and Samaria were not Christians, and they were the first ones called to the task. The Jewish concept of *tikkun olam*, a Hebrew phrase that means repairing or healing the world, likewise suggests that as humans we have a shared responsibility is to transform the world through social action in the pursuit of social justice. Many other faiths have similar calls to work for a better world. The vision of Jesus requires the involvement of people everywhere—people of every faith and people of no faith at all. The role of the Christian church should be to point toward this great vision and to bear witness to it, but if the church refuses to respond to the kingdom, or tries to domesticate it, or continues to mislead people about its centrality in the message of Jesus, then the conspiracy of God will still move forward without the involvement of the church.

Theologian Harvey Cox (b. 1929) observes that in his experience, people of all faiths are often drawn to Jesus because they find something fascinating and admirable about him—his exemplary courage, his compassion for the disinherited, and his willingness to stand up to corrupt political and religious authorities.

> But, what attracted them more than anything else was his emphasis on the possibility of another kind of world where gentleness and equality prevail... The possibility of "another world" is always the reason many non-Christians give when they ask Christians to "go back to Jesus." This utopian hope, even when modestly expressed, links Jesus and the prophets to a much wider history of human longing. It is the antidote to fatalism and the corrosive fear that there are no antidotes to the status quo.[17]

Cox later states:

> This possible world... suggests that communities of love and reciprocity, forgiveness and compassion are within our grasp, even if they cannot be fully realized.[18]

So, now, I'll push the metaphor even further. In my opinion, one does not even have to believe in God—at least not in the traditional sense of a supernatural being—to be part of the conspiracy of God. A remarkable document in the New Testament—the first letter of John—introduced a completely different way of thinking about God.

> God is love, and he who abides in love abides in God, and God abides in him.[19]

As far as I know, the New Testament has only three definitions for God: God is spirit,[20] God is light,[21] and God is love.[22] The first definition comes from the gospel of John and the second two derive from the First Letter of John. So these metaphors may derive from the same community. But of all these definitions, love represents the highest, deepest, and most

17. Cox, *Future of Faith*, 48.

18. Ibid., 53.

19. 1 John 4:16

20. John 4: 24, "God is spirit, and those who worship him must worship in spirit and truth."

21. 1 John 1:5, "God is light and in him there is no darkness at all."

22. 1 John 4:7–8, "Beloved, let us love one another, because love is from God; everyone who loves is born of God and knows God. Whoever does not love does not know God, for God is love."

powerful force in human life. It is the energy that fosters human growth and change. Love is the impulse behind empathy and concern, and the fuel that drives compassion and justice.

In Greek, *God is love* is *theos ein agapē* (*theh'-ohs ayn ag-ah'-pay*). *Agapē* (*ag-ah'-pay*) is one of four different Greek words which we translate into English as love. *Philia* (*fil-ee'-ah*) refers to loyal friendship or a brotherly love; *eros* (*err'-ohs*) is used to describe passionate erotic or romantic love; and *storgē* (*stor'-gay*) is used in relation to the natural affection of family love, like the love of a parent for a child. But, *agape* implies a *selfless love*, a *self-giving love*, often an *unconditional love*. It is a love directed toward others, putting the needs of others ahead of one's self. This is the kind of love people saw in Jesus. And for the early Christian writers, it described the love of God.

When the Bible declares that God is love, it means that these two language symbols—*God* and *love*—are identical. If God is love, then the converse is also true: Love is god. Therefore, the word *God* is a name we give to the spirit of selfless love found at the depths of our humanity and experienced in the relationship of human love toward one another. Thus *God* can be seen as a language symbol that personifies compassionate love as a divine entity. For millennia, humans have projected this image of God onto a supernatural being. However, according to the First Letter of John, God is not a loving being. God is love itself.

When we say that love is God, the divine is no longer seen as a transcendent reality somewhere outside of the known universe (supernatural theism), nor is God viewed as an impersonal creative reality woven through the fabric of the cosmos (panentheism), but instead God becomes an immanent reality within our hearts, within our minds, within our relationships, and in our actions. Selfless love is a divine reality that animates us, empowers us, and transforms us from self-centered and selfish individuals to self-giving people.

Love, bound up in human flesh, is the manifestation of God in the world. This is another way of looking at divine incarnation. For the early church, Jesus embodied the image of a God of love, revealed in his words and deeds. Therefore, some saw him as the incarnation of God on earth. However, the radical message of the New Testament is that God is no longer an external being who dwells in heaven; God has come to dwell among us, not just in the person of Jesus, but within every human being. Indeed, God has always—and only—been a part of humanity, located deep within human consciousness and projected as a divine actor in the human story. God, in the form of compassionate love, is a latent presence within each of us, but this God remains hidden until humans outwardly express love toward others. Loving one another is the full expression of God on earth.

*No one has seen God, but if we love one another, God lives in us and God's love is brought to full expression in us.*[23]

If you don't believe in the reality of God—particularly in a traditional supernatural theistic image of God—you can still affirm the power of love as a dynamically transformative force in the world. Love changes people, and love has changed societies through nonviolent action for freedom and equality. Whether God is real or imagined, it ultimately makes no difference. Acts of love make the God of love present among us.

This equation of God and love opens up the kingdom of God to everyone, no matter what their image or their understanding or their definition of God, because it can be understood as the kingdom of love, or the reigning of love, or the ruling style of love, or the governing mode of love over against our domination systems. It answers the question "What would the world be like if unselfish love ruled our families, societies, and nations?" The reign of love involves love for the victims of oppression and love toward the perpetrators of injustice. It is a movement of love that wants not only transformation of the system itself, but a transformation of those who control the system.

So, I have now begun to favor the phrase *the conspiracy of love* as a new metaphor for the reign or reigning style of God that comprehends a *vision*, a *transforming activity*, and a *people committed to change*. It suggests that the governing style of love is the vision that guides us, but that the daily work toward that vision is in the form of conspiratorial action. The conspiracy of love is a movement to disturb and confound the domination system and its rampant politics of selfishness with a new possibility—a domination-free society based on love, compassion, equality, and community. That was the message and mission of Jesus.

In *What Would Jesus Deconstruct?* John D. Caputo writes:

> *What then is the kingdom of God? Where is it found? It is found every time an offense is forgiven, every time a stranger is made welcome, every time an enemy is embraced, every time the least of us is lifted up, every time the law is made to serve justice, every time a prophetic voice is raised against injustice, every time the law and the prophets are summed up by love.*[24]

23. 1 John 4:12
24. Caputo, *What Would Jesus Deconstruct?* 138.

God's kingdom is not established by domination, coercion, or violence. It is open to all and is offered as an invitation. But it relies on a profound change of heart and a radical change of life to enter. Entrance requires a change in priorities—from self-interest (What will I eat? What will I drink? What will I wear?)[25]—to a compassionate interest about the least in society (What will they eat? What will they drink? What will they wear?).[26] The kingdom involves feeding the hungry, clothing the naked, visiting the imprisoned, caring for the sick, accepting the unacceptable.

This is the conspiracy of love initiated by Jesus—people of compassion and good will engaged in the unending transformation of themselves, their families, their communities, their nations, and the world at large. This book proposes that the vision of Jesus can best be described in the words of philosopher Charles Eisenstein as "that more beautiful world our hearts know is possible."[27] Not only does Jesus envision a more beautiful world, it is more peaceful and just as well. It promises the poor of the world access to the fundamental means of life—food, clothing, shelter, health care, and education for a better tomorrow.

The conspiracy of love for a better world is not just a Christian pursuit; it is a fundamental human task. Regardless of what happens within institutional Christianity, the call of Jesus reaches out to all people. We are all citizens of the world and we are all in this together.

The good news announced by Jesus is that a vast conspiracy is rising up to challenge the unjust systems of the world. Although a community of *shalom* (*shaw-lome'*)—Hebrew for peace, prosperity, well-being, wholeness, health, and safety—was an integral image woven throughout the Hebrew Bible, Jesus believed it was time to fulfill that ancient dream, and he called the people of his day to engage in the creation of the age-old vision. The task he set before his early followers remains before us today, as urgently as ever. After centuries of obscuring the central message of Jesus, the church founded in his name has a decision to make if it is to survive—commit to the vision of Jesus or get out of the way and leave it to those who stand outside the doors of the sanctuaries.

## a conspiracy of love

In 2012, Cory Booker (b. 1969), the junior Senator from New Jersey and former mayor of Newark, spoke to the graduating class of Stanford University,

25. Matthew 6:25
26. Matthew 25:35–36
27. Eisenstein, *More Beautiful World*, 58.

his alma mater. Booker had played football at Stanford, where he earned a Bachelor of Arts in political science and a Master of Arts in sociology. He then received a Rhodes Scholarship to attend Queens College at Oxford where he earned an honors degree in U.S. history. Finally, he attained a law degree at Yale University. Booker told the students that his success in life was only possible because of a vast "conspiracy of love"—countless acts by countless people who laid the groundwork for his achievements. He described the consistent message he had learned from his father, who at his own graduation said to him,

> Boy, you need to understand that who you are now, you are the physical manifestation of a conspiracy of love. That people whose names you don't even know, who struggled for you, who fought for you, who sweated for you, who volunteered for you—you are here because of them. Do not forget that. [28]

Coming from the African-American community, Booker's parents were well aware of the many sacrifices made by those who went before them and those who walked beside them to transform America into a more just, decent, and humane society. Booker's father realized that a vast conspiracy of love and courage had paved the way for his family to sit at integrated lunch counters, ride in the front of buses, and to have the right to vote. He and others had struggled to overcome barriers and open doors so that his family could attend college, get good jobs, and move into decent neighborhoods with quality schools. Cory Booker was given opportunities that had been denied to others before him. As a young man, he took good advantage of his situation, achieving success in football and in education. But, he said that if he became too proud of his accomplishments, his father would remind him:

> Boy, don't you dare walk around this house like you hit a triple, when you were born on third base! You need to understand something—you drink deeply from wells of freedom and liberty and opportunity that you did not dig. You eat lavishly from banquet tables prepared for you by your ancestors. You sit under the shade of trees that you did not plant or cultivate or care for. You have a choice in life, you can just sit back, getting fat, dumb, and happy, consuming all the blessings put before you, or it can metabolize inside of you, become fuel to get you into the fight, to make this democracy real, to make it true to its words that we can be a nation of liberty and justice for all.[29]

28. Booker, "Conspiracy of Love," 2012.
29. Ibid.

During his final year at Yale, Booker lived in Newark, New Jersey, where he wanted to do legal advocacy work and run for the city council after graduation. There, he met Miss Jones, the tenant leader of a high-rise housing project in a neighborhood filled with poverty, violence, and drugs. She taught him that to make a difference in such a context, one has to see beyond the dark realities of the situation and see the world with the eyes of hope.

> You need to understand something—that the world you see outside of you is a reflection of what you have inside of you. And, if you see only problems and darkness and despair, that's all there's ever gonna be. But, if you're one of those stubborn people who every time you open your eyes, you see hope, opportunity, possibility, love—even the face of God—then you can help me make a change.[30]

Booker eventually moved into the projects himself and as he shared the life of the residents, he witnessed small groups of dedicated people who conspired to improve the life of their community. He observed that these conspirators had three characteristics in common. First, they did not seek a comfortable life, but instead embraced discomfort when it was necessary to make a difference. They got out of their comfort zones and went to where the challenges were. Discomfort is a precondition to service, Booker said. Secondly, these conspirators demonstrated continual faithfulness. In spite of the many challenges they faced, they remained faithful to the task in front of them, day in and day out. They did not succumb to cynicism or despair. They did not let their spirits be crushed by the overwhelming odds that they faced. They faithfully persevered. Finally, the third characteristic of these conspirators is that they showed up.

> They just show up. And what do I mean by that? I mean that we go through life all the time but we don't always show up. We may be there in body but we're not there in spirit. And we begin to erode the truth of who we are, we fail to live our authenticity . . . I've learned that what you think about the world says less about the world than it does about you. And when you show up in this world and have the courage to tell your truth in moments big—but more importantly, in moments small—then you are the architect, not only of your own destiny, but you're the architect of transformational change.[31]

30. Ibid.
31. Ibid.

Booker said that many of the conspirators he encountered had these three characteristics in common. But he added that they could not succeed unless they joined with others to work together for change, often with others who were quite different politically, religiously, and economically. The important thing is to be co-conspirators, working toward the same goal while supporting and encouraging one another. Booker quoted Dr. Martin Luther King, Jr who said that we are caught in an "inescapable network of mutuality, tied in a common garment of destiny that injustice, anywhere, is a threat to justice everywhere."

As he ended his address, Cory Booker challenged the students to become conspirators of love in their own lives.

> Join the conspiracy, and love with all of your heart and all of your courage. Let your love be defiant. Let your love be rebellious. Join the conspiracy and make change in your life because change will not roll in on the wheels of inevitability, it must be carried in on the backs of lovers.[32]

The people that Booker described did not solve world hunger. They did not broker a peace agreement between the Israelis and the Palestinians. They did not even put an end to gang violence in Newark. They simply did what they could in their neighborhood. When they got too frustrated with the conditions of poverty, they cleaned up vacant lots, swept their streets, painted over graffiti, organized activities for children, worked to improve their schools, and comforted victims of violence. These are signs of the presence of the kingdom of God. The vision that Jesus described is all around us and we often do not recognize it, perhaps because we are looking for something glorious, something powerful, something successful.

## small acts of love

I had already crafted the metaphor and decided on the title of this book when I came across Booker's speech. He clarified with real examples what I saw as the essence of following Jesus—seemingly insignificant actions by countless ordinary people that can change the world.

I recently saw this quote from the film *The Hobbit: An Unexpected Journey*—based on J. R. R. Tolkien's book—in which the Lady Galadriel (Cate Blanchett) turns to Gandalf the Wizard (Ian McKellen) and asks "Why the halfling?" She was referring to Bilbo Baggins, a small, comfortable,

32. Ibid.

middle-aged Hobbit chosen by Gandalf to go on a dangerous, seemingly-impossible quest. Gandalf replied:

> *Saruman* [the chief of the Middle Earth wizards] *believes it is only great power that can hold evil in check, but that is not what I have found. I found it is the small everyday deeds of ordinary folk that keep the darkness at bay . . . small acts of kindness and love. Why Bilbo Baggins? I don't know. Perhaps it is because I am afraid and he gives me courage.*[33]

Jesus called people to follow him in a way of living. He did not require his followers to accept a catalog of religious beliefs or adopt a set of spiritual practices. Rather, he offered them a new way to live their daily lives. As a result, the earliest members of the Jesus movement were known simply as followers of the Way. They represented not just *any* way, but a way of life dedicated to selfless love in the midst of a selfish, unjust, and violent world. The way of Jesus puts love for others ahead of one's own ego-centricity, resulting in a lifestyle of compassion toward those in need that sets one apart from societal norms of self-interest, self-concern, and selfishness. The way of Jesus is simply the way of love toward others in the world.

It is time to change our lives and begin transforming our communities at a fundamental level. It is time to save our corner of the world from the reigning spirit of indifference, greed, exclusion, and violence. It is time to assist in the birth of a better world that our hearts know is possible.

> *The decisive time has arrived, for the conspiracy of love is rising up to challenge the unjust systems of the world. Change your whole way of thinking and living, and risk everything for this radical message of hope.*[34]

---

33. Peter Jackson, dir., "The Hobbit: An Unexpected Journey," New Line Cinema, MGM, WingNut Films (2012).

34. My paraphrase of Mark 1:14–15: "Jesus came into Galilee, proclaiming the gospel of God, and saying, 'The time has come, the kingdom of God is at hand; repent and believe in the good news.'" See also Matthew 4:17: "From that time Jesus began to preach, saying, 'Repent, for the kingdom of heaven is at hand.'"

# PART 2

# Jesus and the Christ

CHAPTER 5

# the prophetic Jesus

---

*Learn to do right; seek justice.*
*Defend the oppressed,*
*Take up the cause of the orphan,*
*plead for the widow.*[1]

—The prophet Isaiah

*Blessed are those who hunger and thirst for justice.*[2]

—Jesus of Nazareth

JESUS WAS BORN IN a time of empire and rebellion. First-century Palestine was not a peaceful idyllic setting where Jesus cradled little lambs in his arms, patted children on their heads, and strolled quiet paths with his disciples sermonizing on ethereal ideas. It is misleading to assume that Jesus primarily focused on otherworldly things—inspiring people to make inward decisions affecting their eternal souls and assuring them of a blessed and peaceful life after death. Instead, his mission was about adopting a radically different lifestyle in the present. It centered on economic justice, social cooperation, community inclusion, and nonviolent resistance to domination. And it was framed against a background of economic exploitation and struggle for daily survival.

At the time of Jesus' birth, the Jews of Palestine were a conquered people. For over five hundred years, they had been the victims of empires. First,

1. Isaiah 1:17
2. Matthew 5:6

71

it was Assyria, then Babylon, then Persia, then the Greeks. One great power after another had imposed its will over them. For the past six decades, it had been Rome.

The Romans conquered and colonized Palestine in 63 BCE. In accordance with their policy of appointing native rulers in their colonies, the Roman Senate named Herod, the most powerful claimant, as king of Judea in 37 BCE. Due to the major construction projects he initiated, including the expansion of the massive Temple complex in Jerusalem, Herod became known as Herod the Great. He ruled with political shrewdness and ruthless cruelty. His costly building programs—new cities, palaces, and fortresses— and the tribute he paid to his masters in Rome resulted in increased taxes on the peasants. For poor farmers and fishermen, survival was an enormous struggle to begin with. But now, the economic burden required to support the comforts of the Jewish aristocracy and the greed of the Roman Empire was overwhelming. In 4 BCE, Herod the Great died after 33 years on the throne.

The Roman emperor Augustus divided Herod's kingdom among three of his sons based upon Herod's last will. At age 19, Herod Archelaus was given the largest area, the southern regions of Idumea, Judea, and Samaria, including the city of Jerusalem; 17-year-old Herod Antipas received the non-contiguous central regions of Galilea (Galilee) and Perea; and Herod Philip, just 16 years old, took possession of the northerly regions of Gaulantis, Batanea, Trachonitis, and Auranitis. Herod's sons were not given the title held by their father—that of *basileus* (*bas-il-yooce'*) which is Greek for *king*—instead, Archelaus was called an *ethnarchés* (*eth-nar'-khace*), meaning a *ruler of the people*, and Antipas and Philip were given the lesser title of *tetrarchés* (*tet-rar'-khace*), meaning a *ruler of a quarter*. They were client rulers who represented their patron in Rome.

The claim of Herod Archelaus to Judea was opposed by his brother Herod Antipas—who had been bequeathed that territory in an earlier version of Herod's will—and his claim was supported by many other Jewish leaders who feared Archelaus' reputation for ruthless cruelty. They sent a delegation to Rome to protest his appointment. Herod Archelaus prepared to submit his claim to Caesar Augustus, but before setting out for Rome, he demonstrated his brutal character in an exceptional way. In Jerusalem, during the spring celebration of *Pesach* (*pay'-sahk*) or Passover, commemorating Israel's liberation from slavery in Egypt, crowds became agitated, protesting the oppressive rule of Rome and its client kings. Overlooking the walls of the enlarged Temple compound, Herod the Great had constructed the Antonia fortress—a Roman barracks—for his masters. From its tower, Roman and Herodian troops could observe the temper of the large number of pilgrims who attended the Jewish religious festivals. When an angry crowd began stoning Roman troops during this Passover festival, Herod Archelaus responded with a massive show of force. His infantry and cavalry slaughtered nearly 3,000 people in the city and forced many more into the surrounding hills. This incident provided a trigger for the repressed anger of the Jewish peasantry throughout the region. Archelaus then sailed for Rome, leaving Judea under the control of a Roman proconsul named Sabinus.

At the feast of *Shavuot* (*sha-voo'-ot*), or Pentecost, seven weeks later, thousands of Jewish peasants streamed toward Jerusalem. They besieged the Roman troops in the temple and fortress, clashing with the troops under the Temple porticos. Sabinus, in response, burned the Temple and plundered its treasury, enraging the people. A battle for liberation from Roman rule was fully engaged.

## messianic rebellions

A massive peasant rebellion began in all regions of Herod the Great's territories. Three lower-class leaders arose to lead revolts in the regions of Judea, Perea, and Galilee. Each leader challenged the kingship of Herod's sons as legitimate rulers of the people. Like Saul, David, Jeroboam, and Jehu—all popular leaders of Israel's history—these revolutionaries were acclaimed by their followers as anointed or *messiah* kings.

In Judea, a shepherd named Athronges and his four brothers led an armed band of guerrilla fighters against the forces of Herod Archelaus and his Roman overlords. Athronges declared himself as "king of the Jews" and successfully waged war against the Romans for a long period.

Herod Antipas was faced with two rebellions. In Perea, a former royal servant named Simon was proclaimed king by his followers and led a revolt against the royal palaces and estates of the wealthy. In Galilee, the rebellion was led by a tall, handsome man named Judas. He was the son of Ezekias, a popular bandit hero who had been executed by Herod the Great forty years earlier. The revolt in Galilee centered on Sepphoris (*sef'-uh-ris*), a walled city of about 30,000 people that served as the center of Roman government in that region. Judas and his followers attacked the city, armed themselves from Herod's arsenal, and looted the royal palace. A Pharisee named Zadok joined forces with Judas to create a revolutionary party known as the Zealots. The Roman garrison located at Caesarea Maritima on the Mediterranean coast of Galilee could not put down the popular uprising.

Relief came from Syria to the north where Publius Quinctilius Varus (46 BCE – 9 CE) ruled as the Roman governor. Known for his harsh rule and high taxes, Varus led three Roman legions (18,000 troops) to quell the rebellion.[3] He marched south through the country, methodically subduing the peasant revolutionaries. Finally, outside the walls of Jerusalem, he crucified 2,000 of the rebels as a warning. Crucifixion was the method of capital punishment that the Romans reserved for the lower classes—for rebellious peasants and slaves. The bodies were left on the crosses to rot and be scavenged by birds and dogs. The 2,000 crosses were a sign to the populace of the awesome power of Rome. In Galilee, the Romans burned the capital city of Sepphoris (*sef'-uh-ris*) and took all of its inhabitants into slavery.[4]

In Rome, Augustus Caesar approved Herod Archelaus' rule in Judea—at least for the moment—but nine years later in 6 CE, Caesar removed him from the throne and formed the Province of Judea under direct Roman rule. The Judean province became a satellite of the Province of Syria, and was therefore ruled by a procurator, not a governor. The capital of Judea was established at the city of Caesarea Maritima on the Mediterranean coast. Two decades later, Pontius Pilate was appointed as the fifth procurator of Judea, ruling the territory with an iron fist from 26 to 36 CE.

## a child is born

Just four miles south of the destroyed city of Sepphoris, across a fertile valley and up in the rolling hills of the Galilee highlands, lay the small village of Nazareth. There, in the midst of this armed conflict and tension, Jesus was born to a poor peasant family. Rebellions and crucifixions were the bookends of his life.

We do not know exactly when Jesus was born. Scholars cannot specifically place the month or year. He was most likely born sometime before the spring of 4 BCE when Herod the Great died. (That would make him about ten years old when the census of Quirinius occurred in 6 CE, which is the date Luke proposes for his birth. Matthew's gospel places Jesus' birth while Herod the Great still ruled. If Matthew is to be believed about Herod slaughtering male infants up to two years old in Bethlehem, Jesus could presumably be born as early as 6 BCE, putting a 12-year discrepancy (6 BCE in Matthew and 6 CE in Luke) as to the birth year of Jesus.

---

3. Publius Quinctilius Varus is mostly known to history due to a massive military defeat. In 9 CE, he lost three Roman legions and his own life in the Battle of the Teutoburg Forest against Germanic tribes.

4. Although Josephus reports this event, archeologists have not confirmed the destruction and burning.

In spite of what Matthew and Luke contend, Jesus was probably born in the village of *Natzeret* (*nat-zehr'-et*) or Nazareth, not in the village of *Beit-Lechem* (*bate-leck'-em*) or Bethlehem that was located five miles south of Jerusalem. Situated in the region of Galilee, Nazareth was a small community nestled in a hollow in the hills at the site of an ancient spring. It was surrounded by olive orchards and cypress trees. Archeological evidence suggests that the village was less than 200 years old in the first century. It stood at an elevation of about 1,200 feet and commanded a panoramic view of its small corner of the world. Its population was probably just over 200 people.

Jesus was probably the first child of an itinerant construction worker named *Yosef* (*yo-safe'*)—Joseph in English—and his wife *Miyram* (*meer-yawm'*)—Miriam or Mary. When Yosef had Jesus circumcised, eight days after birth, he named his son after Moses' successor, Joshua. In Hebrew and Aramaic, the name is *Yehoshu'a* (*yeh-ho-shoo'-ah*), which means "Yahweh helps" or "Yahweh saves" or "Yahweh is salvation." In those days the name was usually shortened to *Yeshu'a* (*yeh-shoo'-ah*) or even to *Yeshu* (*yeh-shoo'*), which is how Jesus was popularly known. The Hebrew Bible records Joshua as a mighty warrior who led the destruction of the city of Jericho and defeated the Canaanites by convincing God to halt the sun's passage in the sky and send hail upon his enemies to turn the tide of battle. Yeshu was a common name in the first century. To the Jews, the name meant salvation, liberation, and possession of land.

## domination

As he grew into manhood, Jesus experienced three despotic structures of government organized for a privileged few at the expense of the common good of the majority. Galilee was a monarchy ruled by Herod Antipas. After the removal of his brother Herod Archelaus by Rome in 6 CE, Judea was ruled directly by a Roman Procurator who reported to the governor of Syria. However, the day-to-day operations were entrusted to a wealthy oligarchy (meaning *the ruling few*) of the Sadducees (*sad'-dzhoo-seez*), sometimes referred to in the gospels as "the leaders of the people," or "the chief priests and the elders." In conquered territories, it was always Rome's practice to find indigenous collaborators to rule on their behalf. And they always chose people from the wealthy class who saw it in their personal interest to support power when it advantaged them. On top of these structures was an emperor in Rome who was essentially a self-appointed dictator. So Jesus was confronted by a monarchy in Galilee, an oligarchy in Jerusalem, and a dictatorship in Rome.

People living under the oppression of a domination system generally respond to the situation in one of four ways. They may become part of the establishment; but that course is only available to a few of the most wealthy and powerful. They may simply try to cope or compromise to some degree with the ruling authorities—go along to get along—in order to survive. Others may emigrate or withdraw from society in isolated communities. The fourth option is to take up arms and revolt. The people of first-century Palestine certainly fit this pattern of multiple responses. There were several different influential groups or parties active in the culture: Sadducees (establishment), Pharisees (compromise), Essenes (withdrawal), Zealots (revolution). Except for the Sadducees, the other three groups all hoped for a political savior to drive out Rome and set up a new rule.

These parties were notable factions with various political impacts, but they represented only a small minority of the population. Except for the Zealots, they were mostly composed of more-or-less literate elites who had the luxury of engaging in overt positions of political and religious co-operation or opposition. The majority of the people were subjugated and defeated peasants who were buffeted by political winds and degraded by poverty. They just tried to survive until events pushed them to the point of subversive action and rebellion. According to the Talmud, these uneducated peasants were commonly known as *am ha'aretz* (*ahm hah-ahr'-etz*), meaning *the people of the land*. This was a derogatory term suggesting that they were ignorant and uneducated rubes. In John's gospel, they are referred to as the "rabble who know nothing about the law."[5] The peasants found it hard to make any significant response to oppression when they were trying to eke out an existence from the land. But as some saw their lives spiral out of control and they lost lands, homes, and employment, violent rebellion must have been a tempting option. Jesus was born into this class of peasants.

## exploitation

In an agricultural economy, land is the only real source of wealth. The Hebrew people considered the land of Palestine to be a gift from God. The stories of the Hebrew Bible recount the invasion and conquest of the land under the leadership of Joshua and the subsequent division of the land among the twelve tribes and their families. The land was considered a patrimony to be passed down from generation to generation. Inherited land was not to be sold, since the land belonged to God alone. However, land could be lost through indebtedness. The misfortunes of illness and drought, or the

5. John 7:49

flaw of personal failings, could result in the need to borrow money against the land. Foreclosure by lenders was a tool commonly used to extend the property holdings of the wealthy. The pervasiveness of indebtedness was a major issue for first-century Jewish peasants.

By the first century, the globalization of empire was transforming the economic landscape. The Roman economy of commercialized agriculture was impoverishing the peasants of Palestine at an alarming rate. For centuries, the Hebrews had a traditional agrarian economy, raising sustenance crops on small farms. In this type of economy, the Hebrew elites who lived in the cities and who controlled the Jerusalem Temple took about 30 to 50 percent of agricultural production from the peasants in the form of religious tithes and political taxes. But when the Romans introduced commercialized agriculture, the elites took the land itself. Commercialized agriculture depends upon consolidation of farms and pastures into large estates, so that agricultural production becomes more efficient. The benefits go to a small number of wealthy landowners in greatly increased profits, resulting in a luxurious lifestyle at the expense of those who work the land as tenants.

The wealthy elites needed cash to support their lifestyles, so they looked for agricultural exports that could be traded in the economy of the wider Roman Empire. They converted small farms into extensive vineyard estates and shipped wine back to Rome. Only the rich had the means to establish large vineyards because they required tending for at least three years before they produced a usable crop.

When peasants no longer possess their own land, they cannot grow food for their own subsistence. As a result, they must work for wages to buy the food they need. But a commercialized agricultural economy does not support as many people as a traditional one. It creates a large class of expendables, people who are simply superfluous to the economic system and who must compete with one another for meager resources. Large numbers of peasants were forced to become bandits and armed revolutionaries out of desperation.

Freshwater fishing was also becoming commercialized under Rome. Archeologists have discovered the ruins of fish processing plants around the Sea of Galilee. In these facilities, fish was either salted or pickled, or prepared into a kind of salsa for shipment to Roman markets. The commerce was again controlled by wealthy elites who controlled the market for fish and set prices.

The poor fishermen and agricultural laborers to whom Jesus spoke were faced with these dehumanizing realities. They needed some good news because all the news they had was increasingly bad and getting worse.

## the wilderness prophet

The years during which Jesus preached—perhaps somewhere between 24 and 30 CE—were moments of relative calm at the eye of a political hurricane. Jesus lived in a time between rebellions. But the pot was simmering. This was the seething social context when Jesus met the wilderness preacher known as *Yohanan* (*yo-haw-nawn'*) or *Yochanan* (*yo-khaw-nawn'*) *ben Zkaryah* (*bane zek-ar-yaw'*)—John, the son of Zechariah—whom we know as John the Baptizer.

Matthew's gospel tells us that it was John the Baptizer who introduced Jesus to the message of the kingdom of God.

> *In those days John the Baptist appeared in the wilderness of Judea, proclaiming, "Repent, for the kingdom of God is at hand."*[6]

John's prophetic message was a simple one: God was angry with the chosen people and planned to punish them, unless a dramatic change took place. The Hebrew Bible declared that God had acted previously in Jewish history using the armies of foreign empires as God's means of national punishment. God's anger was not due to individual sins, or even over a nation that had turned away from the worship of God. Instead, John declared that the issue that angered God was a lack of social justice, as prophets of earlier times had also proclaimed. John was a social prophet in a long line of social prophets who called the nation of Israel to reaffirm the just society required by their covenant with God.

Peasants were losing their land. Poor people were going hungry. Children were suffering from illness and deprivation and many were without adequate clothing. In a dog-eat-dog society, people refused to help one another in the face of desperate circumstances. Those who had more simply congratulated themselves, closed their eyes, ears, and hearts, and were indifferent to the needs of those who had less. It was an oppressive and unjust society with no system of communal support for those who suffered the most. Judean society exhibited a disregard of the ancient covenant of a contrast society, no commitment to the common good, no obligation to being one's brother's or sister's keeper.

In John's vision, God's judgment would bring massive destruction. John pictured these events as a great forest fire before which the snakes of the forest flee, in which trees and chaff are burnt, and in which people are engulfed in a baptism of fire.[7] He also made use of the metaphors of the

6. Matthew 3:1
7. Matthew 3:8–11

axe and the winnowing fan used to separate wheat from chaff. There is no reason to think that John was referring to a burning hell in the afterlife. The forest fire he described is an image of hell on earth. He foresaw not the cataclysmic end of the entire world, but the Roman destruction of Jewish life, culture, and political hopes in Palestine.

It did not take special insight to see that the Jewish people were on the verge of a suicidal uprising against the Roman Empire. Recurring episodes of violence were leading toward a dramatic confrontation with the most powerful military force on earth. The shadow of catastrophe hung over the land and the signs could be clearly seen for those who paused long enough to read them.

Change or be destroyed, John cried. When confronted with John's dramatic words of impending doom and a call to personal conversion, the people asked, "What then shall we do?" John's response was that religious rituals could not save them. Only acts of charity and justice could avert God's anger and wrath.

> And the crowds asked him, "What then should we do?" In reply he said to them, "whoever has two coats must share with anyone who has none; and whoever has food must do likewise." Even tax collectors came to be baptized, and they asked him, "Teacher, what should we do?" He said to them, "Collect no more than the amount prescribed for you." Soldiers also asked him, "And we, what should we do?" He said to them, "Do not extort money from anyone by threats or false accusation, and be satisfied with your wages."[8]

These are the words of charity that John addressed to those who came to hear his message. But the call for justice was addressed to others who were far away, living in luxurious homes and palaces. In Jerusalem, it was the Sadducees and the aristocratic families they represented who needed to change. Closer to hand, it was Herod Antipas, the ruler of Galilee and Perea, who required a new heart. John believed that it was these uncaring rulers of the people and their economic system of domination that must embrace justice for the poor to forestall a simmering peasant rebellion and a massive Roman military suppression.

Jesus was attracted to the message of John the Baptizer. He traveled to the Judean wilderness along the Jordan River where he was baptized by John and became one of his disciples. While camping nearby, he met several others who were attracted to John: Simon Peter, Andrew, Philip, and Nathanael. They would soon become followers of Jesus.

---

8. Luke 3:10–14

When John began to criticize the aristocracy, Herod Antipas arrested him and had him beheaded. The Jewish historian Titus Flavius Josephus (37–100) wrote: "Herod, who feared lest the great influence John had over the people might put it into his power and inclination to raise a rebellion, (for they seemed ready to do anything he should advise,) thought it best, by putting him to death."

## Jesus, the prophet of justice and hope

After John's arrest and execution, Jesus picked up the mantle of leadership from his mentor. He not only carried on John's message of the kingdom of God, but it became the center of his message and mission.

> *Now after John was arrested, Jesus came to Galilee, proclaiming the good news of God, and saying, "The time is fulfilled, and the kingdom of God has come near; transform your lives, and trust in the good news."*[9]

As he carried on John's work, Jesus began to form a new vision. John was right, of course. If the situation did not change drastically, many people would lose their lives in a futile struggle against the power of Rome. The suffering of many poor and oppressed peasants would only increase. The institutions and culture of the Jewish people would be wiped out and replaced with Greek culture and Roman institutions. And the worship of Yahweh would be replaced by or absorbed into the pantheon of Roman gods.

Unlike John, Jesus did not feel called to save Israel by bringing everyone to a baptism of repentance in the Jordan. He decided that something else was necessary, something that had to do with the poor, the sinners, and the sick—the peasants who were the lost sheep of the house of Israel.

It appears that Jesus and John had different images of God. John saw God as a judge who was angry about human injustice. Jesus saw God as a compassionate and nurturing parent who was constantly forgiving and accepting. As a result, Jesus modified John's message of catastrophe. Jesus began to find a new way to address the coming devastation. He developed an alternative vision, a way out, a way to avert violent confrontation.

John preached actions of justice, but with his emphasis on the coming catastrophe, these actions would have been motivated by fear of judgment. Jesus no longer preached John's message of doom. Instead he preached a vision of the way things could be, the way they would be when God's rule was established on earth. Like John's message, it had to do with acts of

---

9. Mark 1:14–15

compassion and justice. But the way of Jesus was based on hope, not fear. Jesus believed that the reign of God operates by invitation, not coercion. Unlike John's vision, which seemed to associate the kingdom of God with judgment, Jesus proclaimed that God's coming reign was "good news."

Jesus suggested that if people would begin living out the just, compassionate, and nonviolent values of God's in-breaking reign today, the inevitable destruction of violent confrontation could be avoided. It was not necessary to eliminate Roman armies to live justly. An armed rebellion would not accomplish the kingdom of God. Jesus now saw clearly the way God's ruling style could be implemented among human societies, and it began with a message of love and compassion for the least in our midst.

Jesus gathered the timeless hopes of humanity for a world of peace, justice, and equality. In words and actions, he demonstrated that the time had come for a new way of living together. The mission Jesus now embarked on was to make his vision of God's new reign clearly visible to the people of his day, and to invite them to enter as participants. John the Baptizer had relied upon a baptism of conversion and expected fruit worthy of that conversion in the lives of his followers. In a similar way, Jesus looked to the transformed lives of individuals to bear fruit in transformed homes, communities, and societies.

## a political vision

If we take our spiritual blinders off for a moment, we can begin to see Jesus in a new light. Imagine him in the context of a struggle for social and economic equality similar to the struggles of Gandhi and M. L. King as they addressed their respective domination systems. According to Luke's gospel, Jesus began with an inaugural speech in Nazareth—his "I have a dream" speech.

> When he came to Nazareth, where he had been brought up, he went to the synagogue on the sabbath day, as was his custom. He stood up to read, and the scroll of the prophet Isaiah was given to him. He unrolled the scroll and found the place where it was written:
>
> The spirit of Yahweh is upon me,
> because he has anointed me
> to bring good news to the poor.
> He has sent me to proclaim release to the captives
> and recovery of sight to the blind,
> to let the oppressed go free,
> to proclaim the year of Yahweh's favor.

*And he rolled up the scroll, gave it back to the attendant, and sat down. The eyes of all in the synagogue were fixed on him. Then he began to say to them, "Today this scripture has been fulfilled in your hearing."*[10]

Jesus announced that he had come to establish the ancient Hebrew concept of the Jubilee year in which the economic debts of the poor were forgiven, debt-slaves were released, and land that had been taken in foreclosure for peasant indebtedness would be returned by rich landowners to the dispossessed. Jubilee offered an economic amnesty for the poor who had lost everything to debt. Jesus essentially announced that he saw himself as an agent for change, transformation, and liberation. Yet he never claimed the messianic role of a military liberator who effects regime change through violence, but rather he established himself as a voice for radical nonviolent social and economic reformation. Jesus proclaimed himself to be a prophet, not a messiah.

When Jesus announced the coming of the kingdom of God, he was announcing a social revolution. Jesus saw himself as the messenger chosen by God to deliver the good news of God's powerful new activity in the world. God's kingdom of justice was coming to replace the authority of ingrained systems of domination. The kingdom of God, as proclaimed by Jesus, was clearly political. Its very name implies the politics of God. So, at the synagogue in Nazareth, Jesus announced he was launching a political movement to bring relief to the suffering and dispossessed peasants and to re-establish God's reign of justice in Roman Palestine.

Jesus was not naïve. He knew that the call for Jubilee restoration would be rejected by the rich and powerful. It had little chance of succeeding if it required the willing participation of those at the top of society. So he addressed the domination system in a different way—a revolutionary way of living by those at the bottom of society. Jesus rejected the politics of violent revolution. Instead, he developed a nonviolent approach. He would not try to overthrow the kings and oligarchs. Instead, he and his followers would create alternative communities—a new social order in the midst of the old. And, Jesus taught, the kingdom of God was beginning immediately, starting with powerless groups at the bottom of society. The poor and the outcasts

10. Luke 4:16–21. The liberty that Luke takes with the Isaiah text is interesting. Of course, the anonymous author who wrote the gospel attributed to Luke was not an eye witness to the event, if it even happened. In first-century Palestine, nearly all people of the peasant class were illiterate, so it is unlikely that Jesus could read the text of Isaiah. It is estimated that perhaps only 3 percent of the population could read and write. Everyone else lived and learned in an oral culture where memory transmits the essence of a text, not a literal word for word rendition.

THE PROPHETIC JESUS 83

would model life in the kingdom of God for the wealthy and powerful. The least would be the greatest in the kingdom, the last in this world would be the first to arrive. The poor would welcome the change, but the wealthy would not.

> Then he looked up at his disciples and said: "Blessed are you who are poor, for yours is the kingdom of God. Blessed are you who are hungry now, for you will be filled. Blessed are you who weep now, for you will laugh . . . But woe to you who are rich, for you have received your consolation. Woe to you who are full now, for you will be hungry. Woe to you who are laughing now, for you will mourn and weep."[11]

## a movement for change

Jesus quickly formed a political movement to create an alternative social reality. The coming of God's new social order requires a committed people with a new vision and new values. The founding of a new social reality is not a threat to the status quo when it is only a vision in the head of one person. Jesus knew that his call for Jubilee economic redistribution would threaten the rich and powerful, and would likely result in a violent reaction. He also knew that it would be relatively easy to silence a single voice. But a movement empowered by a shared vision is much more difficult to stop. When a movement galvanizes the hopes and aspirations of a larger community, authorities begin to worry. Movements can quickly get out of control.

Jesus gathered a core team of 82 disciples, with twelve in a leadership role. (Imagine King's Southern Christian Leadership Council.) Then he sent 70 of them out to the villages and towns of Galilee to prepare for his forthcoming political campaign tour to engage the peasants in a grassroots effort of social change. In Luke's gospel we read,

> After this the Lord appointed seventy others and sent them on ahead of him in pairs to every town and place where he himself intended to go. He said to them . . . "Whenever you enter a town and its people welcome you, eat what is set before you; cure the sick who are there, and say to them, 'The kingdom of God has come near to you.'"[12]

11. Luke 6:17–25
12. Luke 10:1–9

Sharing food, healing the sick, and announcing the kingdom of God: these were the three assignments to the disciples as they carried the Jesus movement to the villages and towns of Galilee.

The message they shared was that God's economic justice was arriving, and it was important for every individual to get on board. How? By living out the vision of a new economic and political reality immediately. Jesus taught his followers to trust God, to create a compassionate community to provide for each other's needs, and to respond when called upon to care for and share their resources with their brothers and sisters. He taught his followers to reject selfish concerns and to pray for sufficiency—just enough for tomorrow, "our daily bread." The kingdom of God creates a social safety net for the poor, the hungry, and the homeless. The community that gathered around Jesus formed what is known as a "fictive family," not connected by blood ties, but by a common vision. Jesus claimed that they were now his new brothers and sisters—no longer friends, acquaintances, or neighbors, but family.

Jesus began to model the new society for his followers and critics. For Jesus, the beginning of community was the sharing of food. But Jesus emphasized that the sharing of meals was intended to go beyond close family and friends. His table fellowship included the outsider and the marginalized, the despised and those who are socially-defined enemies. Since Jesus had no home, no wealth, no banquet table, and no food to offer, he modeled inclusive table fellowship by publicly accepting invitations to dinner from others—often from those considered "sinful" people.

Jesus began to teach others the ways in which the kingdom of God would be radically different from normal society. Love and compassion were at the center of his political reality.

> I say to you that listen, love your enemies, do good to those who hate you, bless those who curse you, pray for those who abuse you. If anyone strikes you on the cheek, offer the other also; and from anyone who takes away your coat do not withhold even your shirt. Give to everyone who begs from you; and if anyone takes away your goods, do not ask for them again. Do to others as you would have them do to you.[13]

13. Luke 6:27–31

## the march to Jerusalem

According to the synoptic gospels (Matthew, Mark, and Luke), sometime in his third year of healing and teaching in Galilee, after building the core of his movement, Jesus set his sights on Jerusalem in Judea. He decided to go here to confront the Sadducees—the rich and powerful rulers of the people—at their symbolic seat of power. He would interrupt the operations of the Jerusalem Temple with a popular demonstration for economic justice.

Jesus clearly understood that arrest and death are always potential and likely consequences of the pursuit of justice in an unjust society. He cautioned his followers that in order to follow him, they must be willing to risk public execution on a cross—the penalty for civil disobedience and insurrection by common people. It was a time of decision. Jesus was heading towards a confrontation with power that risked his life and the lives of his followers.

Jesus' entry into the city on the Sunday before Passover was a noisy demonstration that attracted wide attention. According to Mark's story, Jesus was hailed as a messiah with leafy branches cut from date palm trees and strewn in his path.

> Then those who went ahead and those who followed were shouting, "Hosanna!"[14]

Hosanna was originally a Hebrew cry for help meaning "save us now!" As an exclamation of adoration it became more of an expression of thanks— "our salvation has arrived!"

On Monday morning, Jesus headed straight for the Temple and created a public disturbance in the Court of the Gentiles in full view of the Sadducees and the Roman garrison in the Antonia Fortress. The earliest gospel recounts the episode this way:

> And he entered the temple and began to drive out those who were selling and those who were buying in the temple, and he overturned the tables of the money-changers and the seats of those who sold doves; and he would not allow anyone to carry anything through the temple. He was teaching and saying, "Is it not written, 'My house shall be called a house of prayer for all the nations'? But you have made it a den of robbers."[15]

On the surface, Jesus seems angered about commerce in the Temple precincts. Some interpreters think that Jesus disapproved of the Temple's

14. Mark 11:9
15. Mark 11:15–17

use of animal sacrifice. Still others believe that his demonstration was against the Temple as a symbol of the Jewish religion itself, as if Jesus was rejecting the religion he was raised in and was replacing it with a new one based on himself as the center of devotion. But most likely, this demonstration at the Temple was a demonstration against the people who managed it and benefited from it—the Sadducees,

The Sadducees were a small group of affluent aristocratic families that formed the ruling upper class in Judea. They were enormously wealthy and lived in great luxury and splendor. Included in their ranks were the high priests of the Jerusalem Temple and a few families of great political influence. The chief priests lived off a Temple tax and the tithes collected from the peasants. By the first century, the lay nobility in Jerusalem had gained ownership of much of the arable land in Judea and other regions—the key to wealth in that agrarian economy.[16] Together with the chief priests, they were in charge of the Temple treasury—essentially the national bank. Thus, they controlled the entire economy. Members of the elite Sadducee party also formed the *Sanhedrin* (*san-hee'-drin*), the high court and legislative body of the Jewish people. Although Judea was now ruled by a Roman procurator, the day to day operations were entrusted to this wealthy oligarchy (*ruling few*) of the Sadducees.

The Sadducees were given a free hand to rule the local population as long as they were loyal to Rome, maintained order, and collected the tribute due to the emperor. They cooperated closely with the Roman governor and kept a tight lid on any potential liberation movements in the country that might threaten the status quo and their own privileged positions. There is no question that the Temple was an instrument of the state as was the case in any other ancient temple-state where priest and king are allied.

Peasant indebtedness was the tool by which the wealthy acquired land for their large estates. Small farmers needed money, not crops, to pay the taxes collected by both temple and state. During times of drought or poor harvests, they were often forced to borrow from the wealthy elites who loaned money to them at interest, which was a clear violation of the traditional Hebraic laws.[17] Their patrimonial land was often given as collateral on these loans. When the farmers could not pay their debts, their property was taken from them. The debt records for all of these transactions were kept by the elites in the Jerusalem Temple, providing us with a clue to

---

16. Nolan, *Jesus Before Christianity*, 27. Also, Jeremias, *Jerusalem in the Time of Jesus*, 147–232.

17. Exodus 22:25, Leviticus 25:37, Deuteronomy 23:19–20

Jesus' angry criticism of those who controlled the temple precincts when he entered it.

All of the objects of Jesus' anger in his demonstration were legitimate operations in the huge Court of the Gentiles that surrounded the central areas reserved for Israelite women, men, and priests alone. The Temple required bird and animal sellers on site so that pilgrims would be able to offer sacrifices that were ritually acceptable. Money changers were required to change foreign currencies into the approved coinage for payment of the temple tax. Jesus upset these operations by driving out those who were selling and buying and not allowing "anyone to carry anything through the temple." But the real objects of his protest were not low level functionaries.

We are told that Jesus addressed the crowds in the Temple with these words:

> Don't the scriptures say, "My house is to be regarded as a house of prayer for all peoples"? But you have turned it into a hideout for crooks.[18]

Jesus was not condemning the Temple as a place of robbery, but as a hideout for the robbers. A den is not where the robbers rob, it is the place where they count their ill-gotten gains. It was not a few moneychangers or dove sellers who were the target of Jesus anger, but the thieves, robbers, and brigands at the top levels of society who perpetuated a system of economic injustice, who robbed people of their land, their wealth, and their livelihoods. But the governing Sadducees understood his message clearly.

The Sadducees had decided that they needed to shut Jesus up before he instigated a rebellion, either violent or nonviolent.

> So the chief priests and the Pharisees called a meeting of the council, and said, "What are we to do? This man is performing many signs. If we let him go on like this, everyone will believe in him, and the Romans will come and destroy both our holy place and our nation." But one of them, Caiaphas, who was high priest that year, said to them, "You know nothing at all! You do not understand that it is better for you to have one man die for the people than to have the whole nation destroyed." . . . So from that day on they planned to put him to death.[19]

When Jesus was arrested late on Thursday night and brought before the chief priest on Friday morning, the Sadducees sought evidence for a capital crime. The chief priest asked Jesus if he was the messiah—a warrior

18. Mark 11:17 (Scholars Version)
19. John 11:47–53

king intending a violent revolution. When brought before Pilate, Jesus was asked if he claimed to be king of the Jews. In both cases, Jesus turned the accusations back on the accusers and never answered directly. He was charged by the Sadducees with blasphemy, but Rome executed him for sedition. On the cross was a sign that listed his anti-government crime—king of the Jews. The cruelty of his crucifixion revealed what imperial authorities do to one who attempts to subvert the domination system. For those who witnessed this event, the cross was not a symbol of divine sacrifice or the taking on of unmerited suffering—it was the price of resistance to the social and economic devastation of empire.

Six agonizing hours after his crucifixion began, on a spring afternoon in the year 30 CE, Jesus died. His heart stopped beating and his brainwave activity ceased. The spirit of life that had animated him at birth, left his body. The biblical tradition says that the body was then removed from the cross and placed in a tomb, sealed with a large stone. But, the Roman practice of crucifixion did not usually allow for burial. The corpses of lower class criminals or revolutionaries were not buried. Instead, the naked bodies of crucified victims were left hanging on the cross, to rot as they were exposed to the elements, and be eaten by carrion, a meal for crows and hungry dogs. In any event—whether he was left on the cross or buried in a tomb—we simply do not know what eventually became of Jesus' corpse. In the gospel accounts, the women who went to the tomb on Easter morning were unable to find it. It was never seen again. The earthly Jesus, the pre-Easter Jesus, was gone from history. But he was not to be forgotten.

## the resurrection as an uprising

The resurrection accounts of Jesus in the New Testament are not stories about a resuscitated corpse. What the first disciples of Jesus experienced was far more than an earthly body that was revived. What they experienced was something completely new and different. The resurrection was a mystical experience of the living presence of Jesus among those who knew him, loved him, and followed him.

The wealthy and powerful thought that the execution of Jesus would eliminate the threat he posed. But the movement he created did not end with his death. In a very real sense, Jesus was resurrected in the people who believed in his message of hope and justice and who followed his example. They felt his presence among them, and this presence gave them the courage to transform their lives with passion, zeal, and courage for the sake of the world. They began a small but passionate uprising in the confident hope that they could create a better world. Clarence Jordan (1912–1969), a New Testament scholar and translator of the "Cotton Patch Gospels" once wrote:

> *The proof that God raised Jesus from the dead is not the empty tomb, but the full hearts of his transformed disciples. The crowning evidence that he lives is not a vacant grave, but a spirit-filled fellowship; not a rolled-away stone, but a carried-away church.*[20]

The political nature of the Jesus movement and its threat to the status quo of empire is unmistakable. Blasphemy and sedition were frequent charges aimed at the followers of Jesus in the first three centuries after his death and capital punishment was the fate of many of the key leaders of the movement. According to tradition, Peter was crucified in Rome and Paul was beheaded there by the emperor Nero (37–68). The Jewish historian Josephus (37–100) reports that Jesus' brother James (the Just) was stoned to death by Temple authorities in Jerusalem. Legends reported by Christian historians Hippolytus of Rome (170–235) and Eusebius (263–339) say that four other disciples met similar fates: Andrew and Bartholomew were crucified, Stephen was stoned, and James, the son of Zebedee was beheaded. Something was going on in the early Jesus movement that clearly threatened authorities of the domination system.

## the political stance of Jesus

So, did Jesus have a particular political stance? I think that if one reads the gospels in the context I have just described, the answer is "yes." The kingdom of God that Jesus announced is a political reality that is meant to be lived in the present. This is the core of the gospel *of* Jesus. But the gospel *about* Jesus declares all of this to be irrelevant. For in that gospel, it is only what happened that fateful weekend in Jerusalem that really matters: Jesus was crucified for our sins, not for his dedication to a cause.

It is wrong to simply view Jesus as a spiritual savior with a heavenly goal. He was concerned about our lives in the here and now, not in the hereafter. He had a political vision for how society should be structured and what values it should embody. He taught about the coming new reality and he modeled it in his own life. He created a movement to carry it on after his death, and the early church continued to live out his vision of communities of sharing and equality for many decades, perhaps even centuries, after his crucifixion.

20. Jordan and Lee, *The Substance of Faith*, 29.

When Jesus announced the kingdom of God, he was putting forth a vision of a world governed by love—more peaceful, more compassionate, more equitable, and more just. Planted deep in our hearts, this dream defines our mission as followers of Jesus. We are called to transform the hearts, minds, and politics of our cities and towns, our states and nations, and the entire global community so that children everywhere will be fed, clothed, healed, and educated.

# CHAPTER 6

# the apocalyptic Christ

---

*And on the way Jesus asked them, "Who do people say I am?"*
*And they answered him, "John the Baptist; and others, Elijah;*
*and still others, one of the prophets."*
*Jesus asked them, "But who do you say I am?"*
*Peter answered and said, "You are the Logos, existing in the*
*Father as His rationality and then, by an act of His will, being*
*generated, in consideration of the various functions by which God*
*is related to his creation, but only on the fact that Scripture speaks*
*of a Father, and a Son, and a Holy Spirit, each member of the*
*Trinity being co-equal with every other member, and each acting*
*inseparably with and interpenetrating every other member, with*
*only an economic subordination within God, but causing no divi-*
*sion which would make the substance no longer simple."*
*And Jesus said, "What?"*[1]

OUTSIDE OF PALESTINE, a dramatic transformation of Jesus began within a few years after his crucifixion. Greek-speaking Jewish communities of the Jesus movement began shifting their attention away from the teachings of Jesus and focused instead on the significance of his death. Spreading quickly through the Mediterranean trading cities of the empire among Jews and Gentiles who were attracted to Judaism, this Hellenistic Christ cult soon became the predominant form of the growing faith.

Beginning just a few years after the death of Jesus—most likely in Antioch in northern Syria—a religious cult began to develop around the figure of Jesus as the *Christ*.[2] The book of Acts records:

1. Commonly-used joke for Trinity Sunday, source unknown. I have been unable to trace this particular trinitarian formula.

2. Mack, *Who Wrote the New Testament?* 75. Burton Mack believes that the transformation of the Jesus movement into the Christ cult most probably began in Antioch and then spread through Asia Minor into Greece. The *Acts of the Apostles* indicates that

*It was in Antioch that the disciples were first called "Christians."*[3]

These Greek-speaking Christians were convinced that Jesus had been transformed at death into a divine spiritual presence. They developed rudimentary theological formulas, rituals, prayers, and hymns that they shared when they gathered together in the name of Jesus, the Christ.

In Damascus in southern Syria, a young Hellenistic Jew named Saul of Tarsus—soon to be known as the Apostle Paul—was introduced to this strain of Christianity. He later shared what he had learned from these communities in his letter to the church at Corinth in Greece:

> *For I handed on to you as of first importance what I in turn had received: that Christ died for our sins in accordance with the scriptures, and that he was buried, and that he was raised on the third day in accordance with the scriptures, and that he appeared to Cephas [Peter], then to the twelve. Then he appeared to more than five hundred brothers and sisters at one time, most of whom are still alive, though some have fallen asleep. Then he appeared to James, then to all the apostles. Last of all, as to someone untimely born, he appeared also to me.*[4]

These Hellenistic Christians began to praise Jesus in worship. It was here that the first creed, "Jesus is Lord"—*Iésous kurios* (*ee-ay-sooce' koo'-ree-os*)—was proclaimed. In antiquity, the term *lord* (*kurios*) was a courtesy title for social superiors, but its root meaning was *ruler*. This creed was a counter-cultural and insurrectionist statement within the Roman Empire where all citizens were required to confess that "Caesar is Lord"—*kaisar kurios* (*kah'-ee-sar koo'-ree-os*). Claiming Jesus as their lord was a rebellious statement of shifting political allegiances. As a result, these emerging Christian communities were viewed with suspicion as atheists and traitors by Roman authorities. For the high priest in Jerusalem, the followers of Jesus needed to be weeded out in order to suppress potential rebellion and keep the peace. The Sadducees thought that Jesus had been dealt with effectively. Now, it appeared that he was being viewed as a martyr by a newly emerging cult. Saul had been one of those appointed to the task of arresting the ringleaders. Instead, he became fascinated by possibilities of their faith, especially their image of a dying and rising messiah.

---

Saul went to Syria to persecute the followers of Jesus. It was on the road to Damascus that he had his epiphany and began his transformation into the Apostle Paul. So Hellenized Roman Syria was probably the breeding ground of the Christ cult.

3. Acts 11:26

4. 1 Corinthians 15:3–8

Paul spent three years immersed in learning and contemplating the ideas of this cult, both in Damascus and in the Arabian Desert. During this period, he reflected on the implications of the death and resurrection of Jesus in the context of the popular Greek mystery religions that attracted many people throughout the Roman Empire. Cults from Greece, Asia Minor, Egypt, and Persia focused on the death and rebirth myths of Demeter, Orpheus, Dionysus, Adonis, Cybele, Osiris, and Mithras. Central to each of these mystery religions was a symbolic reenactment of the natural cycle of growth, death, decay, and rebirth, experienced when plant life is renewed each spring and dies each fall. Each cult was centered in a similar myth in which a deity returns to life after death or descends to the underworld and returns every spring. They were called mystery religions because they involved clandestine ceremonies, often in connection with an initiation rite that imparted secret knowledge. Only initiates were allowed to observe and participate in rituals. The rites were structured to lead worshippers toward heightened feelings and emotions, sometimes guiding them to a religious ecstasy that expressed the beginning of a new life through the mystical experience of dying and being reborn with the deity. More importantly, the mystery religions offered some kind of redemption or salvation in the present life and the promise of immortality in an afterlife.

Paul was a product of two contrasting cultures—the ancient Hebraic tradition of Israel and the Hellenistic civilization of the Roman Empire that had far greater dominion, power, and importance. He spent his adult life trying to find a way to bring these different traditions together in some new fashion. Judaism held an ethical appeal for the Gentile pagans known as "God fearers" who were attracted to Jewish synagogues. It was a faith that drew people in, yet held them apart with requirements of strict dietary laws and circumcision. Paul envisioned a religion that could bridge these broad ethnic and cultural divisions, creating a unified culture for the future of humanity.

## an apocalyptic mystery religion

Through Paul's evangelistic efforts over the next several decades, the emerging Christ cult that he encountered in Damascus began to spread throughout the major trading cities of Asia Minor, Greece, and Rome. As the cult grew and spread, the Palestinian-centered communities of the Way declined as the primary form of the faith. Thus the Hellenistic apocalyptic mystery religion developed by Paul became the foundation of orthodox Christianity.

During the next century, Greek concepts about the dualism of body and soul as distinct entities eventually replaced the Jewish idea of an integrated, inseparable personhood that ended at death. The Pharisaic belief in an earthly resurrection of the dead became incorporated with the Greek idea of an eternal soul existing beyond death. The combination of the two eventually became a belief in an afterlife in heaven—something which would have been very foreign and strange to Jesus.

Like the popular mystery religions, a rite of initiation (in this case, baptism) became part of the Christ-cult observances. The shared common meal of the early Christian communities soon became a distinctly ritual meal, the Eucharist—from the Greek *eucharistia* (*yoo-khar-is-tee'-ah*), which means *thanksgiving*—a meal that commemorated the death of Jesus and recalled his last supper with the disciples. Pagan spiritual practices like ecstatic speech (speaking in tongues) were sometimes incorporated. The trappings of a real Greco-Roman religion began to develop around the cult of the mystical Christ.

As time went on, mythical stories grew up around Jesus. He was known in Palestine as a healer and exorcist, but new stories gave Jesus miraculous power over the elements of nature. For a century after the death of Jesus, his teachings were blended with Jewish apocalyptic and Greek Gnostic thought. Words that Jesus never spoke were attributed to him by later generations seeking his word for their social context and life situation.[5] He was rapidly transformed from a teacher of wisdom, a radical social critic, and a voice for justice into an apocalyptic preacher who proclaimed the end times. His obvious failure as a militaristic and nationalist messiah was corrected by the claim that he would soon return in great power and authority to rid the earth of evil and violently destroy the persecutors of the new faith. The nonviolent prophet was quickly transformed into an avenging warrior king.

In 325 CE, after centuries of debate about the nature and substance of the risen Christ, a council of bishops convened by the emperor Constantine (272–337) took a vote and elevated Jesus to divinity. Jesus became God. But Jesus never claimed to be God. He never claimed to be an exclusive son of God. In fact, he never even claimed to be the Hebrew messiah or Christ. He never made any exalted claims about himself. If he used any self-referential term, it was the son of man.

5. The further the gospels were written from the time that Jesus lived, the more the authors promoted the evolving ideas of the early Christian communities over the authentic words of Jesus. These writers and their communities saw revelation as an ongoing process and they freely put words into the mouth of Jesus which spoke to their current situation in life (*Sitz im Leben*).

## the anointed one

In ancient Israel, the leaders of church and state—kings and high priests—were anointed with olive oil as a ceremonial sign of their new office. The oil was an outward and visible sign of a new status—a consecration for an important task. The practice was common throughout the Near East. Egyptian paintings show the pharaoh being anointed with oil. The biblical stories state that when both Saul and David were anointed, the spirit of Yahweh came upon them powerfully.[6] Of all the individuals who were anointed for their offices, the king was in a special sense *Yahweh's anointed one.*[7] In Hebrew, the word for anointed is *mashiach* (*mah-shee'-akh*). The Greek translation is *christos* (*khris-tos'*). From these we get our English words *Messiah* and *Christ*.

Kings and high priests were anointed, but so were other key figures throughout the history of the Hebrew people. Prophets—those social critics who called upon the nation and its leaders to change their political and economic direction—were also sometimes anointed and would therefore be considered messiahs. The messianic role in Israel could thus be that of prophet, priest, or king. If Jesus is to be considered the messiah in any sense, it would have to be as a prophet. He was never chosen and appointed as a priest of the temple or as a head of state, nor did he seek these grandiose roles. Instead, he was a critic of both institutions—a force for social and religious transformation and change. Still, we have no biblical record that Jesus was ever anointed with oil for his prophetic task nor did he seek the title of messiah in any of its Hebrew contexts.[8] But that did not stop his followers from thrusting that title on him.

Early on, some followers of Jesus began to believe that he was the Jewish messiah. Perhaps that idea took shape even before his death. Certainly that is the image that presents itself in the gospel of Mark, written about four decades after the crucifixion. According to Mark, as Jesus walked toward the city of Caesarea Philippi that lies north of the Sea of Galilee, he asked

6. 1 Samuel 10:9–11, 1 Samuel 16:13. This image is repeated when Jesus is baptized at the Jordan by John the Baptizer.

7. Psalm 20:6. "Yahweh will help [save, deliver, rescue, give victory to] his anointed."

8. All four gospels present a story in which Jesus was a guest for a meal when a woman entered the room and anointed him with an expensive perfume. In two accounts, he is anointed on his head and in two accounts on his feet. The details, including the location and the identity of the woman vary from account to account. See Mark 14:3–9, Matthew 26:6–13, Luke 7:36–50, and John 12:1–8. In Mark's and Matthew's accounts, the anointing on his head is to prepare Jesus for his burial, not for his messianic task.

his disciples, "Who do people say that I am?" Some of the disciples replied, "John the Baptist." Others said "Elijah" or "One of the prophets"—all references to contemporary and ancient prophets, not regal or military figures. Jesus persisted: "But who do you say that I am?" Only Simon Peter answered him: "You are the messiah." In both Mark's and Luke's gospels, Jesus declines to confirm or deny Peter's confession.[9] He simply orders his disciples not to discuss this conversation with anyone.[10] Matthew, however, expands the episode—first having Jesus praise Peter and then claim that this confession would become the basis of his future church—and then sternly ordering the disciples to tell no one of this revelation. Why keep this belief a secret? Because it was a dangerously seditious claim. The messiah was not a spiritual or religious figure, but a decidedly political one.

It was only at the synagogue in Nazareth as portrayed in Luke's gospel that Jesus alluded to himself as a messiah, and then did so specifically in the language that the prophet Isaiah had used to refer to himself—as a messianic prophet. Other than that single instance reported in only one gospel, Jesus never spoke of himself in that term—but as indicated in all the synoptic gospels, at least Peter believed Jesus fulfilled the role. In the end, Jesus was executed because powerful figures in Jewish society were frightened that a messianic figure—whether self-proclaimed or acclaimed by others—could lead to civil strife if he incited a popular messianic movement aimed at violent revolution. For the Apostle Paul, Jesus was also seen as the messiah. His writings predated the gospels and greatly influenced their theology. Writing in Greek, Paul called Jesus "the Christ"—sometimes using his name and title so tightly linked ("Jesus Christ" and "Christ Jesus") that the Christ was no longer simply a title or role, but part of Jesus' resurrected identity.

The word *messiah* (*mashiach*) appears only 39 times in the Hebrew Bible and in most cases it refers to the current ruler of Judah or Israel, although there are a few other variations. In Leviticus, the term is applied to the high priest.[11] In Psalm 105, the entire Hebrew people are called "God's anointed."[12] And when the Persian king Cyrus the Great (c.600–530 BCE) released the Hebrew people from captivity in Babylon soon after 538 BCE,

---

9. Interestingly, the majority opinion was that Jesus was a prophet, not the messiah. Not just any prophet, but one of the great one's from Israel's past—Elijah—and a renowned contemporary—John the Baptist.

10. Mark 8:27–33. See parallels in Luke 9:18–22 and Matthew 16:13–23. This story is not found in John's gospel. In Matthew's version, Jesus commends Peter and declares that he will build his church on Peter's confession. This is one of only two references "the church" in the gospels. It is surely a later addition.

11. Leviticus 4:3

12. Psalm 105:12–15

the prophet Isaiah called him a messiah, in the sense that he was acting as God's agent to liberate the people from captivity and oppression.[13]

But it was King David who became the Hebrew prototype for all potential messiahs. David, who lived from about 1040 to 970 BCE, held a special place in the hearts and minds of the people of Israel.[14] In the biblical narrative, David—an acclaimed warrior—defeated the Philistines, and was crowned king over the united kingdom of Judah and Israel, establishing Jerusalem as his capital. He ruled the nation for four decades as their first great king, and before his death, he laid out the plans for the first temple in Jerusalem, built by his son Solomon. Yahweh promised David that his offspring would rule the nation forever.

As a result, David became the model of the messiah for later generations. As his royal line stretched out over the next four centuries, with varying results, the term messiah began to refer not just to the present anointed king, but to an ideal king. When the Davidic line ended during the Babylonian captivity, messiah became a code word for a new king from the "root of Jesse," a reference to David's father. For the next six centuries, the messiah was seen as a future political and military leader who would reclaim the throne of David, save the people from foreign oppressors, and restore the nation to its former glory.

## a failed messiah

When the title *messiah* or *christ* was applied to Jesus by his Jewish and Greek followers, some confusion is sure to ensue if one examines the historical job description of the ideal king and conquering hero. Although he met the definition of a messianic prophet—challenging the injustice of his society and speaking truth to power—his prophetic ministry began not with anointment, but with a baptism in the Jordan River. In any event, Jesus repeatedly rejected the roles of both priest and king, even though the gospel writers tried to suggest the kingly role for Jesus at his trial and execution and the writer of the New Testament letter known as Hebrews later cast Jesus in the role of great high priest.[15]

13. Isaiah 45:1

14. Interestingly, until recently there has been little archaeological evidence that affirms the existence of David. If he was the leader of a great kingdom, the surrounding nations paid little notice.

15. Hebrews 4:14

John's gospel has the disciple Nathanael declare to Jesus, "Rabbi, you are the Son of God! You are the King of Israel!"[16] This passage links the title "son of God" with the role of the messiah as the "king of Israel," indicating that both are clearly political terms. But Jesus never became the king of Israel or of Judea or of anywhere, even though he was executed with the sign "King of the Jews" above his head. On one occasion, he reportedly fled from a crowd because he believed they were about to force him into that role. This happened after the story of feeding five thousand people in the wilderness:

> When the people saw the sign that he had done, they began to say, "This is indeed the prophet who is to come into the world." When Jesus realized that they were about to come and take him by force to make him king, he withdrew again to the mountain by himself.[17]

The people see a prophet and want to elevate him to the role of king as a challenge to Rome. Any charismatic person could conceivably fill the bill as long as people would willingly follow him to battle. Rather than overthrowing the present kingdom and establishing a new one, Jesus announced that God's kingdom was already present—spread out upon the land—yet hidden. And Jesus saw God as the ruler, never himself. Like David and Judas Maccabeus, Jesus was a peasant, but unlike them, he did not become a military leader. He modeled servanthood, not domination, and he taught the way of peace and forgiveness. But most importantly, he was executed by Roman authorities. This could not be the fate of someone who was expected to overthrow the enemies and oppressors of the Jewish people and establish a great kingdom with authority over other nations. Rome and their Judean collaborators squashed Jesus like a bug, He clearly failed the test of the long-awaited victorious messiah.

And yet, some of Jesus' followers declared him to be the anointed one. That could only be true if the term messiah was completely redefined in prophetic terms, or if his messianic role was somehow to be played out supernaturally after his death.

## a second-chance messiah

As the early church tried to put the life and death of Jesus into the context of Jewish history, the role of messiah somehow needed to be redefined if Jesus was to fill the role. Certainly, prophets had been anointed in the past, and

16. John 1:49
17. John 6:14–15

although that technically made them messiahs, the major role of *the* messiah was still expected to be a military leader and king, not a social critic. The people were looking for a liberator. They weren't looking for someone to free them from iniquity or sin; they wanted freedom from Rome. Moreover, the peasants were looking for freedom from debt and the oppressive economics of the wealthy aristocracy. The pre-resurrection Jesus did not fulfill these expectations of the messiah, but a post-resurrection Jesus had the opportunity to fulfill the hopes and dreams of the people in a spectacular fashion. As Paul and other New Testament writers looked back at Jesus, they were convinced that his resurrection gave him a second chance. He didn't fit the role of messiah in his lifetime, so the role was projected into gloriously imagined future events. And for Paul, it was an impending future. The transition from the human Jesus to the cosmic Christ was dependent on this shift in perspective.

Imperial power and glory are very seductive forces—certainly more impressive than the apparent feebleness (at least in many culturally-bound male eyes) of compassion, forgiveness, and nonviolence. I imagine there were some in the early Jesus movement who couldn't see God's presence in any form of perceived human weakness. The life of Jesus ended in a humiliating defeat on a rebel's cross, and though Paul saw the resurrection as a vindication by God, for many Hellenistic Christians in a world dominated by Roman reverence for Augustus Caesar this was apparently not enough.

These followers believed that Jesus had ascended to heaven and hoped that he would soon return to earth to get the job done properly. Therefore Jesus was confessed as the messiah, not on evidence from his past life, but on belief in a future role. What these followers anticipated and what they fervently desired was the quick return of Jesus in power, majesty, and glory administering the violence of God upon all evildoers and oppressors of the Jewish people.

The mythology of the victorious Christ developed into a militaristic image of Jesus descending from the clouds in splendor and might to defeat the powers of the present age and to put all nations under his control. They believed that Christ's kingdom would become the greatest empire in history and would last for a thousand years. A messianic age of peace will be ushered in, but it is a peace that is only achieved by violence. The humble and nonviolent kingdom of God is replaced with the image of a glorious kingdom ruled by Christ.

This mythology became a central motif in Christianity over the centuries. But the whole concept of the second coming of Christ, makes a mockery of everything Jesus stood for. It attempts to remake the image of Jesus into the image of Augustus Caesar.

## the son of God

The Apostle Paul believed that Jesus was appointed the *son of God* after his resurrection from the dead.[18] For Paul, this newly elevated status reflected a vindication by God of Jesus' humiliating death and seeming defeat on the cross. This metaphor was not intended as a literal claim about the biological parenthood of Jesus. Paul certainly never believed that Jesus had the genetic matter of Yahweh in his being, or as was stated in a creed over three centuries later that Jesus was "one substance with the Father." It would have been absurd and abhorrent to a first-century Jew to believe that a finite human could also be the infinite God of the cosmos, or conversely that a transcendent God dwelling apart from creation would take on a human form—although this was commonly accepted in Greek and Roman religions, and centuries later in Christianity as well. Instead, Paul's metaphor was a statement about the intimate relationship that Jesus had with God.

Two different Greek words are translated as *son* in English. The first, *teknon* (*tek'-non*), refers to a child of either sex by physical descent—a biological son or daughter. The second, *huios* (*hwee-os'*), is a legal descriptor for an heir, often by adoption. When the New Testament writers speak of Jesus as the son of God, they employ the Greek phrase *huios theou* (*hwee-os' theh'-oo*)—*theou* meaning God. Thus, Jesus is the *adopted* son of God. Similarly, the plural version of the phrase, *huioi theou* (*hwee-oh'-ee theh'-oo*), is used for the followers of Jesus who are called the adopted "sons of God" (or "children of God," if you prefer). Singular or plural, it has the same meaning about the relationship to God. Divine paternity is purely a metaphoric relationship, not biological. Paul stated that anyone who is led by the spirit of God becomes God's adopted child.[19]

In most ancient temple-states—like those of Sumer, Akkadia, Egypt, Babylonia, Assyria, and Israel—the ruler was considered an earthly representative of the national god, often regarded as the appointed or adopted son of the god. In some cases, the ruler was seen as a living manifestation of the god, but this was not the case in Israel. Throughout the ancient world, the expression "son of God" was not a term of divinity—it was a label for a political leader. In ancient Hebrew culture, the term "son of God," referred primarily to the anointed king of Israel.[20] For instance, Psalm 2 was written

18. Romans 1:4

19. Romans 8:14

20. Although this was the primary understanding of the phrase, the term was not used exclusively to refer to the king. Elsewhere in the Hebrew Bible, the term "sons of God" refers to angels or members of the heavenly court (in Genesis), and the phrase "son of God" was used to describe all the entire people of Israel (in Exodus). It was also

for the coronation of a king at Mount Zion, the prominent hill located at the center of ancient Jerusalem. [21] This was a song written for an adoption ceremony. In this poem, the psalmist has Yahweh declare:

> I have anointed my king on Zion, my holy mountain. I will pro-claim the decree of Yahweh: You are my son; today I have become your father. Ask of me, and I will make the nations your inheri-tance, the ends of the earth your possession. You will rule them with an iron scepter; you will dash them to pieces like pottery.[22]

The son of God in this poem is envisioned as a mighty warrior who is destined to become an iron-fisted ruler of the surrounding nations. In a temple-state, consummate military and political power was seen as a neces-sary prerequisite for divine sonship. Who else would be worthy of the title? As one Roman writer pointed out, certainly not a peasant born in a stable.

The image of Jesus as a warrior king is forcefully portrayed in the last book of the New Testament, the apocalyptic book of Revelation, which was written somewhere around 90 CE. Within sixty years after his death, Jesus had been transformed into an agent of God's vengeance. The author of Rev-elation pictures Jesus—metaphorically referred to as the Word of God, and dripping in blood—leading the armies of heaven in a consummate blood-bath on the earth. Obviously, the language is symbolic, but the essence of retribution is clear.

> From his mouth comes a sharp sword with which to strike down the nations, and he will rule them with a rod of iron; he will tread the wine press of the fury of the wrath of God the Almighty. On his robe and on his thigh he has a name inscribed, "King of kings and Lord of lords."
>
> Then I saw an angel standing in the sun, and with a loud voice he called to all the birds that fly in mid-heaven, "Come, gather for the great supper of God, to eat the flesh of kings, the flesh of captains, the flesh of the mighty, the flesh of horses and their riders—flesh of all, both free and slave, both small and great" . . . and all the birds were gorged with their flesh.[23]

---

used to describe an individual who practices justice toward the poor (in the book of Wisdom, which is not included in the Protestant Bible).

21. Psalm 2 has often been associated with King David (c. 1000 BCE), but may also date from a later period in Israel's history after the Babylonian exile (c. 538 BCE). In any event, the association of the term "son of God" with the anointed king of Israel is an early and well-known Hebrew tradition.

22. Psalm 2:6–8

23. Revelation 19:11–21

This is one of the most disturbing images in the bloody battle in Revelation—the call for birds to "gather for the great supper of God" where the flesh of kings, military leaders, and the mighty will be consumed. Carrion will feast on the flesh of God's enemies! If that's not an image of unbridled revenge, I don't know what is. The great supper of God! What a dramatic and horrifying contrast to the celebratory banquet images found in the parables of Jesus.

Because, the term *son of God* was generally used to refer to a king or an emperor, it carried a powerful political significance. In Paul's hands, calling Jesus the son of God was a clear political critique of the Roman Empire and of its current leader, whether it was Augustus, Tiberius, Caligula, Claudius, or Nero, all of whom ruled during Paul's lifetime.

In 42 BCE, two years after the death of Julius Caesar (100 – 44 BCE), the Roman Senate declared the assassinated Roman dictator to be *Divus Ilulius* (*dee'-voos ee-loo'-li-oos*) or the "deified Julius," elevating him to the status of a god. Later, his adopted son Octavian (63 BCE – 14 CE) was deemed by the Senate to be *Divi Filius* (*dee'-vee fee'-li-oos*), or "son of the divine one." When Octavian became the first Roman emperor, known by the title Augustus Caesar, he ushered in an era of peace and stability—the *Pax Romana* or Roman Peace—which allowed the devastated lands and economy of Rome to flourish once again. As a military leader, Octavian had ended a disastrous civil war by defeating his political rivals through a decisive military victory. In response, the Senate of Rome awarded him the title *Augustus* (*ow-goos'-toos*) a religious description meaning "the illustrious one" or "the revered one." Due to his immense military and political power, and in recognition of the benefits that he had restored to the social fabric, Augustus soon became the central character in a Roman imperial religion. He was worshipped and revered throughout the Roman Empire as the son of god, the king of kings, the lord of lords, the prince of peace, and the savior of all humanity. As we know, these terms were later applied to Jesus, beginning with the writings of the Apostle Paul and amplified in the book of Revelation.[24]

When Paul called Jesus the Son of God, he was making a decidedly anti-imperial statement that contrasted the servanthood and nonviolence of this peasant prophet to the militaristic power and iron-fisted rule of the

24. Revelation 17:14: "the Lamb will conquer them, for he is Lord of lords and King of kings." The title "prince of peace" comes from Isaiah 9:6: "For a child has been born for us, a son given to us; authority rests upon his shoulders; and he is named Wonderful Counsellor, Mighty God, Everlasting Father, Prince of Peace." 1 Timothy 4:10 parallels the "savior of humanity" claim: "For to this end we toil and struggle, because we have our hope set on the living God, who is the Savior of all people, especially of those who believe."

emperor of Rome.[25] In contrast to the Pax Romana, Jesus offered humanity a different kind of peace—one found in a lifestyle of love, generosity, and forgiveness. It was a peace achieved through nonviolence and compassion, not through warfare and domination. It was a peace which could be found in a close-knit and inclusive community that demonstrated a special concern for the weakest and most vulnerable members in their midst. Jesus called his followers to a different kind of life, a qualitatively richer and deeper life, a more profoundly authentic human existence. In Paul's mind, if anyone was to be called the son of God, it should be Jesus, because Jesus reflected and revealed the true character of a compassionate God, while the emperor of Rome did not.

Paul expressed his belief that Jesus became the adopted son of God at his resurrection in the mid-50s CE. If we follow the development of this idea through the subsequent Christian writings in the New Testament, we see the divine sonship of Jesus moving back earlier and earlier in his life as the metaphor took root and grew. Fifteen to twenty years later, Mark's gospel (written c. 70) moves Jesus' adoption as a son of God back to his baptism in the Jordan River.[26]

> In those days Jesus came from Nazareth of Galilee and was baptized by John in the Jordan. And just as he was coming up out of the water, he saw the heavens torn apart and the Spirit descending like a dove on him. And a voice came from heaven, "You are my Son, the Beloved; with you I am well pleased."[27]

Another fifteen years later, Matthew and Luke (c. 85) place it at his birth, and in fifteen more years, the gospel of John (c. 100) elevates Jesus to a divine role in the creation of the universe.[28]

> In the beginning was the Word [logos], and the Word was with God, and the Word was God.[29]

This represents a remarkable transformation of the status of Jesus from the adopted son of God to a divine being in less than five decades.

---

25. Paul's letter to the Romans 1:1–5 reports that Jesus is "declared to be Son of God with power according to the spirit of holiness by resurrection from the dead." Additional Pauline references to Jesus as the "son of God" are found elsewhere in Romans, 2 Corinthians, Galatians, Ephesians, and Colossians.

26. Mark 1:9–11

27. Mark 1:9–11

28. Matthew 1:18–23, Luke 1:26–35, John 1:1–5

29. John 1:1

## the son of man

Jesus did not speak of himself as either the messiah (the Christ) or the son of God—which we have seen are similar references to a military conqueror and ruler. These were titles created for him by others. According to the gospels, the only self-referential title he used was the *son of man*. No one else calls Jesus by this term. It was an image he apparently claimed for himself, but which the church has generally dropped in favor of son of God. However, where the phrase *son of man* is used in the gospel accounts, modern English translators often capitalize it as Son of Man to ensure that we will understand the use of the term in a very specific context—as a reference to a seemingly supernatural figure found in the book of Daniel in the Hebrew Bible. In Daniel's dream, this figure comes before God on the clouds of heaven and is given dominion over a never-ending empire on earth. The Son of Man fits nicely with the exalted image of Jesus in that other apocalyptic New Testament book—Revelation. But the phrase *son of man* has other connotations in the Hebrew Bible.

For a better understanding of this term, it is helpful to look at Walter Wink's groundbreaking book, *The Human Being: Jesus and the Enigma of the Son of the Man*. Wink explains that in much of the Hebrew Bible the term *son of man* or *ben 'adam* (*bane aw-dawm'*) was used to describe a specific human being or humanity in general—conveying the connotation of ordinary human mortality and weakness. (The Hebrew word *'adam* (*aw-dawm'*) can be translated as either *man* or *Adam* depending on the context.) The phrase *son of man* simply means a human being. Many scholars insist that when Jesus used the term, he meant he was just one of the boys, a regular fellow. Of course, the phrase comes across as very male-oriented, and it is. Wink suggests that if we prefer, we can translate it as *child of the human*, *humanity's child*, or *the human one*. When rendering *ben 'adam* in English, translators sometimes use *human being*, *mere man*, or *O mortal* as substitutions. We see this usage in translations of the book of Ezekiel in the Hebrew Bible, where Yahweh employs the term to refer to Ezekiel, to whom Yahweh appears in a bizarre vision. There are 107 occurrences of *ben 'adam* in the Hebrew Bible, 93 of which are found in the book of Ezekiel. And they all mean "human one."

The apocalyptic book of Daniel was written four hundred years later than Ezekiel, sometime around 167 BCE. Their latest foreign ruler, King Antiochus Epiphanes IV (*an-tee'-ohk-ohs ep-if-an-ace'*) of the Seleucid (*sih'-loo-cid*) Empire, had outlawed Hebrew religious rites and traditions and ordered the worship of Zeus as the supreme god. The Jewish people were being forced at the point of a sword to convert to paganism. It was a time of severe crisis that led to widespread martyrdom and the Maccabean revolt.

The author of the book of Daniel has a series of dreams in which he sees "one like a son of man" coming on clouds of heaven before the throne of God—the Ancient One—to receive universal and everlasting dominion on earth.

> As I watched in the night visions,
> I saw one like a son of man
> coming with the clouds of heaven.
> And he came to the Ancient One
> and was presented before him.
> To him was given dominion
> and glory and kingship,
> that all peoples, nations, and languages
> should serve him.
> His dominion is an everlasting dominion
> that shall not pass away,
> and his kingship is one
> that shall never be destroyed.[30]

Although some biblical scholars and theologians suggest this points to the second coming of Jesus, the verses that follow explain that the *son of man* in Daniel is not a supernatural or divine individual, but is rather a metaphor for the people of Israel.

> The kingship and dominion
> and the greatness of the kingdoms under the whole heaven
> shall be given to the people of the holy ones of the Most High;
> their kingdom shall be an everlasting kingdom,
> and all dominions shall serve and obey them.[31]

## the *son of man* in the gospels

There are 81 instances of the *son of man* sayings in the four gospels, although many of these are parallel repetitions. Wink contends—as Marcus Borg has suggested—that some sayings of Jesus in the gospels are pre-Easter and others are post-Easter, meaning that some derive from the historic Jesus and others derive from the later church. Jesus spoke in Aramaic. He would have used the phrase *bar enash* (*bar en-awsh'*) to refer to himself as a son of man.

30. Daniel 7:13–14
31. Daniel 7:27

The Greek New Testament texts use the phrase *ho huios tou anthropou* (*ho hwee-os' too anth'-roh-poh-oo*), literally *the son of the man* with the second definitive article included.

In the gospels, the *son of man* sayings fall into three categories. The first are proverbs about the role and authority of the son of man in Jesus' Galilean context. The second group describes the passion of the son of man—his suffering and death in Jerusalem. The third collection points to a future return of the son of man on the clouds of heaven.

Group one includes sayings like:

> *Foxes have holes, and birds of the air have nests; but the son of man has nowhere to lay his head.*[32]

> *The son of man has come eating and drinking, and you say, "Look, a glutton and a drunkard, a friend of tax-collectors and sinners!"*[33]

These sayings could refer to both Jesus and his followers.
Group two sayings include:

> *But I tell you that Elijah* [referring to John the Baptizer] *has already come, and they did not recognize him, but they did to him whatever they pleased. So also the son of man is about to suffer at their hands.*[34]

> *How then is it written about the son of man, that he is to go through many sufferings and be treated with contempt?*[35]

These sayings refer to the likelihood that all social prophets will suffer the consequences of their politically prophetic critique.

Group three sayings are clearly apocalyptic.

> *They will see 'the Son of Man coming on the clouds of heaven' with power and great glory.*[36]

> *When the Son of Man comes in his glory, and all the angels with him, then he will sit on the throne of his glory. All the nations*

32. Matthew 8:20, Luke 9:58
33. Luke 7:34
34. Matthew 17:12
35. Mark 9:12
36. Matthew 24:30

*will be gathered before him, and he will separate people one from another as a shepherd separates the sheep from the goats.*[37]

The first group of sayings may have been uttered by the historical Jesus, while the second and third groups most likely stem from writers of the early church looking back at the passion in retrospect and looking forward to an imminent return of Jesus as a judge and ruler over Israel and the other nations of the world.

The enigma is why Jesus might have used this third-person reference to himself, if he did. He was certainly capable of referring to himself as "I" as is evident in these three gospel parallels.[38]

*Who do people say that I am?* (Mark)

*Who do the crowds say that I am?* (Luke)

*Who do the people say that the son of man is?* (Matthew)

This indicates that sometimes the usage is entirely dependent on the gospel writer.

## Jesus and God

I do not believe that the historical Jesus was God. But Jesus had a relationship with God that was extraordinary. Jesus went beyond a simple belief in God, to live a life completely based on a powerful trust in God's love and compassion. Contrary to sound common sense, Jesus trusted that God's abiding concern for the poor and God's passion for the least among us would someday triumph over the injustice of the world. Against all reasonable odds, Jesus trusted that the power of love and non-violent resistance would ultimately overcome entrenched evil and brutality. In opposition to conventional wisdom, Jesus trusted that human kindness and generosity would eventually transform the status quo of selfishness, greed, and apathy. This kind of radical trust seems truly mad given the realities of a world beset by evil and suffering. It invites one to be an open target for the contempt and dismissal of intimidating political, economic, and religious powers. And it inevitably calls one to become a willing martyr in the ongoing struggle to overturn the unjust systems of the world.

Jesus trusted that the radical change of the reign of God would not come about easily. It would require dedication, risk, and suffering. Jesus

---

37. Matthew 25:32
38. Mark 8:27, Luke 9:18, Matthew 16:13

never promised that the transformation of the social, political, and economic systems of domination would occur overnight. He never proclaimed that a sudden cosmic event would magically change the world in the twinkling of an eye. Neither did he promise that he or his followers would live to see the change he envisioned. Instead, Jesus trusted that a life of compassion and service in a suffering world would make a progressively small difference, one person at a time, one act at a time, just like the action of a tiny mustard seed in a well-tended garden, or a bit of yeast in a large batch of dough. In everything he did and said, Jesus trusted that God would provide the courage and strength to help his followers muddle through the overwhelming odds stacked against the lives of humble people, trapped in poverty and condemned as social outcasts. Jesus trusted that the spirit of God would empower and encourage a powerless people to prevail over oppressive social systems that were created to serve the narrow interests of a privileged few. Jesus calls us to that task. He calls us to that journey. He calls us to that life.

# PART 3

# the path of transformation

CHAPTER 7

# the postmodern world

---

*Come mothers and fathers throughout the land.*
*And don't criticize what you can't understand. Your*
*sons and your daughters are beyond your com-*
*mand. Your old road is rapidly agin'. Please get out*
*of the new one if you can't lend your hand, for the*
*times they are a-changin'.*[1]

—Bob Dylan (b. 1941)

OUR BELIEFS ARE OFTEN shaped by the governing worldview of our culture. The modern age that took root in the Enlightenment is now giving way to a postmodern era. This transformation will change how people view the world, how they understand reality and truth, and how they approach the fundamental questions of life. The postmodern transformation will have a tremendous impact on Christianity. The church has its roots in an ancient pre-modern worldview. Slowly it has accommodated itself to the modern world. But many critics wonder whether it will be able to survive the shift to the postmodern age.

The pre-modern worldview—or what comparative religion scholar Huston Smith calls the traditional worldview—developed during the time of the ancient temple-state, in which an alliance of the ruling class and the priestly class closely intertwined religion and political power. Religion's role was to legitimize the king's rule by providing a moral and religious author-ity for his decrees. The king was viewed as God's representative on earth. He was sometimes spoken of as the "Son of God" (as was ancient Israel's King David), and was sometimes seen as divine himself. To these ancient

---

1. Bob Dylan, "The Times They Are a-Changin'," 1964.

societies, the ruler and the social order reflected the will of their god on earth. The pre-modern worldview was essentially the only worldview from ancient times through the Middle Ages.

This worldview is characterized by an unquestioning acceptance of authority and a belief in absolute truths. Pre-modern people generally believe what they are told by authority figures, both religious and secular. They trust religion to provide the answers to life's mysteries. A half-century ago, in 1960, about 82 percent of the adult American population said just that to pollsters.

The Bible is a product of two pre-modern societies. The scribes of ancient Israel produced the Hebrew Bible or the Old Testament, and evangelists of the early Christian communities produced the New Testament. The pre-modern view of the world represented in these documents was accepted without question by the audiences to which they were written. A pre-modern culture was the context in which Jesus lived and died.

The modern worldview began to bloom and flourish in the Enlightenment of the eighteenth century—at least among the literate. Modernity was founded on the pursuit of objective knowledge and the use of the scientific method. It is characterized by a questioning of authority and the pursuit of truth over tradition. Modernity believes that truth is based on facts. In the modern worldview, people believe only what they can observe. Modernity trusts the power of reason and critical thinking to solve the world's problems. It looks to science, not to religion, to provide the answers to life's mysteries.

In the early eighteenth century, some notable Enlightenment thinkers—including Thomas Jefferson (1743–1826)—felt empowered by scientific inquiry and the new rationalism to re-read the bible. They began to question the literal truth of biblical miracles, the virgin birth, and even the divinity and resurrection of Jesus. In the universities of Germany, biblical scholars began to use the tools of historical research and textual analysis— usually called higher criticism—to separate the Bible's historic elements from what they perceived as later legendary additions. They began to look beyond the Christ of doctrinal faith to the earlier Jesus of history who they believed had been obscured by layers of Christian preaching and teaching, including the accounts found in the gospels. Then, in 1859, Charles Darwin (1809–1882), who studied to be a deacon in the Church of England, published *On the Origin of Species*, introducing radically new ideas about the evolutionary nature of life that challenged conventional Christian belief in the literal truth of the biblical creation story.

By the end of the nineteenth century, the findings of Darwin and the higher biblical critics had been embraced by many educated Christians and by influential figures in the media, universities, and seminaries. The largely upper-class and urban people who accepted the new learning became known as modernists or liberals. Many of them developed an optimistic faith in the gradual progress of humanity through knowledge, scientific inquiry, innovation, invention, and rational thought. Much of that optimism was lost after the horrors of World War I.

The rise of modernity led to the rise of secularism—the two go hand in hand. Secularism is defined as a system of ideas or practices that rejects the primacy of religion in society. In its hard form, secularism is atheistic—it denies the reality of God. But in its softer, more widespread form, secularism accepts God's reality but rejects religious institutions like the church, synagogue, or mosque as controlling forces in the life of the national community. When the United States Constitution declared a separation of church and state, it was in response to and a rejection of the state-sponsored religion of many northern European nations. The major Protestant faiths of the newly-formed United States supported the legal separation because each denomination feared that another might achieve favored status over them. In effect, the modern secularism of America's founders encouraged the growth of a plurality of religious expressions in America not seen anywhere else.

## religious reaction to modernity

The liberal and moderate mainline Protestant churches in the United States slowly adapted to modernity. They embraced higher criticism in their seminaries, and adopted the principles of the social gospel that sought to eradicate the evils of poverty and ignorance. But, millions of other Americans saw their historic faith threatened by the spread of these ideas and began to engage in a great cultural war with modernity and the movement toward secular humanism. Two key groups—evangelicals and fundamentalists—have led the battle against the modern secular worldview.

Evangelicals in the United States represent a broad movement of conservative theology that generally adheres to five core beliefs: a strong belief in the Bible as the authoritative and infallible word of God; a belief that the only way to salvation is through Jesus Christ; a personal conversion experience—being "born again"; a personal relationship with Jesus Christ; and a willingness to tell other people about the message of salvation in Jesus Christ

Church historians trace the roots of evangelicalism to the First Great Awakening in Europe and Colonial America of the 1730s and 1740s, whose leading figures set a revivalist tone that would characterize this movement up to the present day. Throughout the nineteenth century—even as mainline Protestants held the dominant position in society, politics, and culture— evangelicalism remained a vital part of the American religious landscape, sparking periodic spiritual awakenings and helping to fuel social movements such as abolitionism, prison reform, and the temperance movement.

Evangelical thought arose from early nineteenth century American values of the American frontier—individualism, republicanism, free enterprise, and patriotic nationalism—that sometimes stood in opposition to the values of the Eastern establishment. One of the chief characteristics of evangelicals has been their anti-intellectualism—a sentiment of mistrust towards intellectuals and intellectual pursuits. They often seek to frame themselves as champions of the ordinary people against those they view as cultural elites. This may be expressed in various ways, such as attacks on the merits of science, literature, and secular education. For many conservative Christians, secular knowledge and critical thinking is considered dangerous to one's faith. In the late nineteenth century, the pre-modern worldview of evangelicals came into increasing conflict with modern secular thought.

At the beginning of the twentieth century, the fertile soil of the evangelical tradition gave rise to a movement that vehemently opposed modernism and affirmed the literal truth of the Bible. These Christians would come to be known as "fundamentalists" because they affirmed five fundamental beliefs which conservative Presbyterian professors at Princeton University put forth in a series of pamphlets: biblical inerrancy, the virgin birth, the miracles of Jesus, the bodily resurrection of Jesus, and the doctrine of substitutionary atonement. Fundamentalists then began a process of purging their churches of those Christians who were making peace with modernity. In 1922, in response to increasing intolerance toward liberal Christians, Harry Emerson Fosdick (1878–1969), a liberal Baptist pastor who served a Presbyterian church in New York City, claimed that the fundamental thing about fundamentalists was that they were opposed to change, history, and progress.[2]

The clash between modernity and its acceptance of the theory of evolution and the pre-modern worldview with its literal acceptance of the creation accounts in Genesis brought the conflict to a head. The 1925 Scopes "Monkey Trial" in Dayton, Tennessee was a public battle between these two contrasting positions, with Clarence Darrow (1857–1938) representing modern secularism and William Jennings Bryan (1860–1925) representing evangelical fundamentalism. John Scopes (1900–1970), a substitute high

2. Fosdick, "Shall the Fundamentalists Win?" 716–722.

school teacher, was accused of violating Tennessee's Butler Act, which made it unlawful to teach human evolution in any state-funded school. In *Inherit the Wind* (1955), the play and film based on this trial, we see a dramatization of the lop-sided interchange when Darrow questioned Bryan on the stand. Bryan sought to defend fundamentalism and literal creationism, and failed miserably. Still, Scopes was found guilty and fined $100. Henry Louis "H L" Mencken (1880–1956) a journalist, satirist, and cultural critic covered the trial for the *Baltimore Sun*. It was Mencken who coined the phrase "Bible belt" for the southern states of the old Confederacy and it was he who dubbed this event the "monkey trial." Throughout most of the eight-day trial Mencken's reports were syndicated nationally, accompanied by stinging political cartoons that were seen by millions of Americans. A mob almost lynched him after he called the people of Dayton "yokels," "morons," and "hillbillies." But Mencken particularly savaged William Jennings Bryan: "It is a tragedy, indeed to begin life as a hero and to end it as a buffoon."

After the trial, evangelicals and fundamentalists, who were embarrassed by nationwide ridicule and negative publicity, began a period of relative seclusion that lasted for nearly four decades. But during this period, the number of evangelicals continued to grow.

In the mid-twentieth century, evangelical isolation began to lessen. Evangelist Billy Graham (b. 1918) brought evangelicalism back to prominence when he was viewed with respectability by the mainline Christian denominations. Graham preached a simple message: come to Jesus, let him into your heart, confess your sins, and be saved. This re-emergence in the fifties and sixties proved to be a decisive break between more moderate evangelicals and the more rigid fundamentalists who condemned Graham for his generous tolerance, openness, and acceptance—well-known liberal traits. Today, most evangelicals are not fundamentalists. They view the Bible less literally and are more open to reasonable dialog. They find themselves in a strange middle ground. Liberals often lump them with fundamentalists, while fundamentalists see them as far too liberal. Still, both conservative groups share a united opposition to many modern secular ideas and their political and social conservatism has placed them firmly in the camp of the right-wing Christian movement in America.

## the postmodern worldview

A new historical epoch is now unfolding before our eyes. It began about the middle of the twentieth century and is continuing to develop today. For lack of a better designation it is being called postmodernism—the successor of modernism. We are not sure how it will play out in the long term, but some initial observations are being made about its nature.

Postmodernity is a different reaction to modernity. Postmodern people are essentially disenchanted modernists. They are convinced that human reason and cleverness cannot achieve the happiness we seek. They have witnessed the environmental ravages of the industrial revolution, the bloody history of competing twentieth-century nations, and continued misery, poverty, and hunger around the globe. None of these problems have been solved by scientific knowledge or reason. To the contrary, the by-products of science and the industrial revolution have exacerbated many of our human problems. Science has provided cures to disease, but it has also created the threat of global warming and nuclear annihilation. If any event can be said to inaugurate the postmodern age, it was the bombing of Hiroshima and Nagasaki in August 1945 and the resulting nuclear arms race. This may have been the spark that marked the demise of modernity and ignited the rapid rise of a global postmodern culture.

The movement from modernity to postmodernity in America began with the Baby Boomers, born between 1946 and 1964. This was the first generation raised under the threat of nuclear weapons. Boomers knew in their guts that science had created a demon that could destroy the world. They saw the basements of their schools and churches filled with civil defense emergency supplies. They practiced "duck and cover" drills in classrooms and listened to their parents discuss the need for backyard fallout shelters.

Unlike fundamentalists, postmodernists have not sought to return to an earlier time. Nor do they see a return to rigid authoritarian religion as the answer. Postmodernism is characterized by the belief that both religion and science have failed us. Neither can be trusted to resolve life's complex problems.

Postmodern people reject the notion of absolute truth. They no longer trust authority and they reject any institution that claims to have a claim on the truth. They have become highly suspicious of facts. They believe that all truth, even to some extent scientific knowledge, is subjective, biased, and socially constructed. Truth depends on what one's culture regards as truth. Therefore the truth is not really true. In the postmodern worldview, people become their own authority and accept only what they personally experience. There is a sense that feeling is all that counts because, in the end, feeling is all there is. The postmodern attitude is, "If I can feel it, if I can touch it, then it must be true."

Among postmoderns there is a pervasive cultural pessimism that is cynical about political and ideological grandstanding of authorities and institutions. After a century of bombs, holocausts, and ecological disasters, many people have become disillusioned with their inherited faiths, the institutional church, the major political parties, and the political process. In the United States, the Watergate scandal and the Vietnam War created a pervasive anti-institutional mood among Baby Boomers, and it has spread to their children. As a result, voter apathy has been on the rise and church membership on a decline.

## generational patterns

In the developed countries of the Global North, worldviews are changing more rapidly than any time in history. Since 1945, each succeeding generation has exhibited a progression toward postmodernity. In this connotation, a generation is not defined as sets of grandparents, parents, or children, but rather a "cultural generation"—a cohort of people born during the same era and shaped by the same events during their formative years. Of particular importance is what was happening in society and the world as they came of age at about eighteen. Sociologists point out that each generational cohort exhibits a "peer personality" which derives from a common age group, common beliefs and behavior, and perceived membership in a common generation. Each cultural generation generally falls into a time span about eighteen years long.

Sociologist Wade Clark Roof (b. 1940) writes:

> More than just an aggregate of individuals of a similar age, a generation tends to have common, unifying social experiences and to develop a collective sense of identity. Members of one age group define themselves in relation to other cohorts by rejecting or reaffirming one or another set of cultural values, beliefs and symbols; in this way a generation comes to have its own distinctive "historical-social" consciousness. This is likely to occur in late adolescence and early adulthood—the formative years for the shaping of a distinct outlook.[3]

In the 1970s and 1980s, sociologist Morris Massey (b. 1939) produced a series of video presentations that helped corporate managers understand the value differences of various generations in the American workplace. The series began with a video called *What You Are Is Where You Were When*.[4] The premise is that we are all shaped by societal experiences and messages during young adulthood. In his work, Massey described three

3. Roof, *Generation of Seekers*, 3.
4. Massey, *What You Are Is Where You Were When*.

major periods or stages of personality development during which lifelong values are shaped.

According to Massey, up to the age of seven, children are like sponges, absorbing everything around them and accepting much of it as true, especially when it comes from their parents. This is the "imprint period" when children learn a sense of right and wrong, and determine good from bad.

Then says Massey, between the ages of eight and thirteen, older children begin to copy their parents and other significant adults in their lives. During this "modeling period," they begin trying on behaviors, beliefs, and attitudes like suits of clothes, to see how they feel. They may be very impressed with teachers, religious leaders, or other adult influences. This is significant, because around the age of ten or twelve, a child's values begin to lock in.

Between 13 and 21, young adults are more influenced by their peers than by their elders. As they develop as individuals, teens naturally turn to people who seem to share their basic values for affirmation, confirmation, and reinforcement. During this "socialization period," media also becomes increasingly important, especially as it resonates with the values of a peer group. By about age eighteen or twenty, a person's values are finally locked in for life.

Given this process of value development, Massey believes it is important to understand the historical contexts in which each American generation developed—the significant events that have contributed to the shaping of their values—in order to create an understanding of not only how we are different from one another, but more importantly *why* we are different. An increased understanding of our cultural differences may give us greater insight into the societal changes we face in our homes, schools, workplaces, and churches.

As the world has changed, each generation's values have been shaped by the unique events they have experienced in their youth—the Great Depression, World War II, the civil rights struggle, the Cold War, Vietnam, Watergate, the September 11 attacks, the 2008 global financial crisis, et cetera. What is going on in the world around us as we mature has enormous impact on the formation of our values. Massey refers to these influences as "significant emotional events." They can have a profound influence on our view of the world and our reaction to it, making any one generation uniquely different from its predecessor and its successor. According to Massey, what we are now was shaped by where we were then, both historically and geographically.

## the Baby Boom generation (1946–1964)

The 78 million *Baby Boom Generation* was born between 1946 and 1964, an eighteen-year time span that was marked by a significant increase in birth rates. Until the arrival of the Millennial generation, Boomers had the largest population of any generation in history. By the sheer force of their numbers, the boomers were a demographic bulge which remodeled society as they passed through it. In their teenage and college years they shaped the counterculture of the 1960s and 1970s.

They came of age between 1964 and 1982. In their youth they were open-minded and rebellious but many became more conservative in their 30s and 40s. One sociologist observed that during their childhood and rising adulthood they metamorphosed from Beaver Cleaver to hippie to yuppie. Job status and social standing were very important to this generation who created the concepts of "workaholic" and "superwoman." They are sometimes divided into two cohorts because life experiences were very different in the mid-60s compared to the mid-70s.

The Boomer-1 cohort was born from 1946 to 1954, and came of age between 1964 and 1972. Their memorable events were the Cuban missile crisis, the Vietnam War, anti-war protests, social experimentation, recreational drug use, sexual freedom, the civil rights movement, the women's movement, Woodstock, and astronauts walking on the moon. They tend to be free spirited, optimistic, ambitious, experimental, and social-cause oriented.

The Boomer-2 cohort was born between 1955 and 1964 and came of age from 1973 to 1982. Memorable events included the Cold War, Watergate, Nixon's resignation, the oil embargo, gasoline shortages, and raging inflation. Jobs were increasingly hard to find as the oil shock and economic slump of the 1970s coincided with their arrival in the work force. These Boomers are less optimistic, more pragmatic, and are characterized by a general cynicism.

In the 1960s, the older Baby Boomers observed the unmasking of the entrenched racism, sexism, and militarism that pervaded American culture behind the facade of what some conservative commentators see as an ideal time in American life and culture. And some of the Boomers reacted to the status quo with protests and social action. The only authority figures that they truly trusted were assassinated—first John Kennedy in 1963, and then Martin Luther King, Jr. and Bobby Kennedy in 1968.

As the nation confronted all of these agonizing social issues, some Boomers saw the mainline and evangelical churches as tacit supporters of the prevailing popular culture. In 1960, over half of Americans were members of mainline Protestant churches, whose leaders were undeniably white and male and decidedly anti-Catholic and anti-Jewish. These churches reflected the American Establishment, socially, culturally, and politically. Although a small number of religious activists worked tirelessly for civil rights and against the lengthy war in Vietnam, they never represented the mainstream reality in local congregations—which is where many Baby Boomers developed their impressions of the church.

Some in the Baby Boom generation began a search for a more authentic faith, away from established religion and toward experiential spirituality. They began dropping out of church. In the 1960s and 1970s, perhaps as many as 75 percent of these young people left their home churches in their early twenties. Some in the first cohort experimented with meditation, eastern religions, and charismatic Christianity, while some in the second cohort became born-again evangelicals. Most however, began to pick and choose less exotic ideas, beliefs, and practices to form unique personal expressions of their faith.

The older Baby Boomers were divided down the middle by the war in Vietnam, some supporting it, some opposing it. Over time, this division blossomed into what has become known as the "culture wars," between liberal and conservative Americans. As a whole, the Baby Boom Generation has remained widely committed to values such as gender equality, racial equality, and environmental stewardship. But the protests against the war in Viet Nam and the movements for equal justice for women and minorities left other Boomers with a more conservative stance.

One of the key factors dividing the Baby Boom generation in the 1960s was education. Sociologist Robert Wuthnow says that "virtually every study showed that the growing liberalization of American culture in these years was closely related to the rising influence of higher education."[5] The better educated Boomers tended to be more liberal on a wide variety of issues; the less educated tended to be more conservative. The impact on the church was that the more liberal Baby Boomers became less involved with institutional religion, while the more conservative maintained their commitment.

## Generation X (1965–1981)

The 51 million members of *Generation X*, born in the sixteen years from 1965 to 1981, arrived after the baby boom ended. They came of age between 1983 and 1999, and grew up in a very different world than previous generations. Divorce, single-parent families, working moms, and daycare

5. Wuthnow, *Restructuring of American Religion*, 157.

created "latchkey" kids out of many in this generation. They were the first generation with widespread access to television during their early formative years. As they came of age, they witnessed the appearance of most of today's digital technology—PCs and Macs in the early 1980s, digital cell phones in 1988, the rollout of the World Wide Web in 1990, and the introduction of the DVD in 1995. This is the first generation where more women than men obtained college educations. They also delayed marriage and parenthood more than any other generation preceding them.

Their memorable events were the *Challenger* explosion, the Iran-Contra affair, the trickle-down theory of Reaganomics, the Solidarity movement in Poland, the end of the Cold War, the fall of the Berlin Wall, the Desert Storm war, AIDS, and safe sex. They were influenced by George Lucas' *Star Wars* and MTV.

Gen Xers are post-partisans. They dislike the battles between liberals and conservatives. Forty percent call themselves independents, the highest percentage of any generation. They are skeptical of authority, mistrust institutions, and reject rules. Generation Xers are deeply suspicious of grand claims. They see life as complex and they distrust simple solutions. Churches that claim they have the last and final word on everything will find it very hard to attract this generation who cannot believe that there is just "one true way for all." They often look at Christianity as one of the many options that can be considered in a world in which they see each person as finding his or her own truth and meaning. Only 30 percent of this generation belongs to a church.[6] They tend to exhibit the same characteristics as the Baby Boomers—independent thought and suspicion of authority—but to an even greater degree. They distrust institutions and believe that denominations are no longer of much importance.

## the Millennial generation (1982–2000)

The 75 million members of the *Millennial Generation* were born between 1982 and 2000, an eighteen-year time span. The Millennials began to come of age starting in 2000 and will continue until about 2018. They may be the first truly postmodern generation. They are the most diverse American generation ever, with nearly 40 percent from minority groups. They celebrate diversity, are highly tolerant and open toward sexual orientation, and are deeply committed to environmental issues. One-third of the Millennial generation are tattooed and many are pierced in places other than their earlobes.

6. Winner, "Gen X Revisited," 1146–1148.

This generation was raised in the most child-centric time in our history. They are more technically literate than any other generation preceding them and are entering adulthood immersed in digital technology, including mobile phones, GPS systems, laptop computers, iPods, iPhones, iPads, Google, YouTube, Facebook, Instagram, and Twitter. Memorable events so far include the terrorist attacks of September 11, 2001, Hurricane Katrina in 2005, dual wars in Afghanistan and Iraq, global warming and environmental degradation, economic globalization and the exportation of manufacturing jobs, the global financial crisis of 2008, and the first black president.

This generation grew up at a time when there was a need to pull together as a nation. They volunteer at the highest level recorded for youth in forty years. Nearly nine in ten Millennials say it's up to their generation to clean up the environment, reversing the great harm to the planet's future created by previous generations. Sixty-three percent think government should do more to solve the nation's problems. In their political outlook, they are the most tolerant and progressive of any generation on social issues such as immigration, race, and homosexuality.

Recent surveys show that the more progressive people are in their social and political views, the less likely they are to attend church. This is certainly true for the Millennials. The Pew Forum reported in 2012 that 30 percent of Millennials in the United States say they have no religious affiliation or are atheist or agnostic, a vast increase over the 20 percent of Generation X and the 15 percent of the Baby Boomers.[7] Nearly one in five young adults say they were raised in a religious tradition—attending church and Sunday School—but now have disassociated themselves.[8] Only a small percentage of the Millennial generation in the United States is actively religious. Of these, 15 percent are Roman Catholic, 10 percent are Baptist, and 10 percent are non-denominational Christian. After that, the connection of Millennials to mainline or evangelical churches drops off to small single digits.

## the iGeneration (2001–2019)

This brings us to the first generation of the twenty-first century. Labels for this group are still emerging, including the *Internet Generation*, the

7. Pew Forum, "'Nones' on the Rise," (October 9, 2012). Online: http://www.pewforum.org/uploadedFiles/Topics/Religious_Affiliation/Unaffiliated/NonesOnTheRisefull.pdf.

8. Pew Forum, "Religion Among Millennials," (February 2010). Online: http://www.pewforum.org/uploadedFiles/Topics/Demographics/Age/millennials-report.pdf.

*iGeneration*, and the *Digital Natives*. The internet seems to be a connective word in all of these labels. These young children were born after 2001 and are mainly the offspring of Generation X, born into smaller families with older mothers. The oldest will be fifteen in 2016. They are growing up with remote controls and cell phones in their hands and believe that bowling is a game played in your family room on a high-definition television with an Xbox, PlayStation, or Nintendo Wii. It is too early to predict when this generation will conclude, but it's likely that the iGen could run until about 2019. Their values are being shaped now, and the events of the next decade will be very important in their formation.

It is likely that many—if not most—children of this generation will have little experience with the church. It's too early to predict their religious attributes, but based on the trends we have observed in previous generations, they are even less likely to believe in God, identify with a denomination, or have attended worship services. But one thing is certain; within a decade these children will be emerging as postmodern adults.

## living in an era that is over

Generational changes and shifting worldviews are confronting Christianity worldwide. In the postmodern Global North—especially in Western Europe and North America—the institutional church is not faring well. In the pre-modern Global South—predominantly in Africa, Asia, and South America—Christianity is on the rise. What worries me is whether the church can only flourish in a pre-modern culture where people are poorly educated and traditional values are rooted in patriarchy, homophobia, and the supernatural. In America, some conservative evangelicals and most fundamentalists have seemingly staked their futures on that assumption and are inculcating their children in these values. Yet time is not on their side.

A 2013 study reveals that four out of ten adult Americans (38 percent) are theological conservatives, while just half that number (19 percent) are theological liberals. Another 28 percent are theological moderates and 15 percent are nonreligious.[9] But religious liberals and the nonreligious hold many similar views on social and economic matters. According to the authors of the study:

> It is often assumed that, in the American religious landscape, theological conservatives anchor one end of the spectrum and theological liberals, the other. However, due to the growth of nonreligious

9. Jones, "Do Americans Believe Capitalism and Government Are Working?", 25.

*Americans who tend to be liberal on both social and economic issues, the opposite end of the spectrum from religious conservatives is now anchored by a combination of religious progressives and nonreligious Americans. Given this dynamic, the 9 percent advantage religious conservatives have in outnumbering religious progressives is muted by the additional 15% of Americans who are nonreligious and hold similar views to religious progressives across a range of issues.*[10]

Younger generations are increasingly changing this dynamic. The generational movement is leaving the religious conservative viewpoint behind. According to the survey, 23 percent of people aged 18 to 33 are religious progressives, 22 percent are nonreligious and 17 percent are religious conservatives.[11] Through this major generational shift the religious and political landscape of American life will be radically transformed.

Historical epochs are not neatly separated. They are not lined up end to end. It is possible to continue to live in an era that is essentially over. While one era prevails, its successor is already forming, and its predecessor continues to exert influence for a very long time. These three worldviews—pre-modern, modern, and postmodern—co-exist side-by-side today in all parts of American culture. But it is particularly apparent in our churches. Some Christians accept what they are told by religious authorities. Others question traditional church teachings and use reason as a guide. Still others reject institutional religion altogether and trust only their own spiritual experiences. But regardless of generation, culture, or attitude, we all are moving together toward a postmodern world and the movement is rapidly accelerating.

10. Ibid, 33.
11. Ibid, 34.

CHAPTER 8

# the spiritual journey

*Life has no meaning. Each of us has meaning and we bring it to life. It is a waste to be asking the question when you are the answer.*[1]

—Joseph Campbell (1904–1987)

*There is not one big cosmic meaning for all; there is only the meaning we each give to our life, an individual meaning, an individual plot, like an individual novel, a book for each person.*[2]

—Anaïs Nin (1903–1977)

WE ARE CREATURES THAT cannot help wondering about the meaning of life and the universe in which we live. This often gets us involved with spirituality and religion, whether we like it or not. At their essence, both spirituality and religion involve the human quest for life's meaning and purpose, a quest that pulls us from the superficiality of daily activities and immerses us deeply in life's most essential issues. To that point, theologian Paul Tillich (1886–1965) defined religious faith as "the state of being grasped by an ultimate concern, a concern which qualifies all other concerns as preliminary and which itself contains the answer to the question of the meaning of life."[3]

1. Joseph Campbell, source not found.
2. Nin, *The Diary of Anaïs Nin*.
3. Tillich, *Dynamics of Faith*, 1–29.

125

The word *religion* comes to English from the Latin root *religio* (*reh-lee'-jee-oh*), which in ancient Roman culture meant reverence for the gods and a careful pondering of the nature of divinity and the sacred in human life. The exact source of *religio* is obscure, but the Christian theologian Augustine of Hippo (354–430 CE) believed it derived from the Latin word *ligare* (*lee'-gah-reh*), which means to bind, tie, or connect. The combination of *re* (again) and *ligare* (connect) would mean "to reconnect." The implication in *religio* is that something that was broken or has been separated is now being reattached. In relation to the divine, one can imagine the ancients envisioning a vertical connection between human beings on earth and the immortal gods in the heavenly realm. For the Greeks and Romans, religion—rites, rituals, prayers, and sacrifices—provided the means of creating and maintaining that connection. But *religio* as reconnecting does not always have to be a connection with a God or gods dwelling somewhere "up there" or "out there." *Religio* could also imply a reconnection with everything around us—with others, with all living creatures, and with the universe at large. Or it could imply a renewed connection with the deepest part of one's existence, the search for the animating force of love and compassion at the depth of one's being.

The religious search for meaning and purpose can be directed upward, outward, and inward. Thus we get the three fundamental theological ideas about the location of the divine: upward toward transcendent divinity—wholly separate and apart from us and creation; outward toward immanent divinity—part of creation and all living things; and inward toward incarnate divinity—dwelling deep within the human spirit.

Today, we often speak of religion as a belief system such as Christianity, Islam, Buddhism, Mormonism, Scientology, pantheism, animism, secular humanism, and atheism. Each of these competing belief systems offers a general picture of the world as a whole and the role of the individual within it based on a particular understanding of the divine and the meaning of life. They all represent answers to questions about the purpose of life, the proper way to live, and what happens to the individual when life ends.

## first-hand experience, second-hand religion

All religious beliefs have their foundation in personal experience, often in the exceptional experience of a founder who encountered the sacred—someone who was grasped by an ultimate concern in a particular time and place. As a religion takes root and develops, it soon becomes focused on deriving knowledge and understanding from that original experience, sometimes resulting in the creation of a sacred text. In the process of describing the relation of human life to the ultimate concern, emphasis is placed on principles of conduct and behavior. And as a religion matures, stories and ceremonies are used to communicate that knowledge and understanding from generation to generation. Religion, then, often involves the practice of specific beliefs, moral codes, and rituals. When a religion spreads beyond a small religious community and becomes embodied in a larger social group, it can become identified with a particular culture, and for its followers, the religion becomes part of their cultural heritage—just a part of the way things are—dutifully accepted and unquestioned.

What may have begun as a personal first-hand experience often becomes a handed-down tradition. In his book *The Varieties of Religious Experience*, psychologist and philosopher William James (1842–1910) distinguished between second-hand and first-hand religion, the former referring to the public forms of inherited religion and the latter to a direct and immediate personal experience.[4]

## spirituality

A first-hand experience with the divine is what many people refer to as spirituality—an intimate encounter with a spiritual reality at the height and depth of life, sometimes seen as a personal connection with the spirit of God as a living presence. The word *spirit* originally referred to breathing or breath. Our English word comes from the Latin *spiritus* (*spee'-ri-toos*), which refers to the vital or animating force within living beings. It was translated from the Hebrew *ruach* (*roo'-akh*) and the Greek *pneuma* (*nyoo'-mah*), which have the dual meanings of *breath* or *wind*. The second (and earliest) of the two creation stories in the book of Genesis describes Yahweh forming an earthling—in Hebrew *adam* (*aw-dawm'*)—from the clay of the earth—*adamah* (*ad-aw-maw'*)—and then breathing life into the inert form.

> *Then Yahweh formed man from the dust of the ground, and breathed into his nostrils the breath [ruach] of life; and the man became a living being.*[5]

In this ancient Hebrew story, the breath of God is seen as the animating force in human life. It arrives at birth and departs at death.

In this sense, spirituality is often focused on the search to find the life-giving spirit of God within oneself. But more than that, spirituality is having

4. James, *Varieties of Religious Experience*, 24.
5. Genesis 2:7

one's life and being grasped by an ultimate concern. It is a search to discover ultimate reality in the midst of life, to find the true essence of being, to explore the deepest values and meaning by which people live, and to realize what it means to be fully human.

It is also a sense that there is something much bigger than any one of us in all that is. The vast grandeur of nature and the staggering beauty of the universe often draw forth a response of profound awe and wonder—powerful emotional reactions that are often interpreted as religious or spiritual experiences. Spirituality may or may not be about God, but it is often a reverence of the majesty and beauty we encounter in many facets of life—a glorious sunset, a vast seascape, a carefully tended garden, a quiet forest, a lyrical symphony, a magnificent cathedral, a tender moment, the face of a new-born child, or the death of a loved one. It is the sense that in the midst of everyday life, we are standing on holy ground.

## a journey or way

Those who are intentional about spirituality often describe it as a path, a journey, or a quest. Others see it simply as a way of being in the world—a life in touch with the deepest part of reality. At its heart, spirituality is the response to life that moves us at the depths of our existence. And sometimes this experience leads to a responsive action. We often speak of people being moved by the spirit, meaning that they are being driven by a dynamic internal force to speak or act in a powerful way. A first-hand experience with the sacred has the power to transform people. It can change how one sees the daily experiences of ordinary existence. Spirituality and religious faith represent the journey of finding out what one believes through a wrestling with the holy that is discovered in the midst of the mundane. This internal struggle is ultimately reflected in what one does or doesn't do with one's life.

When Paul Tillich defined faith as being grasped by an ultimate concern, he was not describing the codified beliefs of institutional religion; he was describing a first-hand experience, something visceral and moving, felt in the gut and filled with emotion. The religious faith that Tillich spoke of is more than any formal belief system. Faith is different than religion. It deals with an unusual level of trust or commitment, not simply an intellectual assent to some sacred scheme. Faith is ultimately trusting in something to the extent that you would bet your life on it. To be faithful within the context of any religion or culture is to be seized by and devoted to whatever is believed to matter most in one's life.

## the quest for meaning

So, the essence of spirituality is the innate, irrepressible quest for meaning in human life that is at the core of religion. Any quest begins with a question and a search for its answer. Why are we here? What is life all about? Is there a greater purpose to human existence? Is there more to life than meets the eye? Answering these questions is something science cannot do and for increasing numbers of young people, institutional religion fails to adequately do so as well.

Robert C. Fuller (b. 1952), a professor of religious studies at Bradley University, defines spirituality as a wide range of questions and responses to the wonders and meaning of life.

> *Spirituality exists wherever we struggle with the issue of how our lives fit into the greater cosmic scheme of things. This is true even when our questions never give way to specific answers or give rise to specific practices such as prayer or meditation. We encounter spiritual issues every time we wonder where the universe comes from, why we are here, or what happens when we die. We also become spiritual when we become moved by values such as beauty, love, or creativity that seem to reveal a meaning or power beyond our visible world. An idea or practice is "spiritual" when it reveals our personal desire to establish a felt-relationship with the deepest meanings or powers governing life.*[6]

Does spirituality involve a mystical encounter with a supernatural dimension beyond earthly reality, or does it have more to do with an intense personal experience within the natural world, or could it be both? For those who have accepted a modern, secular worldview, spirituality may simply be the belief or the suspicion that something else may lie beyond materialistic existence that science cannot explain, that there may be some other reality beyond that which is observable and verifiable, or that there may be some higher level of existence beyond the limits of our human sensory experiences. In the quest to discover whether there is more to life than meets the eye, some refer to the *More* as a characterization of the object of that quest. Therefore, some have described spirituality as an encounter *beyond* daily life. But most spiritual experiences are very earthy and ordinary—an encounter *within* daily life. Perhaps, then, spirituality can take both forms. The former encounter may involve an extraordinary life-changing event, while the latter can be experienced by looking at ordinary events with new eyes, as a revelation of the sacred in our midst. Many people, in their desire for

---

6. Fuller, *Spiritual, but Not Religious*, 8–9.

an extraordinary mountaintop experience, may miss the profoundly sacred aspect of the ordinary all around us.

## religion and spirituality

In the twenty-first century, we are witnessing a growing distinction between spirituality and religion. Religion is often seen to involve external practices, while spirituality relates to an internal experience and transformation. In relation to each other, some suggest that spirituality is the content and religion the container, or that spirituality is the substance and religion the form. Yet, there is much debate today as to whether a relationship between these private and public concepts is even necessary or required.

Robert Fuller reports:

> Before the 20th century the terms religious and spiritual were used more or less interchangeably. But a number of modern intellectual and cultural forces have accentuated differences between the "private" and "public" spheres of life. The increasing prestige of the sciences, the insights of modern biblical scholarship, and greater awareness of cultural relativism all made it more difficult for educated Americans to sustain unqualified loyalty to religious institutions. Many began to associate genuine faith with the "private" realm of personal experience rather than with the "public" realm of institutions, creeds, and rituals. The word spiritual gradually came to be associated with a private realm of thought and experience while the word religious came to be connected with the public realm of membership in religious institutions, participation in formal rituals, and adherence to official denominational doctrines.[7]

Tillich's "state of being grasped by an ultimate concern" falls under what Fuller describes as the private realm of personal experience, or spirituality.

Author and philosopher Sam Keen (b. 1931) compared religion and spirituality as two different paths moving in the same direction:

> To oversimplify slightly, there are two paths we might take that promise to lead us in the direction of the holy, two different ways to seek answers to the perennial questions that face every human being—the path of the religious pilgrim, and the way of the spiritual seeker.
>
> Religion presents the faithful with an authorized map of life—precepts to be followed, the example of lives of saints, saviors,

7. Ibid., 5.

*and bodhisattvas [enlightened beings] to be imitated, taboos to be*
*avoided, commandments to be obeyed, traditions to be respected*
*. . . Thus, the religious life is a pilgrimage to a known destination.*
*The end is given as well as the means. God is the goal of the search.*
*Church, bible, guru, and the accepted disciplines of the spirit are*
*the means . . .*
      *The spiritual quest is the reverse of the religious pilgrimage.*
*The quest begins when an individual falls into a spiritual "black*
*hole" in which everything that was solid vaporizes. Certainties*
*vanish, authorities are questioned, all the usual comforts and as-*
*surances of religion fail, and the path disappears. A spiritual quest*
*is the effort to discover the meaning of life. It is experimental, an*
*exploration of a country not yet mapped, whose boundaries are*
*not yet known. The spiritual mind lives in and loves the great*
*mythic questions.*[8]

In other words, if spirituality is the quest for meaning, religion—especially institutional religion—is a sanctioned set of answers. Look no further.
The truth is here.

## spiritual, but not religious

When it comes to matters of faith, many postmodern people embrace spirituality but largely reject traditional organized religion. Growing numbers
claim to be "spiritual, but not religious." Robert Fuller reported on a 1997
study done to clarify what people meant when they described themselves
this way.

*Religiousness, they found, was associated with higher levels of in-*
*terest in church attendance and commitment to orthodox beliefs.*
*Spirituality, in contrast, was associated with higher levels of inter-*
*est in mysticism, experimentation with unorthodox beliefs and*
*practices, and negative feelings toward both clergy and churches.*
*Most respondents in the study tried to integrate elements of reli-*
*giousness and spirituality. Yet 19 percent of their sample constitut-*
*ed a separate category best described as "spiritual, not religious."*
      *Compared with those who connected interest in private spiri-*
*tuality with membership in a public religious group, the "spiritual,*
*but not religious" group was "less likely to evaluate religiousness*
*positively, less likely to engage in traditional forms of worship such*
*as church attendance and prayer, less likely to engage in group*
*experiences related to spiritual growth, more likely to be agnostic,*

8. Keen, *Hymns to an Unknown God*, 76–78.

*more likely to characterize religiousness and spirituality as differ-
ent and non-overlapping concepts, more likely to hold nontradi-
tional beliefs, and more likely to have had mystical experiences."*

*Those who see themselves as "spiritual, but not religious"
reject traditional organized religion as the sole—or even the most
valuable—means of furthering their spiritual growth. Many have
had negative experiences with churches or church leaders. For example, they may have perceived church leaders as more concerned
with building an organization than promoting spirituality, as
hypocritical, or as narrow-minded. Some may have experienced
various forms of emotional or even sexual abuse.*[9]

Priest, writer, and educator Barbara Brown Taylor (b. 1951) seems to
have the best insight in her introduction to the book *An Altar in the World*.
She describes her reaction to people who tell her they are spiritual but not
religious when they discover she is a religion professor:

*In that context, people are usually trying to tell me that they have
a sense of the divine depths of things but they are not churchgoers.
They want to grow closer to God, but not at the cost of creeds,
confessions and religious wars large or small. Some of them have
resigned from religions they once belonged to, taking what was
helpful with them while leaving the rest behind. Others have collected wisdom from the four corners of the world, which they use
like cooks with a pantry full of spices. Plenty of them are satisfied,
too, even as they confess that they are sometimes lonely.*

*I think I know what they mean by "religious." It is the "spiri-
tual" part that is harder to grasp. My guess is that they do not
use that word in reference to a formal set of beliefs, since that
belongs on the religious side of the page. It may be the name for a
longing—for more meaning, more feeling, more connection, more
life. When I hear people talk about spirituality, that seems to be
what they are describing. They know there is more to life than
what meets the eye. They have drawn close to this "More" in nature, in love, in art, in grief. They would be happy for someone to
teach them how to spend more time in the presence of this deeper
reality, but when they visit the places where such knowledge is
supposed to be found, they often find the rituals hollow and the
language antique.*[10]

---

9. Fuller, *Spiritual, but Not Religious*, 6. Fuller cites a study by Brian Zinnbauer,
Kenneth Pargament, et al, titled "Religion and Spirituality: Unfuzzying the Fuzzy" reported in the *Journal for the Scientific Study of Religion*, (December 1997).

10. Taylor, *Altar in the World*, xv–xvi.

Pollster George Gallup's 1992 report, *The Religious Life of Young Americans*, stated that most young Americans believe that it is very important that life be meaningful and have a purpose. Yet a high percentage of these same people believe that most churches and synagogues today are not effective in helping people find that meaning. Again, Robert Fuller reports:

> Forsaking formal religious organizations, these people have instead embraced an individualized spirituality that includes picking and choosing from a wide range of alternative religious philosophies. They typically view spirituality as a journey intimately linked with the pursuit of personal growth or development.[11]

This is not a small group. According to a 2009 Newsweek poll, 30 percent of Americans identify as spiritual but not religious to some degree. And among the Millennial generation (those born between 1982 and 2000), the percentage climbs as high as 70 percent. The spiritual but not religious community is growing so much that one pastor compared it to a movement.

This is not to say that *all* those who claim to be spiritual, but not religious have necessarily experienced the deeper dimensions of the spiritual life. Most probably have not. There is a great deal of shallow thinking, frivolous theology, and lightweight belief masquerading as spirituality these days. But, unfortunately, that can also be said for many of the people who tell the pollsters they consider themselves somewhat or very religious. Sadly, most people do not think about spirituality or religion very deeply, if at all. They tend to be consumed by other aspects of life, immersed in time-consuming activities or undemanding mindless entertainment, while the spiritual, sacred, or holy dimensions of reality are pushed into the background. Polling data seems to suggest that as many as six out of ten people who are members of churches have only a mild interest in religion. Religious influence over the way they live is marginal at best.

## types of spirituality

Spirituality can take many forms: some that are inwardly focused and others that are directed toward the world around us. Theologian Philip Sheldrake (b. 1946) gives an excellent overview of spirituality in its many varieties and contexts in *Spirituality: A Very Short Introduction*. He describes four fundamental types: ascetical, mystical, active-practical, and prophetic-critical. *Ascetical spirituality* is a special way of life based on disciplines of self-denial, austerity, and abstention from worldly pleasures as a pathway to

11. Fuller, *Spiritual, but Not Religious*, 6.

enlightenment and moral perfection. Most of us recognize this form in the monastic life and some Eastern religious practices. *Mystical spirituality* often seeks a personal communion with the sacred, a sense of connectedness with the cosmos, or an experience of enlightenment regarding deep mysteries. Mystics don't need to withdraw from everyday life and often find that the mundane is transfigured into something wondrous. Mystical spirituality usually involves commitment to practices such as meditation, mindfulness, and contemplation. The ascetical and mystical forms of spirituality may be thought of as inwardly focused, leading to one's personal growth. In contrast, the next two forms of spirituality are primarily outwardly focused, leading to engagement with the world around us. *Active-practical spirituality* is invested in everyday life as the context for spiritual growth. It seeks to develop a sense of meaning beyond the immediate pursuit of happiness or material success. It emphasizes the spiritual value of such human virtues as acceptance, forgiveness, compassion, charity, social responsibility, and freedom from egocentrism. It promotes service to others as a chief form of spiritual practice. *Prophetic-critical spirituality* goes beyond offering charitable service to challenging the fundamental causes of social inequality and injustice as a spiritual task. It is the spirituality of justice. We see this spirituality in the writings of the Hebrew prophets Amos, Isaiah, and Jeremiah (from about 760 to 690 BCE), and in the words and deeds of Jesus of Nazareth and Francis of Assisi (1182–1226). In the last century, we have witnessed prophetic-critical spirituality in the lives of Mohandas Gandhi (1869–1948), Dietrich Bonhoeffer (1906–1945), Martin Luther King, Jr. (1929–1968), and Óscar Romero (1917–1980).

Jesus did not practice an ascetical spirituality. In fact, he was condemned for being a glutton and a drunkard in contrast to the asceticism of John the Baptizer and his disciples. He was not much of a mystic either. Instead, Jesus proclaimed an active-practical spirituality among the poor and illiterate peasants and fishermen who represented the majority of the population in first-century Roman Palestine. He modeled a spiritual life immersed in everyday commonplace realities that consisted of a teaching and ethic that went beyond egocentric attention to one's own well-being to a life lived in service toward others. Jesus was one of those rare individuals who had an immediate experience of the divine that transformed his life and filled him with a spirit of passion, zeal, and courage. As he shared his insights with others, he described a counter-cultural way of living that was based on love, acceptance, forgiveness, compassion, charity, and social responsibility through communities of mutual welfare. However, Jesus did not stop there. He moved beyond this active-practical spirituality to the far more dangerous arena of prophetic-critical spirituality, personally challenging the social inequality, widespread poverty, and economic injustice of his society. For this, the Roman government and wealthy Jewish elites had him arrested, beaten, and executed. After his death, some of his followers began to model their lives on his. They became filled with the same spirit of passion, zeal, and courage that had motivated Jesus. They too boldly stepped forth to challenge the religious and civil authorities who controlled the domination system of their day. Their lives reflected a path of spiritual growth from religious and social conformity to radical activism.

## the path of spiritual development

We instinctively distinguish between the stages of physical human growth: infancy, toddlerhood, childhood, adolescence, young adulthood, middle age, and old age. Each stage is common to all human beings, although our personal experience of each stage is unique. A fundamental understanding of the changes we commonly experience in each stage helps us to recognize that we are not alone in our growth and development—the things we personally experience are part of the normal human experience.

A person's spiritual growth can also follow a series of fairly predictable stages of development. But spiritual growth is not necessarily aligned to physical growth, age, or maturity. We are not all at the same place as we develop, and some never grow beyond a childhood or adolescent faith. As M. (Morgan) Scott Peck (1936–2005), the author of *A Road Less Traveled* and *The Different Drum* writes:

> *Our unique human capacity for change and transformation is reflected in our human spirituality. Throughout the ages, deep-thinking people looking at themselves have come to discern that we are not all at the same place spiritually or religiously. There are different stages of spiritual growth or religious development.*[12]

For most religious people, growth often begins by being enculturated in an inherited tradition starting in late childhood and early adolescence. It is a time of unquestioning acceptance of second-hand religious beliefs. Because our parents and their friends and other authority figures say that certain things are true, we take them at face value at this young age. During late adolescence or early adulthood, some people will move to a period of questioning non-acceptance. The degree to which this happens is often related to one's level of education and the ability or courage to step back and look at one's faith and culture critically. At this phase, many ideas are

12. Peck, *Further Along the Road Less Traveled*, 119.

examined in a search for a more personal faith. Many previously cherished beliefs are rejected and abandoned. This may result in a period of intense struggle, which some have called "the dark night of the soul." If one is able to move through this stage, a new understanding of faith may emerge, leading one to see God and the world in new ways and to experience mystery within and beyond everyday life. Sometimes this transformation can lead to a more intimate relationship with the sacred. Sometimes it leads to the public role of a prophet for social change. A number of authors have described different models of the stages of this faith journey, and although they differ in terminology, they usually follow the broad pattern I just outlined.

## stages of the faith journey

James Fowler (1940–2015), author of *Stages of Faith*, is a pioneer in the study of this field. His research discovered that in any religious context, the human stages of faith development are amazingly uniform. He describes different six stages that are possible throughout life. Fowler's first two stages describe the development of the personality in infancy and childhood. Although these are important phases in the development of basic religious concepts and an image of God, it is the four stages of adult spiritual growth that I want to focus on. Fowler's four adult phases of faith are labeled 1) synthetic/conventional, 2) individuative/reflective, 3) conjunctive, and 4) universalizing. His work became the basis for the thinking of other thinkers.

Marcus Borg identified the first three of Fowler's four adult stages as Pre-critical Naiveté, Critical Thinking, and Post-Critical Naiveté. He described Pre-critical Naiveté as the stage that begins in early childhood in which we take for granted whatever authority figures tell us to be true. For example, believing that miraculous Bible stories are literally true. Critical Thinking is that stage where we make decisions about how much of what we were taught as children we are going to carry with us into adulthood. Some people will retain their childhood faith and others will decide to move on. Some will become skeptical about religious faith altogether, while others may find another path to stay connected to their religious tradition with intellectual integrity. Post-critical Naiveté is the ability to hear the childhood stories once again as metaphorically true, even though they are not factually true. It is the ability to accept the underlying universal truths found in myth as Joseph Campbell (1904–1987) has shown.

Scott Peck also focused on Fowler's adult stages and modified them to reflect his experiences as a psychotherapist. He writes:

*Over the course of a decade practicing psychotherapy, a strange
pattern began to emerge. If people who were religious came to me
in pain and trouble, and if they became engaged in the therapeutic
process so as to go the whole route, they frequently left therapy as
atheists, agnostics or at least skeptics. On the other hand, atheists,
agnostics, or skeptics came to me in pain or difficulty and became
fully engaged, they frequently left therapy as deeply religious
people.*[13]

Peck's model begins with people who are deeply disturbed, so his
stages are labeled 1) chaotic/antisocial, 2) formal/institutional, 3) skeptical/
individual, and 4) mystical/communal.

A third model of faith development comes from the work of pastor and
educator John Westerhoff (b. 1933). His work confirms the essential path
outlined in the other models. However, Westerhoff uses a tree-growth analogy of development, radiating out in concentric circles. Some of the other
models assume a kind of hierarchy of stages. At the center of an individual's
faith journey, Westerhoff proposes a central core of 1) experiential faith, representing what is experienced in infancy and young childhood. Surrounding
that core is the layer of 2) affiliated faith, which translates into one's inherited
faith tradition experienced in childhood and adolescence. Next comes 3)
searching faith, which is the period of doubting and questioning we have
seen in the other models. At the outer layer is 4) owned faith, in which one
takes ownership for the mature faith one chooses to live out.[14]

At a risk of doing a disservice to these authors, I will propose that
we think primarily of the stages of the faith journey as 1) religious conformity, 2) skeptical deconstruction, 3) spiritual reformation, and 4) radical
transformation. The following descriptions are based primarily on James
Fowler's work.

## religious conformity

The stage of religious conformity is where a majority of the population
find their permanent home. Usually arising in childhood, it is characterized by conventionality and certainty. We tend to internalize the beliefs of
the people around us as children. These religious ideas are commonly part
of an inherited second-hand faith where tradition and culture play important roles. One finds one's identity by aligning with the religious group and
theological perspectives of our parents or other significant adults, without

---

13. Peck, *Different Drum*, 188.
14. Westerhoff, *Will Our Children Have Faith?*

critically reflecting on their ideology. Those who have different opinions are seen as separate—not "one of us." In conformity religion, religious authority is usually top-down and is confirmed, endorsed, and supported by a majority opinion of those with whom we associate. This is a stage of religious safety, comfort, and security. If significant questions arise, they are often suppressed by community or peer pressure. However, certain situations may create a crisis of faith and cause one to question one's continued participation in this second-hand faith. These might include institutional and interpersonal situations including internal clashes and disputes within a worshipping community, the revelation of hypocrisy by authority figures, or significant changes to the policies and practices that were previously considered sacred. People in the stage of religious conformity want a consistent and stable structure. They often become very upset if their rituals are changed, their liturgies are altered, or new hymns are introduced, because it is precisely these enduring traditions that have sheltered their lives from the chaos and change of contemporary life. On the other hand, the spiritual crisis may be caused by a newfound critical reflection on inherited belief systems. In some cases, as one grows in knowledge and understanding, and feels empowered to question authority and tradition, the conformist theological perspective just stops making sense. Disillusioned, a person may transition to the next stage of the spiritual journey.

## skeptical deconstruction

Deconstruction is primarily a period of angst and struggle, in which one must face difficult questions regarding one's religious identity and beliefs. Often occurring in adolescence, this stage is marked by doubts and questions regarding the inherited tradition. Those who enter this stage gradually detach themselves from the religious group that formerly provided their identity. Religious authority is questioned. Scott Peck says of these skeptics, "They will then begin—often to their parents' utterly unnecessary horror and chagrin—to fall away from the church, having become doubters or agnostics or atheists." People in this phase realize—perhaps for the first time—that as an individual, it is necessary to take personal responsibility for one's beliefs and feelings. Concepts that were once unquestioned are now subjected to critical scrutiny. Deconstructionists begin the task of asking the hard questions about life, religion, and reality. They become seekers of truth. Brian McLaren sees this as a desert or wilderness experience. Often the seeker is working through this stage alone, but sometimes finds comfort in a small group of people who are also questioning and searching. One may settle into being a rational skeptic and agnostic, and move on with life. Some who find their inherited tradition to be without any validity may become atheists. For many, however, this phase is not a comfortable place to be. It is a rejection of certainty, but does not necessarily embrace uncertainty about ultimate concerns.

Some people who enter this stage sense that not only is the world far more complex than the conformist worldview had proposed, it is even more complex than the agnostic rationality of the current phase allows. Disillusioned with conformist religion and uncomfortable with unresolved religious angst, the questioner may be inspired to move to the next stage—a new understanding of the sacred in the secular world.

## spiritual reformation

The spiritual reformation stage moves from a coldly rational skepticism to the acknowledgement that reality may be far more complex and interconnected than one realized. The individual begins to realize that there are some things in the world that seem to defy logic or intuition, and that there are some things that may lie beyond the ordinary range of perception—a dimension of mystery and unknowing. This appreciation for ambiguity, paradox, uncertainty, and mystery can lead to a period of spiritual and personal transformation and insight. At this point, a person sometimes experiences a new awareness of the sacred in the midst of the mundane and a new openness to the subtle voices of one's deeper self. This stage makes room for mystery within a secular modern worldview that has pushed God aside, but without recourse to a naïve belief in a supernatural dimension. It creates opportunities for new depths of spirituality and religious revelation in the natural world. This can be an overwhelming, ecstatic stage in which one is radically opened to new experiences of awe and wonder and an embrace of the spiritual depths of humanity.

Barbara Brown Taylor has said:

> My life depends on engaging the most ordinary physical activities with the most exquisite attention I can give them. My life depends on ignoring all touted distinctions between the secular and the sacred, the physical and the spiritual, the body and the soul. What is saving my life now is becoming more fully human, trusting that there is no way to God apart from real life in the real world.[15]

---

15. Barbara Brown Taylor, *An Altar in the World*, xvii.

Seen from a fresh perspective, ideas that once had been rejected as false are now found to be true at a deeper metaphorical or symbolic level. Old ideas are integrated into a new vision of faith and reality. This is what Westerhoff spoke of as an "owned faith." One may begin to grasp the depth of reality behind the symbols, myths, and rituals of one's inherited faith, and may see value in the symbols of other belief systems. Because one has begun to see a bigger picture, the walls of culture and tradition that separate us from others may begin to erode. This stage is open to universalizing ideas about faith and spirituality. McLaren says that in this stage, "The seeker finds a unity in the essential things, but is open to diversity in non-essentials."

A larger picture sometimes comes into view—a vision of the unity of humanity, a sense of oneness with creation, and a connection with the spiritual mystery of the universe. Some may feel called to share in the suffering of others and to actively resist the powers of oppression that cause suffering in the world, but may be hesitant to act decisively due to concerns about safety and self-preservation. For the few who find the courage to proceed regardless of consequences, the prophetic stance of radical transformation beckons.

## radical transformation

The final stage of human spiritual growth is a radically transformative faith. Some might call it a stage of engaged enlightenment. The concepts of love and compassion that lie behind all major religious traditions become increasingly clear as the essence of the spiritual life. In this new stage, one becomes an activist for the vision of global human community and a prophetic voice for compassion and justice on behalf of the poor, the marginalized, the excluded, and the oppressed. As one acts on one's beliefs, it is often necessary to step out as a leader for change with passion, zeal, and courage. James Fowler describes it this way:

> Persons described by this stage typically exhibit qualities that shake our usual criteria of normalcy. Their heedlessness to self-preservation and the vividness of their taste and feel for transcendent moral and religious actuality give their actions and words an extraordinary and often unpredictable quality. In their devotion to universalizing compassion they may offend our parochial perceptions of justice. In their penetration through the obsession with survival, security, and significance they threaten our measured standards of righteousness and goodness and prudence. Their enlarged visions of universal community disclose the

*partialness of our tribes and pseudo-species. And their leadership initiatives, often involving strategies of nonviolent suffering and ultimate respect for being, constitute affronts to our usual notions of relevance.*[16]

The movement from spiritual reformation to radical transformation may parallel what theologian Matthew Fox calls "mysticism versus prophecy." He sees both as manifestations of a radical faith. Fox points out that the word *radical* comes from the Latin *radix* (*ray'-dicks*), which means *root*. According to Fox, to be a mystic is to be rooted in the deepest dimensions of life and its mysteries, and to be fundamentally changed as a result. But to be a prophet is to have the courage to "uproot" the status quo of one's culture, to be a voice for change and a force for transformation, to risk everything for the sake of others.[17] Fox understands that true spirituality calls us not to privatized prayer, contemplation, personal growth, and spiritual direction, but to justice.

## the long and winding road

The movement between all of these stages of faith development is not always straight forward. After questioning and struggle, some people may want to return to the certainty of their inherited tradition. The human ability to compartmentalize our lives enables this reversal, separating what we believe on Sunday from what we do and believe the rest of the week. Some who have experienced a spiritual awakening may revisit rational skepticism. Those involved in engaged enlightenment, may go back to the security of seeing the big picture but not acting on it in a radical fashion. Some may shift back and forth between various stages many times. Still, a majority of American adults is comfortably at home in religious conformity, or if they have left the church, are content to work things out as lifelong skeptics and agnostics.

The transformational journey of faith moves us away from a reliance on external authorities—religious or scientific. The transformation of our hearts can lead us from the mediated religion of inherited faith to a more immediate religion of the spirit. As we take ownership of our own life of faith, each of us develops a wholly personal religion, through questioning and honest searching. As we grow from the unquestioning acceptance of our youth to the questioning non-acceptance of mature adults, we become

16. Fowler, *Stages of Faith*, 200.
17. Fox, *Musical Mystical Bear*, 73.

open to experiences of mystery and to a more personal relationship to God or to the divine or to the mystery at the center of our being.

The spiritual journey does not transform us into a state of perfection. It does something much more important. It often enables us to become more fully human. When we are grasped by ultimate concern, we are able to live a more authentic life. That which is transcendent—the sacred, the divine, the holy, the "More"—is no longer external to our lives, sought somewhere "out there." Instead, it is found deep within ourselves. It has truly been within us all along. It only takes a hatching of the heart to recognize it.

## a secular spirituality

As we move into an increasingly secular world where the influence of church-centered Christianity is diminishing, we begin to see how this forms the contours of a religionless or secular spirituality. The word *secular* comes from the Latin *saecularis (say-koo'-lah-ris)*. It is usually defined as worldly, temporal, or profane—standing in opposition to the sacred or the religious. But in Latin it refers to a *saeculum (say-koo'-loom)*, an age or time in history. Specifically, it refers to the present age or the here and now. The active-practical form of spirituality is very much lived in the present amidst daily mundane concerns. But it is a life with a focus on ultimate concern. It certainly has a long history among religious people and groups, but it doesn't have to be a religious form of expression.

The Millennial Generation appears to be more interested in living lives defined by meaning than previous generations. They report being less focused on financial success than they are on making a difference. Social psychologists define *meaning* as the degree to which we feel our lives have purpose, value, and impact.

> Although meaning is subjective—signifying different things to dif-
> ferent people—a defining feature is connection to something big-
> ger than the self. People who lead meaningful lives feel connected
> to others, to work, to a life purpose, and to the world itself. There
> is no one meaning of life, but rather, many sources of meaning that
> we all experience day to day, moment to moment, in the form of
> these connections.[18]

The gospel accounts provide us with an image of what a life lived in the spirit of God looks like. It is a life transformed by the spirit of love, the spirit of compassion, the spirit of generosity, the spirit of forgiveness, the spirit

18. Smith and Aaker, "Millennial Searchers."

of hospitality, the spirit of justice, the spirit of peace. To be spiritual is to embody all of these attributes to some degree or another. The premise of this book is that a life of faith that is honest to Jesus begins when we are grasped by love and compassion. It takes root when we are willing to bet our lives that nothing really matters more in life than the embodiment of self-giving love and the expression of compassion in response to the pain and suffering we see all around us. Deeply-felt compassion is the motivator that drives us to put love into action. When the spirit of God fills our lives, it drives out selfishness, greed, indifference, hatred, exclusivity, and the need for domination. These base human conditions represent the normalcy of the world. Spirituality is much more than an internal quest to discover some kind of personal peace and wholeness. Spirituality is the shaking of the foundations of the status quo, upsetting the normalcy of the world, and transforming the darkness of the human soul into new possibilities for authentic humanity.

When love and compassion become the highest concerns of human life, they bring meaning and purpose to life. This is what people are desperately searching for. There is no great secret to life's meaning. There is nothing esoteric or hidden to be found. There are no arcane disciplines we need to master. When we discover these simple truths about life's purpose—our purpose—then the spiritual journey has led us to a point of both insight and transformation. If, day in and day out, we begin to live our lives—however haltingly—as an expression of love, compassion, forgiveness, generosity, hospitality, peace and justice, then the transformation of the world will begin. We will become agents of radical change within our tiny sphere of influence, and co-conspirators with others in the quiet revolution of God— the conspiracy of love. Our actions may appear as small and insignificant as a mustard seed, they may seem hidden and unnoticed as a tiny amount of yeast in bread dough, but the eventual effects will be seen. Our acts will, little by little, begin to disturb the normalcy of the world. And that is all we can hope for. It is all we can ever hope for. When we take this path—when we embody the love and compassion of God and become more fully human—the true spiritual journey begins.

CHAPTER 9

# cultural nonconformity

---

*Christians were never meant to be normal. We've always been holy troublemakers, we've always been creators of uncertainty, agents of a dimension that's incompatible with the status quo; we do not accept the world as it is, but we insist on the world becoming the way that God wants it to be. And the Kingdom of God is different from the patterns of this world.*[1]

—Jacques Ellul (1912–1994)

*Do not be conformed to this world, but be transformed by the renewing of your minds.*[2]

—Paul, the Apostle

JESUS CALLED ON PEOPLE to change. Not just a little, but dramatically. Mark's gospel reports that Jesus began his ministry with these words:

> *Jesus came to Galilee, proclaiming the good news of God, and saying, "The time is fulfilled, and the kingdom of God has come near; repent and believe in the good news."*[3]

---

1. Jacques Ellul, *Meaning of the City*.
2. Romans 12:2
3. Mark 1:15

144

As we described earlier, the kingdom of God is the term Jesus used to express his vision of a profound transformation of human beings and human institutions—social, political, economic and religious—to fully express the character and nature of God—a God of love. To accomplish this vision, Jesus worked toward the creation of a new kind of community dedicated to values of compassion, generosity, peace, and justice. He was creating a movement for change, a people engaged in a vast conspiracy of love. To lay the groundwork for the dawning of his vision, Jesus called on people to repent and believe in the good news.

Repent and believe. It seems so simple. Traditionally, the listener would assume that Jesus wants us to feel bad about our past sins, resolve to do better, and believe that Jesus brings good news about what the future has in store for us. This assumption regards repentance and belief as a mostly internal experience of the heart and mind—first the emotional response of remorse and then an intellectual affirmation of whatever good news Jesus is announcing, especially if it doesn't demand anything of us. These actions are entirely within one's comfort zone.

Paul's letter to the Romans adds some content to the belief part: "If you confess with your lips that Jesus is Lord and believe in your heart that God raised him from the dead, you will be saved."[4] Of course, Jesus did not agree with Paul on these propositions. The gospels they proclaimed were very different. Accordingly, Paul has led us astray when it comes to the intent of Jesus. When you view Jesus through the lens of Paul's writings, the good news is distorted. The assumption is that we are being saved to experience an eternal life in heaven. This may be standard orthodox teaching, but it is way off the mark in regard to the message of Jesus, and misses his meaning of repentance and belief.

Something has been lost in translation—literally. First of all, Jesus and his followers spoke in Aramaic, an ancient Semitic language related to Hebrew. Paul and the gospel writers wrote in Greek. We of course read these texts in English. We are trusting modern biblical translators to correctly interpret these texts for us, but unfortunately most have an agenda, and that often involves perpetuating orthodox Christian teaching. So let us examine the words *repent* and *believe* in the original Greek to get a better understanding of the real meaning of Jesus' message and see what is missing from our bibles and our theology.

4. Romans 10:9–10

## repent

To our ears, repentance usually conveys a sense of guilt and regret. It is commonly understood as a feeling of remorse, and that is precisely how the church has conventionally used the term.[5] But repent doesn't capture the true meaning of the Greek word *metanoeite* (*met-an-oh-eh'-eet-eh*), a form of the verb *metanoeó* (*met-an-oh-eh'-oh*), as used in the gospels. The noun *metanoia* (*met-an'-oy-ah*) is the more familiar term for many people, meaning a fundamental shift or movement (*meta*) of the mind (*noia*). It is a movement that takes us beyond the mindset of our cultural conformity—our conventional wisdom—into a new way of perceiving and thinking about the world around us. The repentance that Jesus speaks of is a transformative movement, a fundamental change of life that is deeper, more basic, and more far-reaching than our common understanding of the word repentance. It is not about being sorry for the past. It is about thinking differently and changing the direction of our lives for the future. Metanoia essentially means to turn around, to change the form, to take on a whole new identity. It involves a change of orientation, direction, or character that is so pronounced and dramatic that the very form and purpose of a life is decisively altered and reshaped. It means to begin the journey of walking away from the old to the new.

The translation of metanoia as *repent* began when the New Testament was translated from Greek into Latin sometime around 384 CE by Eusebius Sophronius Hieronymus (c. 347–420), better known as St. Jerome. His Latin Vulgate translation used the phrase *poenitentiam agite* (*pay-nih-ten'-see-ahm ah-ghee'-teh*), which means "Go, and do penance" (a voluntary self-punishment). This error was compounded by Martin Luther (1483–1546) when he translated the New Testament into vernacular German in 1522. Luther worked from a 1519 Greek text compiled by Desiderius Erasmus Roterodamus (1466–1536), known to history simply as Erasmus. Luther translated *metanoia* as *büßen* or *büssen* (*boo'sen*), which means to atone, to redress, to do penance.[6] So from the end of the sixteenth century on, Roman

---

5. The confession of sins in liturgical churches reinforces this perception of repentance as being contrite or sorry for sin. The following confession comes from the *Lutheran Service Book* (2006): "O Almighty God, merciful Father, I a poor, miserable sinner, confess to you all my sins and iniquities, with which I have ever offended you and justly deserved your punishment now and forever. *But I am heartily sorry for them and sincerely repent of them*, and I pray you of your boundless mercy, and for the sake of the holy, innocent, bitter sufferings and death of your beloved son, Jesus Christ, to be gracious and merciful to me, a poor sinful being."

6. Luther had earlier used the same understanding of metanoia when he compiled his "95 Theses" (1517) for debate within the Roman Catholic Church. The very

Catholics and many Protestants believed that Jesus was talking about re-gret, sorrow, remorse, or performing acts of contrition, instead of a radical change in thinking and living. One contemporary biblical scholar referred to the substitution of *repent* for metanoia as an utter mistranslation, while another called it the worst translation in the New Testament. So why does it still appear incorrectly in most English translations?

To Jesus, metanoia was a change so dramatic that it implied starting over again through a metaphorical second birth.

> *In reply Jesus declared, "I tell you the truth, no one can see the kingdom of God without being born again."[7]*

Jesus' declaration is not to be confused with what is commonly known as born-again Christianity. The rebirth of metanoia is not about inviting the resurrected presence of the Christ to enter our hearts while remaining firmly rooted in cultural conformity. Jesus was certainly not discussing speaking in tongues or other charismatic gifts often associated with born-again Chris-tians. He was articulating an invitation to a new quality of life in the midst of the old. This is the essence of the life-change that has been traditionally symbolized by baptism. It is a fundamental transformation that enables us to begin the journey of a new life. It is like being reborn with a radically new perspective on the meaning of life and matters of ultimate concern.

The deep-seated change of metanoia that Jesus describes happens through a process of learning and growing. It involves learning a completely new way of thinking about life, being instructed in a new way of seeing real-ity. It means discarding conventional wisdom and traditional common sense for an unconventional wisdom and a transformed sense of purpose. Start by turning around and going the other way, Jesus says to us. You are a captive of your culture and, although you may not be able to see it, you are headed in the wrong direction. You are living in darkness, mired in confusion.

For instance, in America our cultural view of reality is one of climbing an economic ladder. As we climb, we tend to keep our eyes on the rung above, towards those who have more than we do. Because a few are incred-ibly wealthy, we tend to think of ourselves as poorer than we really are. When we turn around, as Jesus calls us to do, we look back down the ladder. Then we are able to see the vast majority of people who have far less than we do, and we begin to understand how incredibly wealthy we really are. It is a change of perspective, a shift of the mind, a whole new way of thinking.

---

first thesis was "When our Lord and Master Jesus Christ said, 'Repent' (Matthew 4:17), he willed the entire life of believers to be one of repentance."

7. John 3:3

If embraced, one's life becomes transformed; it becomes fundamentally altered.

Being born again is not about religion. It is about a way of living. It is a movement from greed to giving, from selfishness to servanthood, from social conformity to insurrection against the status quo. Jesus was talking about shifting allegiances and values away from a mainstream culture of power, domination, and violence to the kingdom values of selfless love, compassion, humility, equality, generosity, forgiveness, justice, peace, service, and inclusive community. This is what it means to be born anew. It is a movement from values that focus solely on "me" to the embrace of values focused on "you" and "us" in a life of mutuality and service.

## believe in the good news

The English verb *believe* is a translation of the Greek *pisteuó* (*pist-yoo'-oh*) which can mean to believe, but more accurately means to trust or to have faith in. It is based on the noun *pistis* (*pis'-tis*) that means faith, belief, trust, confidence, and faithfulness. Normally, belief has the connotation of an intellectual acceptance of a proposition—a certainty that something is true, even in the absence of empirical evidence. Faith, likewise, implies great confidence in an idea. But faith is often a visible and outward expression of what is believed to be true in one's head. Further, faith is a trust in something to the extent that one would be willing to bet one's life on it. To be faithful within the context of any culture is to be seized by and devoted to whatever is believed to matter most in one's life. Belief is a psychological state, while faith is a way of living. We often speak of this visible expression as a faith walk or faith journey.

The good news that Jesus proclaimed was a radical message of hope for people at the bottom of his society—the peasants and fishermen of Galilee. Jesus called on his followers to trust that the way of life he was teaching and modeling had the capability of transforming their lives and ultimately could change the world. He invited them to transform their old ways of thinking, and to shed their culture's conventional wisdom in order to follow him. He asked them to risk their lives for this new way of living when he said, "If any want to become my followers, let them deny themselves and take up their cross daily and follow me." Taking up one's cross in the context of first-century Roman Palestine meant a willingness to sacrifice one's life in an engagement with political and economic power and a challenge to the unjust systems of the world.

So, both *metanoia* and *pistis* involve a committed change—a revolution in one's way of thinking and perceiving, and a life dedicated to that new reality, trusting that this is the right thing to do, that this is the most important thing to do, and that this new way is worth risking everything one has, including one's life.

On the basis of this understanding, I would paraphrase the words in Mark's gospel as:

> *Jesus came into Galilee, proclaiming the good news, and saying, "The decisive time has arrived, for the kingdom of God is at hand. Change your whole way of thinking and living, and risk everything for this radical message of hope."*

This translation describes doing something extraordinary—moving beyond one's comfort zone to a radically different way of life. I do not believe that Jesus calls anyone to a comfortable existence. That was not his message to his first followers. Instead, Jesus calls people to a life of challenge and transformation.

## captivity to culture

Nearly every religion is shaped by its cultural milieu. Cultural variations help to explain why the same religion can look so differently in different settings. For instance, in Afghanistan, the wearing of the *burqa*, which covers the female body from head to toe, is very different from the *hijab*, the simple head covering worn by Muslim women in Western Europe, Egypt, or Iran. Yet both reflect the Islamic ideal of modesty in dress for women. The Quran does not require the *burqa*, but fundamentalist Afghani culture does. Likewise, Christianity can seem widely diverse in different cultural settings. Imagine, for instance, the vast difference between a New England Episcopal high mass and the worship in a backwoods Pentecostal Church of God that practices snake handling. Both are forms of Christian worship that reflect a particular social culture. Christianity, like most other religions, absorbs the cultural values and traditions that surround it.

It generally comes down to whether Christianity exists in a culture shaped by a pre-modern, modern, or postmodern worldview. As a result, Christianity in the modern and postmodern Global North is frequently finding itself at odds with the church in the pre-modern cultures of the Global South. This was revealed most recently in the conflict fomenting in the United Methodist Church over the blessing of same-sex marriages. Several pastors in the United States have had to face censure by ecclesial courts over their participation in this practice. While the American sector of United Methodists—which tends to be moderate to liberal in its theology—is probably shifting towards approving the blessing of gay marriages, the denomination is governed by a global body and its canon law cannot be modified unless all the regions of the church agree. The trouble is that the very conservative Methodist church in the Global South is growing rapidly while the more liberal church in the North is declining. African Methodists will likely outnumber American Methodists within the next decade. Thus, the progressive Methodists are hamstrung by more literalistic conservatives. In our increasingly postmodern culture, American Methodists risk a further alienation of younger generations by their inability to endorse and support equal treatment of all people in loving relationships. Rather than moving forward, the shift in global membership in many mainline Protestant denominations is taking the church backward toward an earlier more conservative position, making it increasingly unattractive and irrelevant to postmodern people.

Culture thus forms the context of a denomination's biblical interpretation, but there is a broader and more subtle issue we must confront if we are to engage in a journey of transformation. We often do not recognize the extent to which our dominant culture has shaped our faith in other ways. Cultural influence is so pervasive we often cannot see it. It is like the air we breathe. In the United States, we live in the midst of a global empire and for the most part American citizens do not recognize it, or in many cases simply do not want to recognize it. In the twenty-first century, we still reflect the cultural captivity of the church by empire that began with Constantine.

## the domination system

As we stated earlier, nearly every society throughout history has favored an elite group of wealthy and powerful individuals and families at the expense of the majority of less-fortunate inhabitants. For thousands of years, economic elites have rigged society in their favor by crafting a system that would benefit their prosperity and ensure their control over the nation's political and economic affairs. They have historically used the economic system to extract wealth from the sweat of slaves, peasants, and laborers, while contributing little to the common welfare. Control has been maintained with violence and military might. These societies have invariably been patriarchies where the authority and desires of men have dominated the lives of women and children. The system has frequently favored one race, tribe, or ethnic group over others. Where temple and state have been mutual partners, religious authority has been employed to justify the entire system and maintain the status quo.

The domination system is all around us. John Dominic Crossan (b. 1934) often uses the term "the normalcy of the world" or "the normalcy of civilization" to refer to the systems of inequality. It implies that this unfair and lopsided system has been around so long that it seems normal to us. It is just the way things are. It is the way they have always been. We are all participants in it and many of us are beneficiaries of it, but the vast majority of the benefits of any domination system go to the super-rich—the elites who through wealth, influence, and power exercise financial and political control in nearly every society.

Walter Wink proposed that the central message of Jesus was a prescriptive remedy to the historic domination system. According to Jesus, the kingdom of God offers a very different set of social and economic conditions. It is a vision of a new way to order human life together—a new system of corporate living, a new type of community—where all are considered of equal value and everyone has enough. Wink's term for what Jesus proclaimed is *God's domination-free order.*

> *Jesus' message offers us more than a set of timeless truths and eternal verities. It speaks to a very specific context, even if, since the rise of the Domination System five thousand years or more ago, it has been essentially the same context. Jesus challenged the Domination System of his day right where it affected men and women in the routine of their lives, in the everyday push and pull of relating to the institutions that shaped their times. His words still challenge the manifestations of the Domination System today . . . In his Beatitudes, in his extraordinary concern for the outcasts and marginalized, in his wholly unconventional treatment of women, in his love of children, in his rejection of the belief that high-ranking men are the favorites of God, in his subversive proclamation of a new order in which domination will give way to compassion and communion, Jesus brought to fruition the prophetic longing for the "kingdom of God"—an expression we might paraphrase as "God's domination-free order."*[8]

All domination systems are based on enduring cultural myths—foundational stories handed down through history—often through oral tradition, but also through institutional means—that explain why things are the way they are and how the world works. Every culture—ancient and modern—has these myths. They help us make sense of the world and the

8. Wink, *Powers That Be,* 63–64.

society into which we were born. Many of our religious ideas in America are thoroughly mixed with the enduring myths of our nation's destiny, the role of the individual, the efficacy of violence, and the source of happiness. These ideas form a backdrop for a widespread generic religious tradition that pervades American society, a component of a broader cultural integration process.

## American civil religion

American popular culture is founded upon a basic belief in God that transcends all varieties of religious expression. Since the 1950s, Gallup polls have consistently reported that about 95 percent of Americans have said they believe in God. Within the last two decades, the pollsters at Gallup have reported a decline in believers to 86 percent.[9] Still, in recent years Pew researchers report that seven out of ten are "absolutely certain" about God's existence.[10]

In addition, many Americans believe that God has a particular role for the United States to play in the larger world. Like everyone else, young people have been raised in the myth of American exceptionalism—America viewed as God's chosen nation with a mission to bring enlightenment and our way of life to the rest of the world, by violence if necessary. Americans have long believed that their nation has been specially chosen by God as a divine instrument because of the virtue of the country's democratic and economic institutions. In the nineteenth century, the term *manifest destiny* reflected the widespread belief that the United States was destined to expand its influence and territory westward across the American continent and later throughout the world. Over the past two centuries, we have gradually created a civil religion that lends divine authority to this premise.

The essential message of this de facto state religion is that God has a special concern for America, and that God guides and protects the United States in an exceptional way. Politicians and religious leaders alike declare that the United States is a nation set apart by God. From John Winthrop (1587–1649) in 1630 to Ronald Reagan (1911–2004) in 1989, America has been pictured as "a shining city on a hill" meant to fulfill God's purposes on

9. Frank Newport, "Americans More Likely to Believe in God Than the Devil, Heaven More Than Hell," Gallup News Service (June 13, 2007). Online: http://www.gallup.com/poll/27877/Americans-More-Likely-Believe-God-Than-Devil-Heaven-More-Than-Hell.aspx.

10. Pew Forum. *Religious Affiliation: Diverse and Dynamic.* U.S. Religious Landscape Survey (February 2008). Online: http://religions.pewforum.org/pdf/report-religious-landscape-study-full.pdf.

earth. [11] This is the foundation of our civil theology. American civil religion affirms that God will continue to guide, bless, and protect the United States as God's instrument for spreading liberty and justice among the nations. These ideas have been expressed in our founding documents, in numerous presidential speeches, in words inscribed on government buildings, on national emblems, and on our money. The pledge of allegiance proclaims that America is "one nation, under God, indivisible." Coinage and currency proclaim "in God we trust." And American presidents now feel obligated to end every major speech with the words, "May God bless America."

There is often a close connection between civil religion and organized religion in American Christianity. In addition to the government adopting religious mottos as part of its national character, many U.S. churches have adopted the American flag as a revered symbol in their sanctuaries. The flag first began appearing in American churches in response to two things: the desire to express an unquestioned loyalty as U.S. citizens and the growing sacredness of the flag in American culture. During World War I, many German-speaking Protestant congregations began placing an American flag in their sanctuaries to declare their national allegiance during a period when any person of German heritage was looked upon with suspicion. The practice increased during World War II. Then, during the "red scare" of the 1950s, it spread across the majority of Christian churches to reflect the nation's opposition to "godless" Communism.

As the American flag has taken on a sacred character—displayed and handled reverently as a holy object—a similarly-designed Christian flag has often been displayed in churches to justify its presence.[12] As early as 1897, a Sunday School superintendent, Charles C. Overton, conceived of a Christian flag which would mirror the design of the national flag. He believed it would bring a nice symmetry to the sanctuary, with the two symbols flanking the altar—the flag of Christianity and the flag of America given equal stature, blending God and country into a single cohesive faith.

---

11. John Winthrop, the founding governor of Massachusetts Bay Colony, had written of the Puritan experiment in 1630, "For we must consider that we shall be as a city upon a hill, the eyes of all people are upon us." His comment was based on Jesus' Sermon on the Mount, "You are the light of the world. A city set on a hill cannot be hidden." (Matthew 5:14).

12. If you have any doubt of the sacredness of the American flag, just observe its handling in a military funeral.

## patriotism as nationalism and militarism

Our civil religion is based on a deep sense of patriotism, that universal sense of pride for and devotion to one's country. It springs from a love of the natural beauty of the land and admiration for the highest ideals of the nation: human dignity, equality, opportunity, and a concern for the common good. Feelings of patriotism run high during international competitive games, but patriotism also has a dark side. Patriotic fervor can create an ugly mood during periods of national adversity. Love of one's own country often goes together with dislike of and hostility towards other countries or people perceived as enemies. This shifts us from patriotism to nationalism, in which persons define themselves primarily in terms of their national identity. It becomes an "us versus them" way of looking at the world. It can become dangerous when nationalists demand unquestioning loyalty as expressed in the phrase "my country, right or wrong." Further, nationalism tends to encourage the embrace of militarism.

Militarism is the belief that a country should maintain a strong military capability and be prepared to use it aggressively to defend or promote national interests. It advocates armed force to gain power and achieve international goals. Throughout history, militarism has been a significant element of the expansionist ideologies of empires. Every empire has sought to possess the strongest military force in the world, more for conquest and control than for protection. After World War II, the United States embarked upon establishing a global sphere of influence through its newly found military might. Historian Howard Zinn (1922–2010) commented on the major militaristic activities of the American government during the postwar period:

> It established military bases in Japan, Korea, the Philippines, and a number of Pacific islands. In the next decades it orchestrated right-wing coups in Iran, Guatemala, and Chile, and gave military aid to various dictatorships in the Caribbean. In an attempt to establish a foothold in Southeast Asia, it invaded Vietnam and bombed Laos and Cambodia.
>
> The existence of the Soviet Union, even with its acquisition of nuclear weapons, did not block this expansion. In fact, the exaggerated threat of "world communism" gave the United States a powerful justification for expanding all over the globe, and soon it had military bases in a hundred countries . . .
>
> After the disintegration of the Soviet Union and the end of the Cold War, terrorism replaced communism as the justification for expansion. Terrorism was real, but its threat was magnified to the

*point of hysteria, permitting excessive military action abroad and*
*the curtailment of civil liberties at home.*[13]

Today, the United States has military bases in 150 countries around the world. U.S. military spending represents 40 percent of the world's total outlay on arms and armies, more than the next thirteen highest-spending countries in the world combined, including potential international enemies Russia, China, North Korea, and Iran. (China and Russia combined spend less than one-third of our military expenditures.) Fifty-four percent of our federal income tax dollars are spent on the military: present, past, and future. The military-industrial complex that President Eisenhower warned the nation about requires the constant identification of an enemy to justify increased levels of spending. Unfortunately, nationalism and militarism are so entwined with patriotism that a rational critique of the nation's military agenda is frequently condemned as unpatriotic or even treasonous. Yet, while we spend enormous sums to prepare for military action abroad, we are clearly not safe from violence at home.

## the idolatry of guns

Apart from those places on the planet actively engaged in civil war or armed conflict, America may be one of the most violent places on earth to live, especially among highly industrialized nations. In the United States, above-average levels of violent crime and particularly high levels of gun violence and homicide define our nation and set us apart from other prosperous developed nations in North America, Europe, and Asia. Way apart.

We live in a "male warrior culture" that is aided and abetted by a deep and abiding love affair with guns. Firearms at Bunker Hill and on the American frontier play a mythic role in our national history. The individual right to keep and bear arms is enshrined in the Bill of Rights of the U.S. Constitution and is often treated as sacred right above all others, including life, liberty and the pursuit of happiness.

Day in and day out, the violent armed male is glorified and celebrated in our media and entertainment. Is there any wonder why a person with mental issues may want to go out in a hail of bullets like one of the fictional heroes of television, film, and video games? Mix a little male testosterone with a touch of depression and anger fueled by alcohol, and you have a gun death in the making. Anger, depression, and guns. It is a perfect storm. The result: the slaughter of coworkers, college students, moviegoers, shoppers,

13. Zinn, "The Power and the Glory"

and young children. Mentally ill people exist in every nation. But emotionally disturbed people with easy access to automatic weapons with great destructive capability is a uniquely American problem.

In 2010—a typical year—the United States experienced 31,513 deaths from firearms, ten times the number of people who perished in the September 11, 2001 terrorist attacks. The firearm deaths include 19,308 suicides, 11,015 homicides, and 600 accidents. Beyond this, the number of non-fatal injuries from firearms is truly significant—from 75,000 to 100,000 every year, including about 20,000 injuries in children aged 0 to 19 years.

According to the Small Arms Survey, roughly 650 million of the 875 million weapons in the world are in the hands of civilians, and one-third of the world's guns (280 million) are in the hands of American civilians. Imagine the scope of this: the U.S. which has 5 percent of the world's population owns 33 percent of its guns. Gun ownership in the United States is unparalleled in the world—nine guns for every ten Americans. (Yemen comes in a distant second.)

Let's break this down. The American population of 317 million people own approximately 280 million privately held firearms. This statistic is more startling when one considers that about 28 percent of the population is under the age of eighteen. Thus, there are fewer adult Americans (228 million) than there are privately held guns (280 million)—resulting in 1.2 guns per adult. But not every adult owns a gun. Surveys of gun ownership reveal that the firearms are actually concentrated in the hands of about 30 percent of the adult population (68 million), averaging four weapons each. This corresponds to surveys that indicate that a third of American households have a gun. Digging a little deeper, some surveys suggest that just 3 percent of the adult population—maybe seven million people—control 65 to 75 percent of the 280 million guns, or about 22 guns apiece. For example, the young man who killed nine people at a community college in Oregon in 2015 had thirteen guns in his household. This small group forms the core of the gun rights movement in America. And less than half of them—three million gun owners—are members of the National Rifle Association, the political lobby for gun manufacturers. They are avid gun owners and passionate defenders of the Second Amendment right of Americans to own guns. Yet, this tiny minority of three million (only 1.3 percent of the adult American population) dominates the national agenda regarding safe control of guns in our midst.

About two-thirds of the 68 million gun-owners say they own their weapons for security. The National Rifle Association claims ad nauseam that more guns in the hands of more people will protect the "good guys" from the "bad guys." Theoretically, the more guns we have, the safer we will be. It is a great sales pitch for the gun industry. Yet, the unfortunate result of gun ownership has been the opposite. Widespread gun ownership brings dramatically increased danger to gun owners and their families. Fear of "bad guys" does not justify the arms sales for protection in this country. Firearm battles among strangers account for just 14 percent of gun deaths in the country. The guns in American homes are predominantly used to kill family, friends, and close acquaintances. And although a majority of the population realizes that firearms in the home bring more danger than safety, gun enthusiasts adamantly refuse to see this threat in spite of the overwhelming evidence.

## the myth of redemptive violence

At the root of militarism abroad and gun violence at home is a global myth that is as ancient as civilization itself. People in nearly every society are enculturated from an early age to believe that violence is a necessary and inevitable part of human life. Evil and violence often go hand in hand. These two forces have always been a part of human history since the rise of the earliest civilizations, and we believe that they will remain a part of human life forever. We are taught to believe that we can never eliminate the presence of evil and violence, but can temporarily hold their powers at bay. But the only way to do that—the only really effective tool, we believe—is more violence, stronger violence, staggering violence.

Walter Wink called this belief "the myth of redemptive violence." At the heart of the myth is a basic story which is retold ad infinitum: A hero (usually male) is overcome by evil forces. They take his possessions, kill his family, beat him savagely and leave him for dead. The hero regains his strength and seeks out the evildoers. He takes revenge in a bloodbath of violence. It is a story told in terms of black and white. The hero, whom we identify with, is always good, while the evil forces are always completely evil. There is no hope for their transformation. The only effective solution to the conflict is their inevitable violent defeat. And yet, in the end, we know that even more evildoers still lurk in the shadows, awaiting their next opportunity to terrorize good and decent people.

We've all seen, read, or heard a multitude of stories based on the myth of redemptive violence. It is found repeatedly in novels, films, children's cartoons, and television programs. Moreover, it is a fundamental belief across all civilizations and religions. It is far more compelling than any religious teaching or belief in Christianity, Judaism, and Islam. As a result, most of us trust violence—not love—to save us. We trust violence—not God—to deliver us from evil. Wink believed that the myth of redemptive violence was more deeply held in America than anything Christianity teaches. And it is probably a more deeply held belief among Christians than anything Jesus said to the contrary.

## racism

Racism is a perpetually insidious cultural myth in America, despite those who would have us believe that we live in a post-racial society. Racism is rooted in the belief that some people are superior to others because they belong to a particular racial, ethnic, or national group. These people embrace racially superior attitudes to boost their own self-esteem or self-worth. Psychologically, however, racism is based on similar thought patterns found in other "isms," like sexism and heterosexism. People of any privileged majority—gender, social, or religious—who benefit from an ingrained social preference for their particular group—are often unable to recognize the collateral damage created by systemic discrimination toward those in the minority.

All social discrimination is founded on the human need to simplify the world through categorization. Thus, people are sorted by classifications of observable differences: gender, skin color, ethnic heritage, religious heritage, sexual orientation, etc. These categories are then assigned stereotypical behavior patterns based on past associations or inherited cultural biases. The use of stereotypes reduces the amount of thinking or processing required when we meet a new person. We logically infer that an individual possesses certain characteristics and abilities that are shared by others in the category we consign them to. Snap judgments are instantly made, though often incorrect.

Over time, pre-judgments become prejudices, often founded on a fear of those who differ from us in physical appearance, religion, customs, values, and ways of living and viewing the world. The tendency toward prejudice becomes particularly problematic when it is acted upon. When we judge people and groups based on our prejudices and treat them differently, we engage in discrimination. Racism stems from discrimination against a group based on the idea that some inherited characteristic, such as skin color, makes them inferior to the privileged group. When organizations, institutions, or governments discriminate against certain groups in order to limit their rights, the result is institutional or systemic injustice. This kind of discrimination is often difficult to recognize and counter, particularly when it is perpetrated by individuals, institutions and governments who do not view themselves as racist.

Some racial, sexual, and religious prejudices are passed down from generation to generation as a part of one's cultural integration. For instance, anti-Semitic prejudice against the Jews has been a part of Western civilization and European culture for more than two thousand years. Sometimes, a fundamental cultural prejudice is overt, while at other times it is concealed, lurking beneath the surface of daily life. These dormant racial and religious hatreds can often be stirred up by charismatic leaders who exploit latent prejudice for their own political ends. Racist demagogues depend upon propaganda and disinformation to achieve their ends, but many are successful because people want to believe that there is a simple cause of their problems and are easily convinced that a certain group is to blame. This demagoguery, known as "scapegoating" is easy to observe in American politics, although politicians often couch their bigotry in code words.

Race and racism in America are undeniably impacted by our history of slavery, particularly in the South. Slavery is an institution as old as civilization itself, because the agricultural economies of many ancient societies were based on slave labor. But ancient slavery was not usually viewed in racial terms. Slaves were most often captives in war, or came from conquered populations. Most slaves in ancient Greece and Rome were of a similar Mediterranean racial background as their owners. If freed, they were easily assimilated into the population. Between the tenth and the sixteenth centuries, the chief source of slaves in Western Europe was the racially similar Slavic tribes of Eastern Europe. In fact, the word *slave* comes from *Slav*.

The transatlantic slave trade that brought over twelve million Africans to the Americas changed the dynamic of slavery. With Native American populations dying off from European diseases, a new source of cheap labor was required. Lasting more than 400 years—from the fifteenth century through the nineteenth century—the African slave trade helped to shape a wide variety of societies from modern Argentina to Canada. In the agricultural South, planters needed a stable workforce to produce crops for export back to England. At first, indentured servants—mostly English and Irish—supplied their needs. But they had to be freed after their time of servitude had expired. African slaves, purchased for life, solved the problem. And as Thomas Jefferson pointed out, because they reproduce, they increase their owner's dividends like no other investment.

To justify the institution of black slavery, the ideology of white supremacy was developed, asserting a natural inferiority of dark-skinned people, even alleging that black Africans were subhuman. (The same thinking was applied to Native Americans when white Americans wanted to expropriate their land.) Although the American Revolution of 1776—and later the French Revolution of 1789—popularized the ideas of liberty and the rights of all human beings, asserting a natural inferiority to blacks was the way that the leading intellectual figures of the time reconciled their ideals with slave economics. After the abolition of slavery in 1865, the ideology did not diminish, but instead found new life in legalized racial segregation and denial of civil rights resulting in another century of discrimination and oppression. Even after the Civil Rights Act of 1965, the ideology of white supremacy remains a factor in the American conscience and an undercurrent in conservative politics.

The corporate ruling class, and the politicians who represent them, regularly exploit competitive fears of working class white Americans in order to deflect attention away from the damage neoliberal economic policies are inflicting on the middle class. The objective is to divide Americans so that blame is misdirected from the rich to the poor over current economic struggles. In the recent immigration debate, demagogic politicians on the right make diametrically opposing claims that illegal immigrants are taking jobs from hardworking Americans and at the same time are relying on government welfare programs because they are too lazy to work. Either way, white anger toward these immigrants in incensed and leveraged for political gain.

## the cult of rugged individualism

In addition to civil religion, a belief in the efficacy of violence, and a mythology of racism, a cult of rugged individualism pervades American culture. At the heart of our nation is the belief in the importance of individual freedom. But the idea of personal success through individual initiative apart from any societal assistance or social obligation adds a mythological layer to liberty. For generations, Americans have been reared on stories describing how strong individuals succeeded on their own and made the nation great. Whether it's the pioneering settler on the prairie or the brilliant entrepreneur creating a new industry with vision and determination, we've been taught there's nothing nobler than the self-made man or woman who succeeds on his or her own. These stories have spawned a belief that individuals can and should succeed on their own with minimal help from society or the government, widely embraced by political conservatives.

In Chicago in the summer of 1893, historian Frederick Jackson Turner (1861–1932) presented a paper at the World Congress of Historians entitled "The Significance of the Frontier in American History." Turner suggested that the American character was unique, and that it came, not from European influences, but from the presence of a great frontier on our continent, which represented the border between "savagery and civilization." He wrote that the individuals who settled the wilderness embodied the qualities that made America special and superior. Americans were a rugged, self-made society, forged in adversity through the pioneering experience, and reborn and purified into a breed unique on earth.[14]

The concept took a further hold on the American imagination when Herbert Hoover (1874–1964) referred to "rugged individualism" in a campaign speech in 1928, one year before the onset of the Great Depression. He argued that individuals should be able to help themselves without assistance, and that government should not involve itself in people's economic lives nor in national economics in general. Referring to the growth of government influence over American life during World War I, Hoover said:

> We were challenged with a . . . choice between the American system of rugged individualism and a European philosophy of diametrically opposed doctrines—doctrines of paternalism and state socialism. The acceptance of these ideas would have meant the destruction of self-government through centralization . . . [and] the undermining of the individual initiative and enterprise through which our people have grown to unparalleled greatness.[15]

Hoover won the election of 1928—largely because his Democratic opponent Alfred Smith (1873–1944) was a Roman Catholic. After the stock market crash of 1929, President Hoover tried to implement rugged individualism as a public policy, insisting that the economy would fix itself and that the government did not need to interfere. Unfortunately, for millions of people Hoover's naïve belief and resulting inaction failed miserably. Still the contrast between American individualism and "European socialism" still reverberates in contemporary political debate.

Since the 1980s, the myth of the rugged individual has been used to divide the electorate. A narrative has evolved in Republican political discourse claiming that the federal government is the enemy of individual freedom and serves primarily to help the indolent poor, transferring tax money from decent hardworking people to subsidize a sub-culture of lazy freeloaders. It is a battle between individualism and "collectivism"—understood as the subjugation of individual rights to the needs of a larger group, even to achieve the common good. In the 1980 presidential campaign, Ronald Reagan—a talented mythmaker—used this narrative to win over the white electorate, particularly in the South, and his Republican successors have continually repeated the mantra, with its thinly disguised racial overtones.

14. Turner later published his ideas in *The Frontier in American History* (1921).

15. Herbert Hoover, campaign speech, New York, October 23, 1928. Online: http://livefromthetrail.com/about-the-book/speeches/chapter-5/herbert-hoover

The underlying message is that the "makers" (industrious middle-class white suburbanites) are supporting the "takers" (non-productive poor urban people of color). This narrative has been effective in delivering a strong block of white votes for Republican candidates at all levels of government. It has also resulted in a middle-class white electorate voting against their self-interest, as Republican tax and subsidy policies shift wealth to the richest 1 percent. The problem we face as a nation, however, is not a transfer of wealth to the poorest Americans; it is the dramatic transfer from the middle class to the super rich that began with the economic policies of Ronald Reagan in 1980.

Obviously, individual initiative is a key factor in one's success. But the current political narrative of "us versus them" is based on stereotypes without much substance in reality. The idea of helping one's neighbor and working together for the common good has been subverted by an orchestrated political deception. As a result, American racial divisions and stereotypes are increasing, political discourse has become poisoned, and governance in Congress is at best ineffective, and at worst destructive.

## free market fundamentalism

As the rich get richer and the poor get poorer, there is no question that middle-class Americans of all colors are experiencing increasing economic stress. In 1970, the United States had the largest and most prosperous middle class in the history of the world, but for the last four decades their earning power has declined significantly. Not since the 1930s have working people faced such insecurity about their economic future. Globalization and loss of manufacturing jobs is one factor. But the heart of the problem is an underlying economic philosophy so pervasive that it has achieved mythic proportions throughout our history.

The myth of a free market has had a profound effect on American culture. Eighteenth-century Scottish economist Adam Smith (1723–1790), founder of the Liberal school of economics, used the metaphor of the "invisible hand" of the market to suggest that the market was entirely self-regulating and did not need government interference. In his 1776 book *The Wealth of Nations*, Smith advocated the abolition of government intervention in all economic matters—no regulations or restrictions on manufacturing, no barriers to commerce, and no tariffs. He called for total unrestricted freedom or *laissez-faire* ("allow to do") in the economic sector—free enterprise, free markets, and free trade.[16]

16. Elizabeth Martinez and Arnoldo García. "What is 'Neo-Liberalism'?: A Brief Definition," Global Exchange (February 2000). Online: http://www.globalexchange.

This free market philosophy became the dominant force in Western economics for the next 150 years. By 1850, the lack of government regulation and oversight led to sweatshop factories in England and the United States—workplaces that were crowded, dangerous, low paying, and without job security. By the end of the nineteenth century, free enterprise had allowed industrial robber barons to amass huge personal fortunes by pursuing anti-competitive business practices. The capitalists of the Gilded Age (1870–1900) helped the United States become a modern industrialized nation, but many American workers were left behind as they struggled to make ends meet in this new economy. Long hours and hazardous working conditions led many workers to attempt to form labor unions despite strong opposition from wealthy industrial leaders. In the Roaring Twenties, unregulated freedom in commerce, investment, and speculation reached a soaring pinnacle. Then, with the onset of the Great Depression, the Liberal school of economic theory fell into disrepute. It soon became obvious that the unregulated free market could not heal itself from its own greed and excesses.

In the early decades of the twentieth century, British economist John Maynard Keynes (pronounced *canes*) (1883–1946) declared that governments had a legitimate and necessary role to play by intervening in the economy in order to maintain levels of employment and to advance the common good. The economic philosophies of Keynes guided Franklin D. Roosevelt's New Deal during the recovery from the Great Depression. As a result, Keynesian economic theory held sway in the United States for the next fifty years, and fostered an economic prosperity sometimes called the "Golden Age of Capitalism" that ran from 1945 to 1970.

But Liberal economic theory was not dead. Thinkers such as Milton Friedman (1912–2006) and others at the Chicago School of Economics sought to resurrect the influence of free market philosophies. Friedman asserted that, "Keynes was wrong on just about everything, and his followers are wrong on absolutely everything." His views gained traction in the 1970s when a combination of high unemployment and inflation, known as "stagflation," sharply ended the long post-war boom in an economic malaise. This led to the rise of a new liberal or *neoliberal* economic ideology. Its proponents wanted to recreate unrestricted market economies by cutting government regulations, slashing public expenditures for social services, privatizing public services, de-unionizing workers, and reducing wages for the working middle class. Initially rejected by mainstream economists, neoliberal ideology was embraced by two key political leaders of the 1980s—Margaret Thatcher (1925–2013) in Great Britain and Ronald Reagan

org/resources/econ101/neoliberalismdefined

(1911–2004) in the U.S. Since the mid-1980s, neoliberalism has become the dominant force in both American and global economics.[17] Rather than delivering prosperity for all, liberal and neoliberal economics have historically benefitted the very wealthy to the detriment of all others. Economist Paul Krugman (b. 1953) recently defined the six decades following World War II as the passage from the "Great Convergence: 1950–1980" where wealth was distributed more equitably in American society, to the "Great Divergence: 1980–2012" where we have witnessed the most massive transfer of wealth to the top 1 percent since the Gilded Age.

## the myth of consumerism

The economy of the United States is sustained by the myth that personal gratification comes through consuming goods and services in ever-greater amounts. We live in a consumer society in which consumerism and materialism are central aspects of the dominant culture, and where goods and services are acquired not only to satisfy basic needs but to secure psychological fulfillment. Consumerism is the faith that meaning, identity, and significance can be found in material consumption, which in turn requires money. It offers short-term ego-gratification for those who can afford consumer items and frustration for those who cannot. But because meaning and self-realization cannot be gained through material goods, and basic psychological needs cannot be met by consumption, consumers remain unfilled and are driven ever on to seek more possessions which requires still more money. All of this is well understood by the marketers of consumerism.

Television, films, and magazines present glamorized lifestyles that are seen as attractive and desirable by consumers. As a result, consumers create personal visions of living such lifestyles, and then behave in ways that help realize the vision. The problem with this process is that the lifestyles most often portrayed are well beyond the means of all but a very small percentage of Americans. Consumers aspire to something that the vast majority of them cannot possibly achieve and then become addicted to a way of living that gradually separates them from the things in life that bring the most joy.

American consumerism as we know it did not just happen. Following World War II, the era of postwar prosperity and economic stability led to a pursuit of happiness through plenty that has become deeply embedded in American culture. The American economy grew dramatically in

17. For more information on the struggle between competing economic philosophies in the twentieth century, see Yergin and Stanislaw, *Commanding Heights*. See also the PBS Frontline series of the same name viewable online.

the postwar period, expanding at a rate of 3.5 percent per year between 1945 and 1970, until it tapered off around 1975. Many incomes doubled in a generation, resulting in millions of factory and office workers being lifted into a growing middle class, enabling them to sustain a standard of living once considered reserved for the wealthy alone. By 1960, a massive population shift from the farm to the city resulted in ever larger numbers of people sharing in economic prosperity. By the early seventies, post-war American consumers enjoyed higher levels of disposable income than those in any other country. It was an age of conspicuous consumption motivated by the desire for prestige and the public display of social status rather than by the practical utility of consumer goods and services. America generated a steadily growing demand for better automobiles, clothing, appliances, family vacations, and higher education.

Today, with a declining middle class, in which relative earning power has not increased since the 1970s, consumer debt has become the fuel for our conspicuous consumption. In addition, women have joined the workforce in record numbers since 1970, when just 25 percent worked outside the home. Today six out of ten women are employed. The increase is partly due to a higher percentage of educated women who seek fulfillment through jobs and careers, but it is also due to the need for additional income in married households to maintain desired patterns of consumption.

Psychologists speak of people having intrinsic motivation (coming from within) and extrinsic motivation (coming from outside). Intrinsically-motivated people are driven by their own values, and do not feel the need for acceptance, approval, or validation by some outside entity. They demonstrate self-acceptance and find meaning in relationships and community. Extrinsically-motivated people are generally seeking acceptance by something or someone outside themselves. They focus on their appearance, social popularity, and financial gain.

Those who are the most extrinsically-motivated, and stay that way for a long time, begin to lose touch with their authentic intrinsic motivations—the things in life that naturally bring them the most joy. Studies show that intrinsically-motivated people are much happier. In the end, money does not buy happiness. Neither does a life of consumerism or materialism. But our society is trapped in a myth that makes us believe that wealth, status, and possessions will bring lasting fulfillment. And powerful cultural forces perpetuate that myth.

## voices of protest

In spite of the overwhelming power of our cultural myths, a handful of social movements and prophetic voices have refused to accept these narratives and have voiced strong protests against the forces that perpetuate them. During World War I, the cultural influences of individualism, unfettered capitalism, nationalism, and militarism were identified by the Social Gospel's most influential spokesman Walter Rauschenbusch (1861–1918) as the four major institutionalized spiritual evils in American culture. Fifty years later, during the Vietnam War, Martin Luther King, Jr. (1929–1968) identified the giant "triplets" of racism, extreme materialism, and militarism as three cultural influences that corrode human society and prevent justice and peace in the world.[18]

Many people would agree that racism and militarism are destructive forces. However, when it comes to a capitalist economy, most Americans cannot see a viable alternative. State-controlled communism has been completely discredited as an economic system. And four decades of neoliberal economics have persuaded many that capitalism can only be successful when it is unconstrained. But the sad results—including the global economic failure of 2009—have shown this philosophy to be a deceptive mythology. The neoliberal brand of capitalism benefits the wealthy, while most people become unwitting victims of a system that works against their best interests.

Nearly fifty years after Dr. King spoke, it was Pope Francis (b. 1936) who identified the current global neoliberal economic system as a spiritual evil. In an apostolic letter named *Evangelii Gaudium* (*ay-van-ghel'-ih-ee gow'-dee-oom*)—"the joy of the gospel"—Pope Francis spoke out against the economic influences that are creating so much suffering and inequality in the world. He does not mince words in his letter. He believes that Christians must say "No!" to an economy of exclusion and inequality, the idolatry of money, the deification of the market, and the prevailing spirit of selfishness and indifference that lie at the core of the neoliberal economic system.

> *In this context, some people continue to defend trickle-down theories which assume that economic growth, encouraged by a free market, will inevitably succeed in bringing about greater justice and inclusiveness in the world. This opinion, which has never been confirmed by the facts, expresses a crude and naïve trust in the goodness of those wielding economic power and in the sacralized workings of the prevailing economic system. Meanwhile, the excluded are still waiting. To sustain a lifestyle which excludes*

18. King, "Beyond Vietnam," April 1967.

*others, or to sustain enthusiasm for that selfish ideal, a globaliza-*
*tion of indifference has developed. Almost without being aware of*
*it, we end up being incapable of feeling compassion at the outcry*
*of the poor, weeping for other people's pain, and feeling a need*
*to help them, as though all this were someone else's responsibility*
*and not our own. The culture of prosperity deadens us; we are*
*thrilled if the market offers us something new to purchase. In the*
*meantime all those lives stunted for lack of opportunity seem a*
*mere spectacle; they fail to move us.* [19]

## the lordship of culture

In spite of the voices of protest, most Christians remain part of the system, little understanding the forces that dominate them and morally indifferent to its impact on others. A theology of personal salvation blends seamlessly with a politics of selfishness and individualism. Rather than standing in contrast to the predominant culture, Christianity is likely to be shaped by the enveloping culture in subtle and profound ways. All of these cultural layers contribute to a life of conformity to social and religious conventions. It was to people such as us—who are shaped by a pervasive cultural conformity—that Jesus proclaimed a new way of thinking and living. The process of transformation that Jesus proposed requires a questioning of all of our deeply held assumptions and inherited beliefs—political, economic, and religious.

Writer and activist Jim Wallis (b. 1948)—founder of the Sojourners publication and organization—has said, "The call to discipleship, the call to follow Jesus Christ, demands a fundamental break with the dominant values and conformist patterns of the majority culture."[20]

*Our most persistent problem is that we try to make the claims*
*of Christ negotiable with the claims and demands of the world*
*. . . The principal way the world system seeks to overcome the*
*church is by trying to squeeze the church into its own mold, to*
*reduce the church to conformity. Therefore, the church must resist*
*the constant temptation to reduce the claims of Christ, soften the*
*demands of the gospel, ease the tension between the church and*
*the world, and allow the ever radical message to be squeezed into*
*more comfortable and congenial forms and styles . . . The commu-*
*nity of believers must expect to find themselves at variance with*

19. Pope Francis, *Evangelii Gaudium*, chapter 2, section 54.
20. Wallis, *Agenda for Biblical People*, 11.

*the social consensus, the political conformity, and the popular wis-*
*dom of their society, for they are witnesses to a whole new order.*[21]

For the early church, the cultural decisions were clear. Jesus called people away from a religion of holiness, the tyranny of economic exploitation, and the oppression of military occupation. But in doing so, he rejected an overthrow of the institutions that perpetuated these repressive ways of living. Instead, he offered an alternative vision of how to live in community, a way to live in the midst of domination with authenticity and courage. He called people to radical non-conformity and non-violent resistance. He called people to transfer their allegiance from the self-serving values of empire to the servanthood values of the kingdom of God. Turn the other cheek, walk the second mile, give up your shirt as well as your coat, forgive seventy times seven, love your neighbor, love your enemy, do to others as you would have done to yourself. These are the words of a non-conformist. And the ethic of love that he modeled is sure to pit us against our culture, our governing authorities, and even our churches.

In the United States, I see Americans falling into four general categories regarding our national culture. First are the *active conformists* who are cheerleaders for the status quo. Among Christians, these are represented by the Religious Right. Second are the *passive conformists* who represent what Richard Nixon called "the great silent majority," those vast numbers of people who do not publically express their opinions. Some are cautious supporters of the status quo; others are simply uninterested and uninvolved. Third are the *passive non-conformists* who are uncomfortable with aspects of the domination system, and are cautious challengers of the current politics of selfishness. But perhaps due to cynicism about the possibility for meaningful change, remain largely inactive. Many clergy find themselves in this group, knowing that justice demands more of them, but also knowing that their pastoral role requires them to be a comforting presence to all their members, including the most conservative ones. Thus, they are extremely cautious in expressing opinions and sometimes uncomfortably dishonest with their parishioners. Fourth are the *active non-conformists* who engage in movements for change. The vision that Jesus painted of the kingdom of God primarily attracts followers from groups three and four, with the loudest prophetic voice coming from the active non-conformists. These are the people who represent the most vocal agents of the conspiracy of love.

The myths of our culture shape us. They shape the way we perceive reality. They shape our religious perspective. And they shape the way we live. To follow Jesus is to begin to see these myths for what they are, to recover

21. Ibid., 17–18.

our sight from a culturally imposed blindness, and to change our lives so that we are no longer captive to the system of domination they sustain.

## living counter to your culture

We are called to follow Jesus in the real world—in a nation where guns are considered sacred, where violence is glorified, where market capitalism is deified, where consumerism is celebrated, and where selfishness is the dominant political value. The life of faith Jesus calls us to is lived in a global arena where two-thirds of the children are forced to survive on less than two dollars a day, where one-third live without shelter, and where thirty thousand children die every minute of every day of malnourishment and preventable disease.

In an interview, Marcus Borg pointed out that Christianity, like most religious traditions maintains that something is wrong with our lives as we typically live them.

> We live our lives much of the time in a self-preoccupied way, in a burdened way that feels cut off from the vital center of energy. And so the central spiritual-psychological issue in the Christian life is the need for internal transformation from a selfish way of being to a way that is free from that. Our central religious issue is an internal transformation that leads to a different way of being in the world.[22]

The way of Jesus is a journey of transformation—a movement beyond the narrow scope of race, tribe, and nation to a wider vision of community. It is a movement beyond a naturally self-centered nature to a spirit of personal humility and concern for the welfare of others. It moves us beyond the spirit of self-reliance, isolated independence, and rugged individualism that separates us from others in order to journey through life in mutual interdependency grounded in compassion, sharing, and service. It is a journey away from violence, militarism, racism, and materialism. For many, it also requires an abandonment of inherited or enculturated religious traditions that are so allied with and so captive to cultural values.

Non-conformity as a resistance to dominant cultural values is the way of Jesus. If we want to change the world, we must begin with ourselves. The Mahatma Gandhi saw this clearly when he reportedly said, "Be the change that you wish to see in the world." This means confronting the ego-centrism that drives us. The desire to follow this path, to turn one's back on selfishness,

22. Marcus Borg, "Beyond Belief," *The Lutheran*, 12.

to live responsibly for the sake of others, is the path of transformation from cultural conformity to new understandings about the meaning and purpose of life.

The Apostle Paul recognized this when he said "Do not be conformed to this world, but be transformed by the renewing of your minds."[23] This act of turning around, of walking in a different direction, of opposing the norms of our society, is an act of revolution. Jesus was calling for a sudden, marked change in cultural values leading to a radical and pervasive change in society. The kingdom of God is a movement of insurgency against unbridled militarism, a rebellion against institutional racism, an insurrection against unfettered capitalism, an uprising against unconstrained materialism, and a revolt against self-centered individualism. The way of Jesus is a rejection of the values of selfishness, greed, and violence that lay at the core of these "isms" of American culture. It is an uprising against the powers that dominate our common life. It is a resistance to the normalcy of civilization through acts of generosity, compassion, forgiveness, acceptance, nonviolence, and distributive justice.

---

23. Romans 12:2

# PART 4

a conspiracy of love

CHAPTER 10

# Bonhoeffer's vision

*If religion is only a garment of Christianity—*
*and even this garment has looked very different*
*at different times—then what is a religionless*
*Christianity?*[1]

—Dietrich Bonhoeffer (1906–1945)

POSTMODERN PEOPLE SEEM TO be heading away from traditional "church" Christianity to some new mode of being a Christian in the world— Christianity developing outside of the walls of a church building. Nearly 70 years ago, Dietrich Bonhoeffer (1906–1945) first conjectured on the possibility of this happening. Bonhoeffer was a German Lutheran pastor and theologian who opposed the state-controlled German Evangelical Church under Adolf Hitler.

## a compromised church

Because the modern state of Germany was created from of a number of small independent principalities and kingdoms in the late nineteenth century, the Lutheran and Reformed (Calvinist) Protestant churches of Germany remained separated as 28 independent regional bodies reflecting their origins as small state-sponsored churches (*Landeskirchen*) with the local ruler as head. In 1922, they formed a loose federation to participate jointly in mission activities, but they did not come together as one unified church until April 1933 when the German Evangelical Church (*Deutsche Evangelische Kirche*) was created under the direction of Adolf Hitler. The

1. Bonhoeffer, *Letters and Papers*, 280.

173

German term *evangelisch* more accurately corresponds to the broad English term *Protestant* rather than to the narrower *evangelical* (in German called *evangelikal*), and was a compromise term in the unification of Lutheran and Reformed bodies in Germany.

Only months earlier, in January 1933, German President Paul von Hindenburg (1847–1934) had appointed Adolf Hitler (1889–1945) as Chancellor of Germany. When Hindenburg died the following year, Hitler combined the offices of chancellor and president and became the nation's dictator. Many Christians in Germany openly welcomed Hitler's National Socialist (Nazi) party to power as a historic moment of Christ's work on earth for and through the Aryan *Volk* (German for *people*).

Like many conservative evangelicals in the United States who believe that America is God's chosen nation, the German people believed that Germany was destined for greatness as God's chosen instrument in the world. As it rose to power in the 1930s, the Nazi message was that in spite of their God-given destiny, the nation was threatened from within by the insidious presence of Communists, Jews, and liberals in their midst, eerily similar to messages espoused today on conservative talk radio and cable TV about the influence on American society by liberals, socialists, feminists, and homosexuals. Hitler told the nation that their duty was to purify themselves of these influences to prepare for their divine vocation as God's anointed nation.

Just a few months after Hitler's rise to power, the German Evangelical Church was founded under the strong influence of an anti-Semitic faction called the German Christians (*Deutsche Christen*) who were proponents of the Nazi party and its belief that the nation could only fulfill its destiny by absolute obedience to a strong leader (*Führer*). This faction, representing about one out of six Protestant clergy, was not alone in its prejudice against Jews. Anti-Semitism had long been a characteristic of many Christians since the Middle Ages, especially in Northern Europe. Even the great Protestant reformer Martin Luther (1483–1546) had contributed to religious hatred in his pamphlet *On the Jews and Their Lies* (1543) in which he called the Jews "those miserable and accursed people" after his unsuccessful attempts at their conversion. In 1933, two-thirds of the population was Protestant (about 40 million members) and the remaining third was Roman Catholic (about 20 million). Less than 1 percent (600,000) was Jewish.

In September 1933, Ludwig Müller (1883–1945), a leader of the German Christian faction, was appointed by Adolf Hitler as Reich Bishop (*Reichsbischof*) of the newly unified church. Müller's task was to bring the church under the absolute control of the Third Reich and its Führer. Hitler was a Roman Catholic but saw Martin Luther as a true German hero and believed that both Protestants and Catholics were necessary components of German culture and therefore of the Third Reich. Hitler believed that religion, along with other cultural elements, needed to be brought in line with the Nazi vision. He ordered members of the Nazi party to demonstrate a powerful religious presence by filling the pews of Christian churches in uniform on Sundays.

Reichsbischof Müller supported a revisionist view of the historical Jesus which proposed that Jesus had been a member of the Aryan race and was not Jewish at all. The German Christian faction envisioned a more "heroic" and "positive" interpretation of Jesus, who was seen as one who battled against corrupt Jewish influences in his society. Müller and others favored a plan to purify Christianity of "Jewish corruption," including eliminating large parts of the Old Testament from the Bible, and focusing only on a revised New Testament. They rewrote the gospels, calling the region of Judea "Jewland" and suggesting that the people of Jesus' native Galilee were of Aryan descent. Under Müller, the church implemented the "Aryan paragraph" of the Nazi-sponsored 1933 Civil Service Law that purged people of Jewish descent and those married to non-Aryan spouses from further participation in government-funded positions. This included clergy of state-supported churches who were considered to be employees and representatives of the state. Non-Aryan clergy were dismissed from their positions.

## the Confessing church

In May 1934, Protestant Christians opposed to the Nazi vision and infuriated by the Aryan Clause, met at the industrial city of Barmen in the Rhineland region of Germany. Known as the Confessing Church (*Bekennende Kirche*), the defiant pastors denounced Müller and his leadership and declared that they and their congregations constituted the true Evangelical Church of Germany. The Theological Declaration of Barmen (*Die Barmer Theologische Erklärung*)—primarily authored by Swiss theologian Karl Barth (1886–1968), with the consultation and advice of other Confessing Church pastors like Martin Niemöller (1892–1984)—opposed the theological ideas of the German Christian faction and affirmed that the church owed its ultimate allegiance to God and not to the leader of any state. They protested that the church was not an organ of the state and needed to be independent of political ideologies to be true to its calling. The declaration stipulated that any state—democratic or totalitarian—was under the judgment of God's commandments. No person and no nation could be above the law of God.

However, to their discredit, the Confessing Church only protested state manipulation of religious affairs. They did not take up defense of the Jews.

During the first six years of Hitler's dictatorship, from 1933 until the outbreak of war in 1939, Jewish citizens felt the effects of more than 400 decrees and regulations that restricted all aspects of their public and private lives. In September 1935, Nazi leaders announced the Nuremberg Laws that excluded German Jews from Reich citizenship and prohibited them from marrying or having sexual relations with persons of German or German-related blood. They were deprived of most political rights, denied the right to vote, and not allowed to hold public office.

It is estimated that there were about 18,000 Protestant clergy in Germany at this time, ministering to 40 million church members. About 3,000 pastors were part of the German Christian faction and about 3,000 participated in the Confessing Church movement. That left the vast majority, about 12,000 pastors, who remained in the Nazi-controlled church and, not voicing strong opinions either way, simply went along to get along. To a great extent, they believed that their calling was a purely spiritual one and thus took an apolitical stance. And so they remained silent in the face of increasing tyranny. For a time, this seemed like a very safe position, but ultimately it was destructive to the life of the church.

Historian, civil rights leader, and peace activist Howard Zinn (1922–2010) titled his autobiography *You Can't be Neutral on a Moving Train*. He meant that, at any given time, history is moving along a clear and observable path. The context of one's life is not a still point in time but a vector—a course or direction with velocity. Opting for the status quo is not a choice to avoid taking responsibility for historical consequences; it means one is moving along with the popular direction of one's time. To be neutral is not neutrality at all. It is to make a decision, to take a side, to support a direction, often a direction that can potentially lead to great evil and repression of people at the margins of society. Elie Wiesel (b. 1928), who won the Nobel Peace Prize in 1986, has said,

> We must take sides. Neutrality helps the oppressor, never the victim. Silence encourages the tormentor, never the tormented.[2]

Only a small minority of German Christians ever spoke out against the growing evil as Nazi ideology overtook their land, infiltrating their schools, churches, and institutions. As Irish statesman Edmund Burke (1729–1797) famously said, "All that is necessary for the triumph of evil is that good men do nothing."

2. Elie Wiesel, Nobel acceptance speech, Oslo, Norway, December 10, 1986.

## the two kingdoms

The majority of clergy in the German church represented a long tradition dating to Martin Luther who held that there were two different "kingdoms" or realms in the world—one spiritual and one political. God was ultimately responsible for both areas of life, but according to Luther, God has delegated the spiritual realm to the church and the political realm to governmental leaders—be they kings, princes, elected officials, or dictators. In turn, as people who rule on God's behalf, the leaders of church and state were considered ultimately responsible to God for their actions. Therefore Luther said, it was the duty of the average Christian to obey the church in spiritual matters and to obey their leaders in political matters. And opting for the status quo is the supreme act of obedience in both arenas.

Seven brief verses of the Apostle Paul's letter to the house churches at Rome (Romans 13:1–7) provided the basis for this idea, and it gave the German Evangelical Church and the Nazi party tremendous authority. The core of Paul's message is this statement:

> Let every person be subject to the governing authorities; for there is no authority except from God, and those authorities that exist have been instituted by God. Therefore whoever resists authority resists what God has appointed, and those who resist will incur judgment.[3]

In the epistle known as First Peter was the further simple injunction, "Fear God. Honor the emperor."[4] As a follower of Jesus, it is often necessary to resist authority, as Jesus did, if one is committed to peace and justice. But in Protestant theology, eight short verses from the epistles have trumped everything in the gospels that Jesus taught about how to live authentically in a world of injustice and violence.

Thus, the vast majority of German Protestant clergy took themselves out of action in the political arena and then looked the other way when it came to Nazi alterations of historic Christian theology and church practice, opting for the status quo in both arenas of life. After all, by 1934, Adolf Hitler and his national vision were wildly popular with the majority of Germans, including the parishioners of most congregations. Most clergy, like most other Germans, believed in the great destiny for their nation, and the importance of duty to those in authority was a deeply-held German value.

In the late 1960s, as I contemplated military service in Viet Nam, I expressed my strong beliefs against killing to my Lutheran pastor. I had

3. Romans 13:1–2
4. 1 Peter 2:17

of course studied the Ten Commandments in catechism, including "Thou shalt not kill" and had read Jesus' teachings regarding love for one's neighbors and enemies, as well as his advice to respond to unjust domination and force with nonviolent resistance. My pastor advised me that in a just war, I would not be under God's judgment for killing another person. If I was following orders, only my superiors would be held ultimately accountable for any homicides or atrocities I committed. Ultimately, only the national leaders were answerable to God for all of the death and destruction affecting combatants and non-combatants alike. Thus, he reasoned, I could do my duty to my country without any moral qualms. If drafted, it was my biblical obligation to obey my government and go to war as ordered. This is the historic Lutheran approach to participation in war and is commonly held by most other churches around the world, but I did not buy it. I chose instead to take a conscientious stand against involvement in the war and declared myself to be a conscientious objector.

## Bonhoeffer's resistance

The situation in Germany in the early 1930s impelled Dietrich Bonhoeffer, among others, to take a conscientious stand regarding his duty to the German state under Adolf Hitler and the German Evangelical Church under Ludwig Müller. At Barmen, Bonhoeffer became one of the founding members of the Confessing Church, which soon asserted itself as the center of the minimal Christian resistance to the Nazi regime.

Bonhoeffer quickly became a leading spokesman of the new church body. In 1935, he was appointed to organize and lead an underground seminary for the Confessing Church at the town of Finkenwald on the Baltic Sea. However, the experiment was short lived; the Gestapo shut it down in October 1937.

Bonhoeffer began to see that the church could not continue to be concerned simply with the purity of its own life and practice. He believed the church was the church only when it lived for others. Therefore, he voiced his distress about the narrow scope adopted by the Confessing Church. He strongly condemned the church for failing to move beyond its very limited concern for religious civil liberties and called on the members to focus instead on helping the suffering Jews. In 1937, Karl Barth admitted, "For the millions that suffer unjustly, the Confessing Church does not yet have a heart."

Years later Martin Niemöller reflected on this great sin of the Confessing Church.

*First they came for the Socialists, and I did not speak out—because I was not a Socialist. Then they came for the Trade Unionists, and I did not speak out—because I was not a Trade Unionist. Then they came for the Jews, and I did not speak out—because I was not a Jew. Then they came for me—and there was no one left to speak for me.*[5]

The Confessing Church was of course suppressed by the Third Reich. As pressure increased, Karl Barth returned to his native Switzerland in 1935, Bonhoeffer's authorization to teach at the University of Berlin was revoked in August 1936 when he was denounced as a "pacifist and enemy of the state," and Martin Niemöller was arrested by the Gestapo in July 1937. In 1940, Bonhoeffer was forbidden to speak in public and was required to regularly report his activities to the police. In 1941, he was forbidden to print or to publish.

By 1941, Germany had been at war for two years. As the war raged on, and oppression of the Jews worsened, Dietrich Bonhoeffer realized he needed to do more.

*We are not to simply bandage the wounds of victims beneath the wheels of injustice, we are to drive a spoke into the wheel itself.*[6]

Bonhoeffer joined an underground resistance movement opposed to Hitler through a brother-in-law who was already involved. He became increasingly engaged in the work of a conspiracy committed to the overthrow of the Nazi government, especially within the *Abwehr* (the German Military Intelligence Office), that planned to assassinate Adolf Hitler and take over the government in order to broker a surrender to the Allies before Germany's destruction was complete. Even though he was committed to nonviolence, Bonhoeffer believed that true Christian discipleship demanded political resistance against a criminal state. He became a civilian member of German Intelligence (exempting him from the draft) and used his position to get deferments for other pastors in the Confessing Church. He drew up a report documenting the treatment of Jews in Germany. He acted as a double agent travelling to ecumenical conferences in Switzerland, Sweden, and Norway, where he shared sensitive information with international church leaders. In 1942, Bonhoeffer met with Bishop George Bell (1883–1958) of the Church of England in Stockholm and asked him to pass a message to British Foreign

5. Martin Niemöller. Different versions of this quotation come from variations in Niemöller's lectures during the early postwar period. This version is from the *Holocaust Encyclopedia* created by the United States Holocaust Memorial Museum, Washington, DC.

6. Bonhoeffer, No *Rusty Swords*, "The Church and the Jewish Question," 225.

Secretary Anthony Eden (1897–1977) sounding out the Allies' response to a potential coup in Germany.

In March 1943, Bonhoeffer was arrested and imprisoned by the Gestapo because documents found in the Abwehr offices linked him to various subversive activities, specifically to his participation in "Operation 7," an undercover activity that spirited fourteen German Jews across the border to neutral Switzerland under the pretext that they were Abwehr agents.

In July 1944, an attempt was made to assassinate Hitler. It failed disastrously, and hundreds of political prisoners were executed afterwards. Bonhoeffer was eventually hanged at the Nazi concentration camp at Flossenbürg on April 9, 1945 only a month before the end of the war in Europe. He was 39 years old and had spent the last two years of his life as a prisoner.

## what does it mean to be religious anymore?

Nearly a year after his imprisonment, in a letter written on April 30, 1944 from cell 92 in Berlin's Tegel penitentiary, Dietrich Bonhoeffer described his thoughts about the state of Christianity to his good friend Eberhard Bethge (1909–2000), who later edited Bonhoeffer's writings.

> *You would be surprised, and perhaps even worried, by my theological thoughts and the conclusions that they lead to . . . What is bothering me incessantly is the question what Christianity really is, for us today.*[7]

In light of the depravity of the Nazi state and the horrific violence of the Second World War, perpetrated by religious people on all sides, Bonhoeffer questioned what Christianity represented any more. Why are Christians so unquestioningly captive to their culture? Why did German Christians not protest the persecution of the Jews? Why were they so unwilling to stand up to evil authorities and unjust laws? Bonhoeffer began struggling with what it means to claim to be religious in any real sense. And he saw a time coming in which religion would prove to be fundamentally irrelevant.

> *We are moving towards a completely religionless time; people as they are now simply cannot be religious anymore. Even those who honestly describe themselves as "religious" do not in the least act up to it, and so they presumably mean something quite different by "religious" . . .*
>
> *And if therefore man becomes radically religionless—and I think that is already more or less the case (else, how is it, for*

7. Bonhoeffer, *Letters and Papers*, 279.

*example, that this war, in contrast to all previous ones, is not calling forth any "religious" reaction?)—what does that mean for "Christianity"?*[8]

Traditional Christianity—the church of Constantine—had proven to be morally bankrupt and incapable of dealing with the evils of the modern world, including violence, oppression, and racism. The religious practices of Christianity had become personal and private and were largely divorced from social ethics and politics. The mainstream churches in the so-called "Christian nations" proved to have no prophetic voice.

Bonhoeffer was disappointed that religious people—lay and clergy alike—were not speaking out or taking a stand, and their social and political struggles were conducted without drawing on their faith—or more likely, that their faith had become so disjointed from social and political conditions that they saw no connection. Eleven years earlier, in 1934, when Adolf Hitler appointed himself as Führer of the German Reich, he held a national referendum to confirm his usurpation of political power. Ninety-five percent of the registered voters went to the polls, and 90 percent of them (over 38 million people), voted "yes." In Germany, the majority of Christians—Protestants and Roman Catholics—fully supported the Third Reich and its policies until the Second World War brought terror and destruction to their cities and homes.

In German churches, the twisted cross of the swastika was proudly displayed as Nazi flags replaced the cross of Christ. Adolf Hitler's manifesto *Mein Kampf* (*My Struggle*) supplanted the Bible on church altars. The song *Die Fahne Hoch* (The Flag on High), written by Nazi martyr Horst Wessel (1907–1930) was included in the German Evangelical Church hymnal. One of its verses declared:

> *Clear the streets for the brownshirts,*
> *Clear the streets for the stormtroopers!*
> *Already millions, upon seeing the swastika, are filled with hope*
> *The day of freedom and bread is dawning!*

In the United States, the same kind of national idolatry was occurring, but to a lesser extent. American flags increasingly appeared next to altars and pulpits, indicating an unwavering support for the country in time of war, but also suggesting that the symbol of the nation had an equal value with the cross, the symbol of the church. Just like their counterparts in Germany, American churches had become chaplains for their nations' political policies and war machines. If religious institutions in every nation were

8. Ibid., 279–280.

willingly transforming themselves into servants of the state, and not raising a prophetic voice for peace and justice, was there another possibility for Christianity in the world? In his prison cell Bonhoeffer questioned:

> *Are there religionless Christians? If religion is only a garment of Christianity—and even this garment has looked very different at different times—then what is a religionless Christianity?*[9]

What would Christianity look like when it is stripped bare? Bonhoeffer began to struggle with what remains when the typical traits of a religion—clergy, religious institutions, sacred rites, orthodox beliefs, and an absolute morality—are eliminated. How would that redefine Christianity? What would be left?

What bothered Bonhoeffer was that a person could confess doctrinally correct beliefs, observe its moral codes, and follow the accepted behaviors and practices of the church, while simultaneously hating and oppressing other human beings. We have witnessed the same thing in the American South—the so-called "Bible Belt"—where for over a century after the Civil War, legalized segregation, harassment, humiliation, persecution, oppression, and lynching of African-Americans were social norms for many mainline and evangelical white Christians. The apartheid system of racial segregation in South Africa was likewise created and enforced by their white Christians of Dutch and British descent.

The question thus becomes "how is it possible that the practice of Christianity can become divorced from loving our neighbors in any real sense?" How is it that religious practice—including word and sacrament—can leave a person ultimately unchanged at the core of his or her being?

Perhaps it is because typical Christian religious practice does not guarantee a transformation of the heart nor does it necessarily provide a personal encounter with the God of love. For many Christians, religion is simply a secondhand experience, passed on by family and tradition, and thoroughly integrated with the prevailing culture.

## a life of contemplation and action

Dietrich Bonhoeffer believed that, in the future, a new form of Christianity, stripped of its religious garments, would be limited to two things: contemplative prayer and righteous action in the world. He described his thoughts in a letter to the infant son of his good friend Eberhard Bethge on the occasion of the child's baptism in May 1944. Bonhoeffer had been asked to be

9. Ibid., 280.

godfather for his namesake Dietrich Bethge[10], a duty he could perform only from a jail cell.

> *Today, you will be baptized a Christian . . . By the time you have grown up, the church's form will have changed greatly . . . Our church, which has been fighting in these years only for its own self-preservation, as though that were an end in itself, is incapable of taking the word of reconciliation and redemption to [humankind] and the world . . . Our being Christian today will be limited to two things: prayer and righteous action among [humanity]. All Christian thinking, speaking, and organizing must be born anew out of this prayer and action.*[11]

I often look at Bonhoeffer's letter as one that could have been addressed to me. I was born less than three years after Dietrich Bethge. With others of my Baby Boomer generation, I have witnessed the increasing decline of institutional "church" Christianity in Europe and North America. Seventy years later, the new form of Christianity is struggling to be born in a secular world.

> *To be a Christian does not mean to be religious in a particular way, to cultivate some particular form of asceticism (as a sinner, a penitent, or a saint), but to be a [human being]. It is not some religious act which makes a Christian what he [or she] is, but participation in the suffering of God in the life of the world.*[12]
>
> *The religious act is always something partial; "faith" is something whole, involving the whole of one's life. Jesus calls men [and women], not to a new religion, but to life.*[13]

Bonhoeffer believed that through contemplation and action, the Christian would learn a new way of thinking and seeing: to view the world from the perspective of those at the bottom of society.

> *It remains an experience of incomparable value that we have for once learnt to see the great events of world history from below, from the perspective of the outcasts, the suspects, the maltreated, the powerless, the oppressed and reviled, in short from the perspective of the suffering. If only bitterness and envy have during*

10. Dietrich Wilhelm Rudiger Bethge (b. 1944) is a cellist in the English Chamber Orchestra.

11. Bonhoeffer, *Letters and Papers*, 299–300.

12. Ibid., 361. This translation was taken from John A. T. Robinson, *Honest to God*, 83.

13. Ibid., 362.

*this time not corroded the heart; that we come to see matters great
and small, happiness and misfortune, strength and weakness with
new eyes; that our sense for greatness, humanness, justice and
mercy has grown clearer, freer, more incorruptible; that we learn,
indeed, that personal suffering is a more useful key, a more fruitful
principle than personal happiness for exploring the meaning of the
world in contemplation and action.*[14]

In the life of Jesus, we can clearly see the two dimensions of religion-less Christianity—contemplative prayer and righteous action. The gospels describe Jesus continually moving between these two polarities. He often withdraws to the wilderness or to a quiet, lonely place to meditate and pray alone. And then he jumps back into the life of the world with healing actions and a bold prophetic voice. Prayer and righteous action were the key features of the life of Jesus. This is where Bonhoeffer believed that Christianity was heading in the future. Religionless Christianity is a life of caring for people and responding in concrete ways to heal wounds and alleviate the causes that lead to people who are hurting. That has been part of the church's mission over the centuries, but sometimes it seems to forget that it is central, not just a peripheral activity.

It will perhaps surprise many to say that the model for a religionless Christianity is Jesus himself. But Jesus did not intend to found a new religion. Christianity as we know it was not his objective. His life, teachings and actions were focused on creating a new kind of personal and community life in the midst of the old. He set out to transform human life in the midst of a great empire and to challenge those forces that oppress and divide people in every society. This is the journey he invites us to take. This is where the example of Jesus leads today.

14. Ibid., 17.

# contemplation and action

*Life's most persistent and urgent question is:*
*"What are you doing for others?"*[1]

—Martin Luther King, Jr (1929–1968)


*You are like no other being,*
*What you can give no other can give*
*To the future of our precious children,*
*To the future of the world where we live.*

*Love will guide us, peace has tried us,*
*Hope inside us will lead the way.*
*On the road from greed to giving,*
*Love will guide us through the dark night.*[2]

—Sally Rogers (b. 1956)


THE NEW TESTAMENT WRITER of the First Letter of John asserts that God is love—in Greek, *theos ein agapē* (*theh'-ohs ayn ag-ah'-pay*). John specifically

1. Dr. Martin Luther King, Jr made this comment to an audience in Montgomery, Alabama on August 11, 1957. "An individual has not begun to live until he can rise above the narrow horizons of his particular individualistic concerns to the broader concerns of all humanity. Every person must decide, at some point, whether they will walk in the light of creative altruism or in the darkness of destructive selfishness. This is the judgment. Life's most persistent and urgent question is, 'What are you doing for others?'"

2. Sally Rogers, "Love Will Guide Us," 1985.

states that God is unselfish or generous love, which is the meaning of the Greek word *agapē*. Therefore, the word *God* is the name we give to the spirit of selfless love found at the depths of our humanity and experienced in the relationship of human love toward one another. God is a human symbol that personifies compassionate love as a divine entity.

Love is primarily an active verb, not an emotional feeling, although many of us usually consider it only in the latter sense. To say that God is love does not mean that God is a loving feeling or a deep emotion; rather, God is love in action. Feelings are transitory, but acts of love have substance and impact. It is not what we feel, think, believe, or say that count in this life. The only thing that really matters is what we choose to do or leave undone. Love becomes a reality in the midst of human life only when we embody it, share it, and live it. Therefore, that which we call *God* is compassionate love expressed in action through human hands and voices.

God as love does not exist as a disembodied reality in the universe. Love simply does not have that character. Love is not a thing, or a being, or even the source of all being. Love is a human relationship, pure and simple. The theological proposition that God is love teaches us that in the relationship of self-giving love, we find the presence of God. It is there—in that humble yet profound human interaction—that we find ultimate reality.

Dietrich Bonhoeffer said:

> Our relation to God is not a religious relationship to a supreme Being, absolute in power and goodness, which is a spurious conception of transcendence, but a new life for others, through participation in the Being of God.[3]

For Bonhoeffer, participation in the being of God was centered in a new life for others. He believed that it is expressed in two key elements: 1) identifying with those who suffer (through contemplative prayer) and 2) acting in solidarity with them, or on their behalf, to achieve justice in an unjust world.

> Our being Christian today will be limited to two things: prayer and righteous action among [humanity]. All Christian thinking, speaking, and organizing must be born anew out of this prayer and action.[4]

3. Robinson, *Honest to God*, 76.
4. Bonhoeffer, *Letters and Papers*, 300.

## contemplative prayer

Bonhoeffer believed that regular contemplative prayer focused on the needs of others was important because it draws forth empathy and concern toward those whom we envision. Commonly known as intercessory prayer, this mental process brings individuals into our conscious mind and helps us identify with the situations they face—their joys and their sorrows, their trials and successes, their fears and their failures—making us more sensitive to their circumstances. Thinking deeply about other peoples' suffering—and not just solely our own particular problems helps put everything into a larger perspective.

Today, contemplative prayer is often defined as centering prayer. In contemporary terms, contemplative prayer is a listening process—opening the mind and heart to God that involves rhythmic deep breathing while focusing on a single word or mantra. But that is not how Bonhoeffer used the term. For him, it was not about achieving a state of consciousness focused on inner peace and tranquility, it was about moving beyond ourselves into the lives of others. In contemplative prayer, Bonhoeffer said, "I move into the other [person's] place. I enter [their] life . . . [their] guilt and distress. I am afflicted by [their] sins and [their] infirmity."[5] Bonhoeffer believed that this sense of identity with the situations of others was the necessary motivating force that would lead us to "act upon and affect the lives of men and women throughout the world."[6] Contemplation is a matter of opening one's heart and letting one's self be moved with compassion. One scientific study showed that motor circuits in the brain lit up when people were feeling compassionate, as if they were getting ready to do something about the suffering they were sensing.

The importance of contemplative intercession is that it can move us to act in real and tangible ways, rather than calling upon an omnipotent God to act in a supernatural way while we sit idly by. Countless people pray daily for God to change conditions in the world. Their prayers may often sound as if they are reminding God what God's job is (to bring peace among warring nations, to bring healing to the sick, to be with those who suffer, etc.). They want to put everything in God's hands and let God deal with the mess we have created here below. This kind of prayer allows the petitioner to sit passively aside, waiting for God to act, ignoring the reality that the God of love can only work through us in the world. Since the human Jesus no longer dwells among us, it is now our duty as his followers to act on his behalf. A

---

5. Bonhoeffer, *Sanctorum Communio*, 133.
6. Spinner, *A Book of Prayers*, 227. Spinner does not cite the original source.

familiar prose poem commonly (but mistakenly) attributed to Saint Teresa
of Ávila (1515–1582), a Spanish mystic, reformer, and writer states:

> *Christ has no body now but yours, no hands, no feet on earth but*
> *yours. Yours are the eyes through which He looks with compassion*
> *on this world. Christ has no body now on earth but yours.*[7]

Bonhoeffer likewise realized that the power we call God can *only*
work through us in the world. It is not appropriate, nor is it realistic, to ask
God to do things in the world independent of us. Contemplative prayer
doesn't ask God to act; it is instead a motivating force for each of us to act in
concrete ways.

How one prays depends on one's image of God. Today, the majority of Americans—56 percent—view God as a supernatural, omnipotent
interventionist. For many others, however, this concept of God no longer
works. One just has to observe the real world of pain, suffering, and evil
that surrounds us to believe that the supernatural God is not all-powerful,
is not in charge of events on earth, and does not act to save those who suffer
most. Instead, the supernatural God of the past has apparently abandoned
humanity and has left the asylum to the inmates.

Bonhoeffer saw God not as omnipotent, but as weak and powerless in
the world. In the human Jesus, he saw weakness and suffering as the way
that a God of love operates among humanity. Theologically speaking, if Jesus is the decisive revelation of what God is like, then the weakness and suffering of Jesus on the cross can be viewed as an image of God's weakness in
the world. Bonhoeffer wrote that instead of intervening, God has forsaken
us and we are left to suffer like Jesus on the cross.

> *God would have us know that we must live as [people] who man-*
> *age our lives without him. The God who is with us is the God who*
> *forsakes us.*[8]

In this letter to his friend Eberhard Bethge (1909–2000), Bonhoeffer
notes the passion narrative of Mark's gospel in which Jesus cries out to God
in Aramaic as he is being crucified:

---

7. A number of scholars have stated that these words are not found in the writings of Teresa of Ávila, therefore she is not the source. Instead, they seem to have
originated in England around 1890 from the ideas of a Methodist minister Mark Guy
Pearse (1842–1930) and later modified to its current form by Quaker medical mission-
ary Sarah Elizabeth Rowntree (dates unknown). The current quote is an abbreviation
of Rowntree's writings.

8. Bonhoeffer, *Letters and Papers*, 360.

*At three o'clock Jesus cried out with a loud voice, "Eloi, Eloi, lema sabachthani?" which means, "My God, my God, why have you forsaken me?"*[9]

Bonhoeffer then comments:

*God lets himself be pushed out of the world on to the cross. He is weak and powerless in the world, and that is precisely the way, the only way, in which he is with us and helps us . . . Christ helps us, not by virtue of his omnipotence, but by virtue of his weakness and suffering.*

*Here is the decisive difference between Christianity and all religions. [Humanity's] religiosity makes [them] look in [their] distress to the power of God in the world: God is the Deus ex machina. The Bible directs [people] to God's powerlessness and suffering; only the suffering God can help.*[10]

The Latin phrase *Deus ex machina* (*day'-us eks mack'-in-ah*) refers to situations in ancient Greek theater in which a crane was used to lower actors playing a god onto the stage. Bonhoeffer uses the term to refer to the common religious hope that God will step in to resolve a hopeless situation like a comic book action hero. Bonhoeffer believed that God does not intervene in history to save us. His view of history from the first half of the twentieth century—two world wars, a global economic depression, and the extermination camps of the Jewish Holocaust—was evidence enough that God does not act in this way.

Bonhoeffer prayed so that he—acting as one of God's agents—would be motivated to change things in the world that he could impact personally. He realized that instead of us waiting for God to intervene, the God of love waits for us to act. Prayer on behalf of others stirs up the compassionate response that drives us to take the necessary action.

Because a God of love acts through us and as us, we are called to solidarity with those who suffer, empathizing with them, and sharing their suffering with them. Bonhoeffer wrote: "[We are] summoned to share in God's suffering at the hands of a godless world."[11] Solidarity with the suffering of the world is the essential Christian stance. Service to the suffering of the world is the essential Christian act.

---

9. Mark 15:34. See also Matthew 27:46.

10. Bonhoeffer, *Letters and Papers*, 360–361.

11. Ibid., 361.

The contemplative prayer that Bonhoeffer describes begins by bringing to mind those for whom we easily feel compassion—friends and family. It should then begin to expand in ever larger concentric circles to include others, not only those we are fondest of, but also those with whom we have difficulty. Contemplative intercessory prayer is not just a practice for religious people. Atheists and agnostics can and should pray for others. This is a compassionate process that works for everyone, whether or not one believes in God's existence. "You can pray for someone even if you don't think God exists," said Gordon Atkinson, a Baptist preacher.

Going beyond friends, family, and acquaintances, our contemplation should bring to mind those who are in need and are suffering in our towns, our nation, and the world. This expanded form of contemplation is really a meditation on the issues and crises of daily life, reflecting the news of the world. It is important to look deeply at current events from one's theological perspective and see how that might inform a compassionate response. Karl Barth (1886–1968) reportedly said, "We must hold the Bible in one hand and the newspaper in the other." He later clarified that one should interpret the news from the Bible's perspective. For me, the teachings of Jesus and the prophets of the Hebrew Bible provide a unique lens on the problems of the day.

Prayer can be an instrument of insurrection and transformation. If it doesn't lead us to begin the task of fundamentally changing the conditions of the domination system that cause massive suffering, then we do not really understand the purpose of prayer. Karl Barth is also reported to have said, "To clasp the hands in prayer is the beginning of an uprising against the disorder of the world."[12] Reformer Mohandas Gandhi (1869–1948) once said something similar: "Prayer is not an old woman's idle amusement. Properly understood and applied, it is the most potent instrument of action." Austin O'Malley (1858–1932), a Dublin football player and teacher, put it this way: "Practical prayer is harder on the soles of your shoes than on the knees of your trousers." These quotes reflect the foundations of an active-practical form of spirituality.

## compassion

Compassion is a feeling of empathy with the suffering of others, the capacity to feel how others feel. The Latin root of the word *compassion* is a compound of *com* (with) and *passio* (suffer), which gives us the meaning *to suffer with*. Compassion is entering into the pain of another. It is feeling the suffering of

---

12. This comment by Karl Barth is frequently quoted, but its source is not cited.

someone else—experiencing it, sharing it, tasting it. It is identifying with the sufferer, being in solidarity with the sufferer.

True compassion is being so moved at a gut level that we are moved to the point of action. Jesus was moved by compassion for the poor. We are told that, "He had compassion on them because they were harassed and helpless, like sheep without a shepherd"[13] And in the parable of the Good Samaritan he demonstrated that the one who loves the neighbor is the one who shows compassion on the one who suffers, even if that person is culturally defined as the enemy.

Marcus Borg has said that, "For Jesus, compassion was the central quality of God and the central moral quality of a life centered in God." The Pharisees represented a theology of holiness, according to Borg, which was based on holiness as a defining characteristic of God: "Be holy for I, Yahweh, am holy."[14] Jesus proclaimed a theology of compassion based on an alternative characterization of God's essence: "Be compassionate as your Father in heaven is compassionate."[15] These differing theologies led them to different ways of living.

## righteous action

The word *righteous* may need some clarification because the common understanding of righteousness is 1) being morally right, or 2) being right with God. These moralistic and relational understandings can sometimes lead the Christian to a sense of superior self-righteousness which is certainly not what a God of love desires. When he used the term *righteous*, Bonhoeffer was not talking about the moral quality of the doer; he is talking about the nature of the deed. Bonhoeffer was referring to a more holistic biblical understanding of righteousness—standing up for what is right, doing what is right and just. Righteousness means seeking justice in human society.

The terms *righteousness* and *justice* are often linked in biblical texts. That is because they are synonymous, redundant terms. In the original languages of the Bible, the word for justice also means righteousness. The Greek word *dikaios* (*dik'-ah-yos*) in the New Testament and the word *tzedakah* (*tze-dah-kah'*) in the Hebrew Bible have this dual meaning. Righteousness implies a personal and individual dimension, while justice implies a social dimension, but they both have the same objectives—acting on behalf of those suffering from injustice and violence.

13. Matthew 9:36
14. Leviticus 11:44
15. Luke 6:36

Compassionate action usually takes three forms: charity, service, and justice. Although some would include service under the first category, charity more specifically involves gifts of money, clothing, food, or other material goods, but does not necessarily involve an investment of our time and talents. Charity is important, but writing a check to a worthy cause does not automatically transform our lives. We remain distant from those we seek to help. Service, however, involves us face-to-face with those in need. It can be an immensely transformative experience that can change us from our natural state of self-centeredness into increasingly selfless people. Perhaps it is the only thing that will. Although generosity sometimes leads to self-satisfaction, service often becomes a very humbling experience.

Charity and service are both personal forms of compassionate action. Their objective is to alleviate the effects of suffering in the world. Justice, on the other hand, seeks to eliminate the root causes of suffering. Martin Luther King, Jr. said:

> We are called to play the Good Samaritan on life's roadside; but that will be only an initial act. One day the whole Jericho road must be transformed so that men and women will not be beaten and robbed as they make their journey through life. True compassion is more than flinging a coin to a beggar; it understands that an edifice that produces beggars needs restructuring.[16]

Justice is focused on transforming the social structures and systems that produce poverty and suffering. Justice is the social form of compassionate action. It is the political form of caring for the least of these. The difference between charity and service on the one hand and justice on the other is this: charity and service seek to heal wounds, while justice seeks to end the social structures that create wounded people in the first place. William Sloane Coffin has said: "The bible is less concerned with alleviating the effects of injustice, than in eliminating the causes of it."[17] Still, all three of these are necessary components of what Bonhoeffer describes as righteous action among humanity.

## charity

Jesus was a radical. And nowhere else is this more evident than in his call for radical charity and generosity. His words are a significant challenge.

---

16. King, *Where Do We Go from Here?*, 198.
17. Coffin, *Credo*, 50.

*Give to everyone who begs from you.*[18]

*Do not refuse anyone who wants to borrow from you.*[19]

*Lend, expecting nothing in return.*[20]

*Do not be afraid, little flock, for it is your Father's good pleasure to give you the kingdom. Sell your possessions, and give alms.*[21]

Jesus challenged his followers to give up everything to follow him. He invited them to step out in a journey of faith with no material security as a safety net. As far as we know, Jesus was homeless and possessionless himself, depending on the charity of others for food and shelter. We are told that he sent his followers out to the villages of Galilee with no money or food, telling them to depend on the kindness of the strangers they met along the way to provide sustenance and shelter.

Matthew, Mark, and Luke all describe a rich young man who came to Jesus to discover what more he could do with his life. He was trying hard to love God and his neighbor. Mark's gospel says that "Jesus looked at him and loved him" for his sincerity and effort. When the young man asked Jesus if there was anything more he could do, Jesus responded:

*Go, sell what you own, and give the money to the poor, and you will be spiritually rich; then come, follow me.*[22]

We are told the young man "walked away sad, because he had great wealth." Jesus was trying to get those who sought to follow him to understand that there are two ways to achieve security in life. The first is to take care of ourselves by accumulating personal wealth. This is what the rich young man had done. The second is to create a community in which we care for each other by sharing our wealth. This is what loving one's neighbor means. And this is what the rich young man could not do. Maintaining his personal wealth was too important. Giving it away was too great a risk. To live this way requires an enormous act of faith.

Following Jesus can be costly, but we are not required to emulate Jesus by abandoning all our possessions and financial security. Instead, the idea that we should pool our resources to help one another is central to the communities that gathered around him. This was how the Jerusalem

18. Luke 6:30
19. Matthew 5:42
20. Luke 6:35
21. Luke 12:32
22. Mark 10:21

community of his disciples structured themselves after the death of Jesus. They maintained their own homes while generously contributing to a common fund in order to care for others as needs arose. There are still models of this radical approach in small monastic communities and house churches today. But more importantly, the way of Jesus involves using our pooled resources on local, national, and global scales to care for those afflicted by poverty and war.

The kind of radical personal charity that Jesus recommended is rare. Regardless of our generosity, most of us are cautious in how we use our funds. We know we can do more, yet we hold back, not wanting to be taken advantage of by undeserving people. But, no matter how generous we are, in the end, charity is only a Band-Aid. It fills the gaps left by an unjust society. Charity is important, but it is not enough.

## service

Serving the needs of others is the path of transformation from ego-centrism to humility. Our captivity to our egos in the context of the present domination system causes us to value success, importance, and praise. But Jesus calls us to deny ourselves—our self-importance, our self-centeredness, our innate selfishness—and by humbling ourselves, serve others in need.

Matthew's gospel recounts the story of two of Jesus' disciples—brothers James and John and their mother—who desired greatness, power, and acclaim.

> Then the mother of the sons of Zebedee came to him with her sons, and kneeling before him, she asked a favor of him. And he said to her, "What do you want?" She said to him, "Declare that these two sons of mine will sit, one at your right hand and one at your left, in your kingdom."

When the other disciples heard this, they became angry with the two brothers.

> But Jesus called them to him and said, "You know that the rulers of the Gentiles lord it over them, and their great ones are tyrants over them. It will not be so among you; but whoever wishes to be great among you must be your servant, and whoever wishes to be first among you must be your slave."[23]

Luke's gospel has a parallel account:

23. Matthew 20:20–28

*A dispute also arose among them as to which one of them was to be regarded as the greatest. But he said to them, "The kings of the Gentiles lord it over them; and those in authority over them are called benefactors. But not so with you; rather the greatest among you must become like the youngest, and the leader like one who serves. For who is greater, the one who is at the table or the one who serves? Is it not the one at the table? But I am among you as one who serves."*[24]

We all have an inborn desire to be noticed, to be affirmed, and to feel significant. But a servant is one who quietly and humbly serves the needs of others regardless of personal recognition. So, if we're striving to be like Jesus, no task should be beneath us, no person below us, and no appropriate sacrifice too great.

There are many ways to serve, but we should be aware of some pitfalls. Professor Rachel Remen (b. 1938) suggests that sometimes our natural inclination to help others and to fix their brokenness can be impediments to real service.

*Service is not the same as helping. Helping is based on inequality; it's not a relationship between equals. When you help, you use your own strength to help someone with less strength. It's a one up, one down relationship, and people feel this inequality. When we help, we may inadvertently take away more than we give, diminishing the person's sense of self-worth and self-esteem . . . Helping incurs debt: when you help someone, they owe you. But service is mutual. When I help I have a feeling of satisfaction, but when I serve I have a feeling of gratitude.*

*Serving is also different to fixing. We fix broken pipes, we don't fix people. When I set about fixing another person, it's because I see them as broken. Fixing is a form of judgement that separates us from one another; it creates a distance.*

*We may help or fix many things in our lives, but when we serve, we are always in the service of wholeness.*[25]

Theologian Jean Vanier (b. 1928) is the founder of L'Arche, a group of communities in 35 countries for people with developmental disabilities and those who assist them. He describes true service as being present with and accompanying another. The word *accompany*, like the word *companion*, comes from the Latin words *cum pane* (*cum pahn'-ay*), which means "with

24. Luke 22:24–27
25. Rachel Remen, "Helping, Fixing, Serving," Awakin.org (May 29, 2000). No pages. Online: http://www.awakin.org/read/view.php?tid=127

bread." Accompaniment implies nourishing each other by eating, sharing, and walking together.

> *Accompaniment is necessary at every stage of our lives, but particularly in moments of crisis when we feel lost, engulfed in grief or in feelings of inadequacy. The accompanier is there to give support, to reassure, to confirm, and to open new doors. The accompanier is not there to judge us or to tell us what to do, but to reveal what is most beautiful and valuable in us.*[26]

Anyone can serve another in this way. A true servant is one who has answered an inner call to show up and be present to what is right before them, and who asks the question, "What can I contribute?" The following quote has often been attributed to Mother Teresa. Regardless of who said it, it is an important thought.

> *If you can't do great things, do little things with great love. If you can't do them with great love, do them with a little love. If you can't do them with a little love, do them anyway.*[27]

## justice

Loving one's neighbor calls us to much more than charity and service; it means working for a just and equitable society. Justice is ultimately the most important factor in loving our neighbors. Philosopher and activist Cornell West (b. 1953) once said, "Justice is what love looks like in public. You can't talk about loving folk and not fighting for justice"[28] So justice is not only the social form of compassion, it is the social form of love. One definition of love is "a choice to do what is best for another person." Consequently, love in a family involves feeding, clothing, sheltering, educating those whom we love. By extension, love in the human family means insuring that everyone gets a fair, equitable access to the means of life.

The word *justice* means different things to different people. For many people, it brings to mind *retributive* justice, which seeks to punish lawbreakers. Some of us think of *procedural* justice, which makes sure that everyone gets fair treatment under the law. However, the biblical meaning of justice is *distributive* justice, which promises a fair share of the necessities of life.

---

26. Vanier, *Becoming Human*, 129.

27. Attributed to Mother Teresa by Ortberg, *The Me I Want to Be*, 141. No source cited.

28. This comment by West is frequently quoted, but not cited.

The Bible teaches that justice is economic sharing. Those who have more, help those who have less. Biblical scholar John Dominic Crossan reacted to the suggestion by some conservatives that the equitable sharing of our resources is nothing more than liberalism, socialism, or communism by suggesting that if we need to give biblical justice an "ism," the best label would be "enoughism."

The pursuit of justice leads us directly into politics. We cannot avoid it. Therefore the command to love our neighbor is always a political command. To follow Jesus and to proclaim the God of justice leads us to a distinctly political stance of looking out for the welfare of the poor and disadvantaged. To avoid proclaiming God's call to distributive justice is to support the status quo of the domination system—which is also a political stance.

Charity, service, and justice are needed in a suffering world. The question is why Christians nearly always favor the personal forms of charity and service over justice. In an unjust world, only the first and more limited responses—charity and service—are acceptable to those in power. The work of faith-based charities is often lauded by government until they try to influence government policies to change the status quo. Television journalist Bill Moyers (b. 1934) has said:

> Charity is commendable; everyone should be charitable. But justice aims to create a social order in which, if individuals choose not to be charitable, people still don't go hungry, unschooled, or sick without care. Charity depends on the vicissitudes of whim and personal wealth; justice depends on commitment instead of circumstance. Faith-based charity provides crumbs from the table; faith-based justice offers a place at the table. [29]

Dom Helder Camara (1909–1999), a Roman Catholic bishop from the poor Brazilian region of Recife said in the 1960s, "When I feed the poor, they call me a saint. When I ask why they are poor, they call me a Communist."[30] And biblical scholar John Dominic Crossan once said, "Charity gets you canonized; justice gets you crucified."[31] In the church, it is easier to talk about charity than justice. That is because justice gets us squarely into politics where we come face-to-face with the institutional selfishness of the

---

29. Moyers, *Faith Works*, xvii.

30. Rocha, *Helder*, 53.

31. I heard Crossan say this at a retreat at the Kirkridge Retreat Center in Bangor, Pennsylvania in 2003. It is found in a slightly different form in *The Birth of Christianity*, 586: "Those who live by compassion are often canonized. Those who live by justice are often crucified."

domination system that we have created. More importantly, it gets us into questions of how to achieve justice.

In the current political realm, conservatives tend to favor charity, while liberals look to justice to deal with issues of suffering. We face a political divide on how to help the poor most effectively. One position holds that it is the role of individuals to voluntarily help the poor to whatever extent an individual feels called to provide from their resources. The other position maintains that as a society we have an obligation to deal with hunger, homelessness, and poverty together through governmental programs wherever possible. The first approach would use free-will offerings, while the other believes that our national treasure allows us to better accomplish societal needs as a people. Ask any major charity in the United States and they will tell you that without government help, charitable contributions fall significantly short of the pressing needs.

In response to suffering, a weak and powerless God of love moves us to action, urging us to transform the human conditions that cause suffering. God's active love expressed in our lives is evident when we pursue justice— creating those conditions that promote life and put an end to suffering. From Deuteronomy to Micah to Matthew, the call is clear:

> *Justice, and only justice, you shall pursue.*[32]

> *What does the Lord require of you but to do justice?*[33]

> *Strive first for the kingdom of God and God's justice.*[34]

In spite of the seeming immensity of the task, there is hope that a just society is possible. As Martin Luther King said, "The long arc of the universe bends toward justice." But as Barack Obama added, "The arc of the moral universe may bend towards justice, but it does not bend on its own." We are the shapers of the moral universe.

As followers of Jesus, we are called to pursue justice on behalf of the vast majority of people all around the world who suffer under the present domination system. Nobel Peace Prize winner Rigoberta Menchú (b. 1959) wrote:

> *We feel it is the duty of Christians to create the kingdom of God on Earth among our brothers. This kingdom will exist only when we all have enough to eat, when our children, brothers, parents*

32. Deuteronomy 16:20
33. Micah 6:8
34. Matthew 6:33

*don't have to die from hunger and malnutrition. That will be the
"Glory," a Kingdom for we who have never known it.*[35]

The reign of God is about doing for the entire human family what we do within our individual families. Loving the whole human family means insuring that everyone gets a fair and equitable access to the necessary means of life: food, clean water, clothing, shelter, education, health care, meaningful employment, safety, and protection from violence. As followers of Jesus, it is up to us to figure out how to live together as a human community, how to love one another, and how to care for the earth and all its creatures.

Acts of compassion, generosity, service, and justice not only help others, they also transform us into better people. As Gandhi said, "Be the change that you wish to see in the world." In becoming better people, we have a chance to create a better world. If we live our lives as co-conspirators with Jesus, if we engage in his conspiracy of love in our time and place, his vision of the inbreaking reign of love will be fulfilled within us and around us one small sacred act at a time. And all we need is love.

35. Menchú, *I, Rigoberta Menchú*, 158.

# CHAPTER 12

# the ethics of love

_Love is the fulfillment of the law._[1]

—Paul, the Apostle

_Love is the ultimate law._[2]

—Paul Tillich (1886–1965)

_Love is all you need._[3]

—Paul McCartney (b. 1942) and John Lennon (1940–1980)

THE 1982 FILM _THE Year of Living Dangerously_ is set in Indonesia during the rule of president-for-life Sukarno in the 1960s.[4] The film reveals an unstable society on the edge of revolution. The disparity between the rich and the poor is appalling.

The diminutive character Billy Kwan (played by actress Linda Hunt, who won an Academy Award for this role), challenges Guy Hamilton, an

---

1. Romans 13:10
2. Tillich, _Systematic Theology_, 152.
3. Lennon and McCartney, "All You Need Is Love," 1967.
4. Peter Weir, Dir., _The Year of Living Dangerously_, Metro-Goldwyn-Mayer, 1982. The film is based on the book of the same name by Australian novelist Christopher Koch, published in 1978. The screenplay was by David Williamson, Peter Weir, and Christopher Koch.

Australian reporter (played by the young Mel Gibson), who like other foreign reporters chooses to stay in a Western compound and separate himself from the suffering masses of the country. On his first night in Jakarta, as they walk through the stalls of a market for the poor on a stretch of wasteland, Hamilton is confronted by the misery and suffering of the poorest people in the city. As a journalist, he believes he must remain detached from the situation, but reacting to the extreme poverty before them, Kwan challenges Hamilton's lack of compassion.

> *Kwan: The people asked him, saying "What shall we do then?"*
>
> *Hamilton: What's that?*
>
> *Kwan: It's from Luke, chapter 3, verse 10. What then must we do? Tolstoy asked the same question. He wrote a book with that title. He got so upset about the poverty in Moscow that he went one night into the poorest section and just gave away all his money. You could do that now. Five American dollars would be a fortune to one of these people.*
>
> *Hamilton: Wouldn't do any good. It'd just be a drop in the ocean.*
>
> *Kwan: Ah, that's the same conclusion Tolstoy came to. I disagree.*
>
> *Hamilton: And what's your solution?*
>
> *Kwan: Well, I support the view that you just don't think about the major issues. You do whatever you can about the misery that's in front of you. Add your light to the sum of light.*

"What then must we do?" is the foundational question behind every ethical system. Tolstoy found the phrase in the third chapter of the gospel of Luke where these words are addressed to John the Baptizer by the crowds who gathered around him at the Jordan River. Warning his listeners that a great catastrophe was approaching, that a time of judgment was coming, John does not advise people to forestall God's action by praying or worshipping or evangelizing the world, but instead tells people to begin acting justly and generously with one another.

Every day we are confronted with the distance between what we *do* and what we *ought* to do. What do we do in the face of injustice? Is it right to be dishonest in a good cause? Or alternatively, is it right to tell the truth if it endangers someone? Is it ever right to take a human life? Should we give money to a homeless person begging on the street, or should we turn away?

Beyond these day-to-day questions, we are faced with global moral issues. Can we justify a lifestyle of conspicuous consumption, using vast amounts of the world's non-renewable resources while polluting the environment and warming the globe? What are our obligations to the other creatures with whom we share this planet and to the other generations of humans who will come after us?

At the root of our ethical responses to life are some even more fundamental human questions. Why are we here? What is our purpose in life? Are we here to achieve happiness or wealth or virtue or love? Are we really meant to be our brothers' and sisters' keeper?

## the ethic of love

At the heart of Christianity is a powerful ethic. It is what the first followers of Jesus called the Way—a way of living based on love and compassion, reconciliation and forgiveness, inclusion and acceptance, peace and nonviolence, generosity and justice. This ethic is what makes Christianity good. Without it, Christians can become rigid and intolerant, self-righteous and condemning, hate-filled and violent, selfish and unjust. In other words, without the ethic of Jesus, Christians can represent the worst humanity has to offer.

Unfortunately, this negative image has all too often become the public face of Christianity. Throughout my life, I have struggled with the label "Christian" because to many people, especially to many younger people, Christians are characterized by hypocrisy, condemnation, and intolerance. They seem to be people who focus on practicing what they believe is correct religion but frequently miss doing what Jesus taught was the right kind of living—a non-judgmental life of acceptance, compassion, and forgiveness. They are people so concerned about believing the right things that will assure a path to heaven when they die, that they miss the importance of living compassionately and justly in the present.

To follow Jesus, we need to practice the ethic of Jesus. And that requires a transformation from a life of selfish individuality to a life centered in concern for others. It requires a major shift of focus from securing a place in the afterlife, to improving life for all in the here and now.

In some ways, it would have been easier for us if Jesus had prepared a new set of rules. It would save us a lot of time and energy we now spend in deciding what to do. If his new set of rules had been sufficiently complete, all we would have to do would be to run down through the moral code until we came to the precept that applied, and "presto!" the decision would be made for us. But the difficulty in this approach is that it undercuts what Jesus was all about. What he wanted to drive home to us was a personal embrace of love toward God and compassion toward our neighbor. For Jesus, this entirely simple but very profound set of relationships formed the basis of the Law and the Prophets—the ethical content of the Hebrew Bible.

Some church teachers claim we cannot build a system of ethics on Jesus' life and teachings because they are simply too radical. They suggest that Jesus' teachings, especially in Matthew's Sermon on the Mount and Luke's Sermon on the Plain, were not intended for the long term. They tell us that this was merely an "interim ethic" until the quickly anticipated arrival of the kingdom of God in all its fullness. However, that brief interim has now stretched to over 2,000 years. If Jesus intended his teachings as a brief interim ethic, he was a bit off the mark in terms of the timing.

Also, some church teachers claim, Jesus and his followers were not in positions of power. They were simple peasants and poor fishermen. Christians today can hold positions of great authority, making decisions that affect the lives of millions of people. Therefore we must base our ethics not on the teachings of Jesus, but instead on some general principle of proper behavior or more commonly on fixed moral laws.

But what if these church teachers are wrong? What if Jesus meant exactly what he said, not just for the short term, but for every time and place?

It's easy to claim that all Christian ethics should be based on the Bible, but the biblical record shows two clearly different avenues: the path of religious rules and the path of compassionate action. Nowhere are they more explicitly presented as competing ethics than in the gospel accounts. Jesus spoke of two alternative paths in life—one narrow and difficult, the other wide and easy. He used the metaphors of doors or gates as well—narrow and wide.

> Enter through the narrow gate; for the gate is wide and the road is easy that leads to destruction, and there are many who take it. For the gate is narrow and the road is hard that leads to life, and there are few who find it.[5]
> Strive to enter through the narrow door; for many, I tell you, will try to enter and will not be able.[6]

Religious people often understand the narrow path as the path of correct beliefs and proper behavior. They see the wide path, which leads to destruction, as incorrect beliefs, even unbelief, and improper behavior that violates absolute moral codes. This was as true in Jesus' time as it is in ours.

Yet, I believe that Jesus understood these two paths very differently from the church. The wide path is the path of conventional religion—of correct beliefs and rigid moral rules. It is easy because one doesn't have to

5. Matthew 7:13–14
6. Luke 13:24

think. One only has to follow the rules. The narrow path is a path encountered by a heart rooted in compassion. It is a path demonstrated by behavior
rather than belief, but it is a behavior which is defined by compassionate
action in ever changing contexts. It is a more difficult path, but says Jesus it
"leads to life."

We are told in the gospels that compassion was the driving motive for
Jesus' actions. What made Jesus unique was the unrestrained compassion he
felt for the poor and the oppressed.

> *He was moved with compassion because they were distressed and*
> *dejected like sheep without a shepherd.*[7]

It was compassion that motivated Jesus to feed the hungry crowds that
followed him:

> *I have compassion for these people; they have been with me for*
> *three days and have nothing to eat.*[8]

What's more, compassion is expressed in his parables. What made the
loving father in the parable of the Prodigal Son so unusual was the excess
of love and compassion he felt for his prodigal (spendthrift) son.[9] Even
though the son had wasted his share of the father's wealth in profligate
living, the father needed no apology, but instead ran to greet his son, and
rejoiced at his return.

> *But while he was still far off, his father saw him and was filled*
> *with compassion; he ran and put his arms around him and kissed*
> *him.*[10]

In the parable of the Good Samaritan, Jesus tells us that the Samaritan
felt compassion for the man left half dead on the roadside

> *But a Samaritan while travelling came near him; and when he*
> *saw him, he was moved with compassion.* [11]

We are told that the Samaritan was moved to the point of action,
became personally involved, was interrupted and inconvenienced, took a
personal risk, and willingly paid for the man's expenses as he recovered.

7. Matthew 9:36, Mark 6:34
8. Matthew 15:32, Mark 8:2
9. Luke 15:10–32
10. Luke 15:20
11. Luke 10:25–37

The ethics of the conspiracy of love are not based on rules. They are based on an understanding of the nature of God as love, and a vision of what this world would be like if the radical values of love, compassion, and forgiveness were lived out among the people of God.

In their desire to be like Jesus, the early Christians looked to his stance of love, inclusion, acceptance, forgiveness, and compassion in establishing a community of equals. They looked to his stance of generosity and distributive economic justice for and among the poor. And ultimately, they looked to his stance in relation to the power of the state—his nonviolent direct action for social change, his willingness to accept arrest as a consequence of his actions, and his execution without recourse to violence. These are the ethical behaviors that Jesus modeled. This is the ethical lifestyle of Jesus we are called to follow. This is the ethic of love, compassion and justice that he believed reflected the very character and nature of God.

## religion and morality

The way of religion has historically included the development of a morality. As long as people have been living together in groups, the moral regulation of behavior has been necessary to the group's well-being. Over time, customary standards of right and wrong behavior evolve into oral and written moral codes. In ancient cultures these codes of conduct were combined with some myth to explain their origin. In the Babylonian tradition, the sun god Shamash presented the code of laws to Hammurabi. In the Hebrew tradition, Yahweh presented the Ten Commandments to Moses on Sinai. Enveloping the morality with the mystery and power of divine origin provided a strong reason for accepting the moral code.

There are two fundamental questions involved in ethics and morality. "What is the right thing to do?" and "Why should I do the right thing?" By connecting morality to religion, the priesthood could answer both of those questions. They could make judgments regarding right and wrong behavior and claim divine approval. By attributing a divine origin to morality, the priesthood became its interpreter and guardian, and thereby secured for itself tremendous social power. In addition to a cooperative relationship between temple and state to punish or absolve transgressors, punishment and reward could be extended to eternity. This link between morality and religion has been so firmly forged that it is still sometimes asserted that there can be no morality without religion.

Today, many people look to religion to provide authoritative rules to conform their decision-making in line with what they regard to be God's will. Quite often, these moral codes have their historical roots in an individual ethical response to a specific situation. But then, over time, that specific response becomes institutionalized as a universal rule which must be applied in all situations. These moral rules are supported and reinforced by consensus within a community and they are transmitted to new members through the pervasive culture or religious heritage of that community, or by decree from religious authorities. Morality is so intertwined with culture that it is generally unquestioned within the culture. It's just part of the way things are. Everyone knows that the accepted behavior is good and right and true. In a multicultural setting, competing cultural mores can lead to confusion and conflict. Still, any law code that gets into regulating specific behavior is out of date almost before it is written. Laws have to be amended and adapted to changing situations. All too often, morality is simply restricted to a process of rule-making and rule-keeping that is irrelevant to changing conditions and may harm innocent people with unintended consequences.

## ethics versus morality

In order to understand the many ethical dilemmas and moral choices we face each day we should examine the closely linked concepts of ethics and morality. A distinction between the two is important. Technically, ethics is the study of moral systems. It explores those values that lie behind our decision-making as we encounter choices in life. Ethical systems attempt to determine principles or standards of human conduct, used to judge whether human actions are right or wrong in a specific circumstance. But in another sense, an ethic represents an individual or personal way of responding to the issues of life based on one's ethical principles, in contrast to a pre-determined morality imposed by others, specifically a rigid code derived from religious custom or authority.

Both ethics and morality have their linguistic roots in words that originally meant *customs*. *Ethics* derives from the Greek term for customs from which we get *ethos*, which refers to the ideals or motivating spirit of a community. *Morality* comes from the Latin root that gives us *mores*, a word that describes the customs of a people. Morality is often the product of a religious system, while ethics are more individual and personal, derived from fundamental principles one chooses to live by. Religious morality is derived from centuries of institutional and philosophical rule-making as a guide for human life. Morality is therefore usually rule-based and determined by others, while ethics are principle-based and are determined by the individual responding to a particular situation in life.

Basically, there are three schools of thought regarding morality and ethics. First, there is *moral absolutism*. This concept affirms that there are fixed objective standards of right and wrong derived from the laws of God. Many Christians throughout history have accepted that certain actions are absolutely right or absolutely wrong, regardless of the situational contexts, the intentions behind them, or the consequences that result. They regard such a moral system as unconditional and unchangeable throughout human history. It is held to be true at any time and in any place, with no restrictions or exceptions. Thus stealing, for instance, might be considered to be always immoral, even if done to promote some other good—such as stealing food to feed a starving family. The Roman Catholic Church regards abortion as a grave moral sin in all cases because it takes a human life. They allow no exceptions for circumstances of rape or incest, or to save the mother's life. In the United States, Roman Catholic bishops oppose abortion's legality under the law and would deny Holy Communion to any Catholic who votes for a politician specifically because of that person's pro-choice stance. Catholic pro-choice politicians are sometimes threatened with excommunication. This is an example of an absolute morality. It makes rules more important than people, and doesn't allow exceptions.

The second approach is *moral nihilism*. Nihilists generally reject the existence of God, and without a God to impose rules on humanity, they believe that every behavior is permitted. They contend that there are no inherent rules for human conduct and that every morality is artificially contrived. Nihilists accept that everyone becomes their own arbiter of the law—a law unto themselves. With the rise of modernity, religion began to give way to science, technology, materialism, and market economics that are not based on moral foundations. They are not immoral, but simply amoral. German philosopher Friedrich Nietzsche (1844–1900), observed the growth of nihilism as a widespread phenomenon throughout Europe and America from the middle of the nineteenth century. Existentialist Albert Camus (1913–1960) wrote that the best example of nihilism taken to its extreme was the Nazi regime and Adolf Hitler's genocides. For Hitler and his followers, the only value that mattered was the glory of the German nation. It was thus right to eliminate anyone or anything that stood in its way. Moral nihilism can lead to complete chaos with no laws at all, and no way of choosing between two courses of action.

The third school of thought is *moral relativism*. This philosophy falls between absolute morality and nihilism. It contends that all conduct is relative to the particular circumstance, but is guided by a fixed moral norm or standard. This view is concerned not with universal rightness or wrongness, but is a personal response to a situation by applying ethical principles. It contends that some foundational criteria must be used to determine one's response to a moral dilemma. The norm of one's ethical system may be a great guiding principle or value like honor or truth or duty or love. But in the end, each individual must decide what is moral or immoral in a given situation. As a result, moral relativism is sometimes referred to as situational ethics.

For most Christians, nihilism is not an option. As a result we generally have two polarities in any discussion of ethics. On the one hand are those who believe that all ethics are situational, and on the other hand those who believe that morality is absolute and cannot be compromised to deal with a specific circumstance. Situational ethics requires the individual to make tough decisions and weigh alternatives in determining an appropriate course of action. Absolute morality, on the other hand, consists of clearly defined external rules which must be followed in all situations, thus freeing the individual from the burden of choice.

Situational ethics is about doing what is right regardless of what we are told, while absolute morality is doing what we are told regardless of whether it is right.

So which ethical path did Jesus follow? In his time and culture, moral law was very clear. The written law in the Torah—the first five books of the Hebrew Bible—includes the Ten Commandments and the 613 *mitzvot* (*mits-vote'*), commandments, rules, and regulations found primarily in the law codes of Exodus, Leviticus, and Deuteronomy. These ancient laws guided a gamut of human social behaviors including topics on diet, clothing, disease, sexual taboos, economic transactions, religious offerings, crime, and retribution. Jesus repeatedly tried to explain to his followers that adherence to a law or rule was not enough. He urged his followers to try to go beyond the external form of the law to discover the intention of God that lay behind the law. Jesus chose to go to the heart of the Hebrew laws and used two fundamental love relationships as a basis of morality. When questioned by a lawyer about the most important commandment in the Hebrew scripture, he replied:

> *You shall love the Lord your God with all your heart, and with all your soul, and with all your mind. This is the greatest and first commandment. And a second is like it: "You shall love your neighbor as yourself." On these two commandments hang all the law and the prophets.*[12]

---

12. Matthew 22:37–40

Loving God and neighbor are not new legal requirements or fixed moral codes; they are relational interactions. They are ties, bonds, and connections. Jesus was declaring that the unwavering law of the Hebrew Bible was superseded by love. He was not describing loving feelings or an emotional devotion toward God and neighbor, but rather love expressed in concrete actions. For Jesus, nothing was more important than loving God and one's neighbor. In the first epistle of John, these two concepts are seen as essentially the same thing.

> Those who say, "I love God," and hate their brothers or sisters, are liars; for those who do not love a brother or sister whom they have seen, cannot love God whom they have not seen. The commandment we have from him is this: those who love God must love their brothers and sisters also.[13]

For Jesus, love of God and neighbor became the ethical principle that every other law or rule or regulation should be subjected to in order to determine a correct ethical response to a moral situation.

The Apostle Paul later declared the same thing:

> Let no debt remain outstanding, except the continuing debt to love one another, for he who loves his fellowman has fulfilled the law. The commandments, "Do not commit adultery," "Do not murder," "Do not steal," "Do not covet," and whatever other commandment there may be, are summed up in this one rule: "Love your neighbor as yourself." Love does no harm to its neighbor. Therefore love is the fulfillment of the law.[14]

The writer of the epistle of James agrees:

> If you really keep the royal law found in Scripture, "Love your neighbor as yourself," you are doing right.[15]

## situation ethics

In 1966, ethicist and Episcopal priest Joseph Fletcher (1905–1991) published *Situation Ethics: the New Morality*. Fletcher rejected an absolute morality. But, he believed it is possible—even necessary—to have an absolute norm or standard at the root of one's ethics while maintaining a flexible

13. 1 John 4:20–21
14. Romans 13:8–10
15. James 2:8

application of the standard to each individual situation. Through situational ethics, Fletcher attempted to find a middle road between legalistic and nihilistic ethics. In his own ethical framework, love became the sole factor in making moral judgments. He declared that moral rules or principles aren't the same thing as doing what is right. Fletcher quoted a Saint Louis cab driver who said "Sometimes you've gotta put your principles to one side and do the right thing." His book ignited a firestorm of controversy.

The type of love Joseph Fletcher referred to is *agape*, the Greek word for a self-giving, often unconditional love. Agape is the kind of love people saw in Jesus. As we said previously, agape love is not a fleeting emotion. It is not a warm feeling of friendliness, a condescending generosity, or a gentle tolerance of the shortcomings of others. Agape love is not a feeling of any kind; it is a verb. Genuine love at its deepest level is an action, an activity, a commitment. True love is self-giving concern for another. One definition is that love is "a choice to do what is best for another person." Love in a family involves caring for those we love—feeding, clothing, sheltering, and educating them. It means providing them with the means of life and growth. Love is giving oneself to nurture another's full humanity, concerned with the other's care, healing, wholeness, growth, and transformation.

Fletcher believed that there are no absolute laws that must be obeyed other than the absolute norm of agape love. He contended that all of the ancient biblical laws were established in order to achieve agape love in the human family. But self-giving love cannot be commanded. It can only be invited, encouraged, and nourished. All the other laws are only guidelines to how to achieve this love, and thus, claimed Fletcher, they may be broken if the other course of action would result in more love for another person.

Fletcher proposed six fundamental principles or propositions regarding love as an ethical norm:

- Love is the only thing that is always good.

- Love and justice are the same. Justice is simply love on a larger scale.

- Love is not liking. Love wills the other person's good, whether we like the other person or not.

- Love as an end justifies the means. The end must be the most loving result. When measuring a situation, one must consider the desired end, the means available, the motive for acting, and the foreseeable consequences.

- Love decides there and then. Love's decisions are made situationally, not prescriptively.

## a universal ethic

At the heart of Jesus' ethic of love is what has been called the golden rule—"Do to others what you would have them do to you." This so-called rule, or its companion version "Do not do to others what you would not want them to do to you," is found in many world religions. (Expressed in the negative form it is sometimes called the silver rule.) The fact that many religions have this simple ethic in common—and a resulting dedication to compassion, peace, and social justice—has led me to wonder why this one element is almost universal but the other aspects of world religions are so very different.

If one looks at the evolution of religions, beginning with primitive societies, one often finds similar patterns. When faced with the unknown and the inexplicable, primitive people developed beliefs about the existence of spirits and gods as explanations for things beyond their grasp. They believed that when bad things happened, they were the result of the actions of evil spirits or capricious gods. To ensure that suffering was minimized and prosperity maximized, taboos were defined to avoid offending the spirits and offerings were made to appease the gods. Many great world religions began in these simple acts. In Judaism, for example, hundreds of purity rules, regulations, and taboos were defined over the centuries to make the Hebrew people acceptable to a God of holiness, and a vast temple system was created to send the barbecued fragrance of animal sacrifice wafting into the sky to obtain God's blessings on the nation. But overlaid on these complex taboos and the ceremonial slaughter of animals was an ethic of compassion, often voiced by the biblical prophets, but found throughout the Hebrew bible.

As in many other religions, this ethic seemingly developed during a six-century transformative period from about 800 to 200 BCE that German psychiatrist and philosopher Karl Jaspers (1883–1969) has termed the "axial age." As explained by Karen Armstrong in her book *The Great Transformation*, similar teachings about love, compassion, and nonviolence arose in China, India, Persia, Palestine, and Greece during this period, fueled by a reaction to the intense violence, domination, and oppression in their respective societies. Particularly in China, India, and Palestine, itinerant sages and teachers developed new religious and ethical ideas, engaged in the quest for human meaning. Among those active during this period were the Jewish prophets Amos, Hosea, Isaiah, and Micah (from about 760 to 690 BCE); Siddhārtha Gautama, also known as the Buddha, in India (c. 583–463 BCE); Confucius in China (551–479 BCE); and Socrates in Greece (c. 469–399 BCE).

The Hebrew book of Deuteronomy was produced during this same period (perhaps between about 625 and 535 BCE). It contains the words, "Love your neighbor as yourself." In every major civilization, religious leaders and thinkers were developing similar concepts. In India, the Buddha (meaning "awakened one" or "enlightened one") sought to eliminate human suffering caused by ignorance, greed, and hatred. He taught a *Dharma*, a particular way of life based on wisdom, ethical conduct, and meditation. In China, Confucius taught an ethic based on empathy and understanding of others. His concept of *Rén* (variously translated as benevolence, goodness, and humaneness) was found in a selfless pursuit of the common good. He was the first to have presented a form of the golden rule, "What you do not wish for yourself, do not do to others," written over five centuries before Jesus. In Greece, Socrates asked (socratically, of course) how men should best live. He described fundamental human virtues such as wisdom, temperance, justice, and courage that he believed could be taught and learned. Socrates proposed that the ideal life was spent in search of "the Good" which would benefit the entire society.

The great spiritual seekers of the axial age emphasized life in the present. They taught that empathy and compassion leading to a life of principled ethics and social justice were central elements of the religious life. As a result, variants of the golden rule are common to many of the world's great faith traditions.

- Taoism: "Regard your neighbor's gain as your gain, and your neighbor's loss as your own loss."
- Buddhism: "Hurt not others in ways that you yourself would find hurtful."
- Hinduism: "This is the sum of duty; do nothing to others what you would not have them do to you."
- Zoroastrianism: "That nature alone is good which refrains from doing to another whatsoever is not good for itself."
- Judaism: "What is hateful to you, do not do to your fellowman. This is the entire Law; all the rest is commentary." (Hillel)
- Christianity: "Do to others what you would have them do to you."
- Islam: "No one of you is a believer until he desires for his brother that which he desires for himself."

This empathy toward the other has become interwoven with each religion's unique revelations, rules, and rituals. When the ethic of compassion and justice is valued and practiced, these religions work for the good of humanity. However, when people of religion ignore their empathic and compassionate tradition, they can become harmful and even dangerous to the life of the world. That is the danger of fundamentalism, whether it is Christian, Jewish, or Islamic. Fundamentalism focuses on what separates us, defining insiders and outsiders. It views people of other faiths as enemies and agents of evil. But concern for the well-being of others focuses on those values we hold in common—uniting us in spite of our historic, cultural, and religious differences. It is this common concern that enables leaders of many religious traditions to join together in efforts to promote peace and justice in the world.

## holiness or compassion?

The way of religion is far too often the way of holiness. This is as true today as it was in the time of Jesus. Many Christian churches—chiefly the more conservative ones—profess and teach a holiness religion. They are the new Pharisees, purveyors of holiness and purity, and condemners of perceived sinners. The central religious issues for them are sin, guilt, and forgiveness. Morality is absolute, unchanging. Yet, in the path that Jesus followed, the central issue was simply love for and compassion toward others.

As Christianity emerged from Judaism in the late first century, the holiness codes and temple worship practices were jettisoned, but the biblical ethic of compassion and social justice was maintained—expressed anew through the life and teachings of Jesus. Although theology and history divides the two religions today, what Christians and Jews have in common is this shared biblical ethic of compassion and justice. However, it should be noted that for many conservative Christians and Jews, the Old Testament holiness codes become more important that the ethic of love and compassion. In the tension between compassion and holiness, compassion often declines. When "correct" doctrine wins, humanity suffers.

The Jesus of the gospels does not provide us with a moral system—a clearly defined universal set of rules for moral behavior. Instead, Jesus provides us with a model of ethical behavior based on a compassionate response to the situations one encounters. The life of Jesus thus becomes the "norm" or standard for our ethics.

The earliest followers of Jesus looked to Jesus as their norm for ethical behavior. They modeled their lives on Jesus. The New Testament is filled with appeals for Christians to be like Jesus. The call to follow Jesus is a call to imitate Jesus and, in doing so, to reflect the essential character of God as exemplified in his life. Christians are told to love as Jesus loved and to serve others as he did. They are admonished to forgive freely as God forgives and to love indiscriminately as God does.

## Bonhoeffer's ethics

Before his arrest and imprisonment, Dietrich Bonhoeffer had begun work on what he considered his most important writing. It was an examination of ethics in response to his experiences in Nazi Germany. He continued to work on it in prison. It was left to his friend Eberhard Bethge to collect his manuscript and notes after his death to publish Bonhoeffer's *Ethics*.

In 1941, Bonhoeffer was encouraged by his brother-in-law Hans von Dohnányi (1902–1945) to join the Abwehr, the military intelligence arm of the German army. This position also enabled him to avoid bearing arms. Interestingly, many Abwehr operatives were anti-Nazi—including Admiral Wilhelm Canaris who headed the agency from 1935 to 1944—and as a result the Abwehr was a center of the resistance against Hitler. Conspirators within the Abwehr plotted a coup to assassinate Adolf Hitler and take control of the government in order to negotiate an end to the war with the Allies. Bonhoeffer was well aware of this plan and assisted the conspirators by becoming a double agent, traveling to neutral countries under the cover of gaining information that would aid Germany, when in fact he was making contacts to garner support by Allied leaders for the coup.

Several years earlier, when he had begun his book on ethics, it was in response to his insight that the question of whether something was right or wrong was the wrong question to ask. For Bonhoeffer, the question was, "What is the will of God?" In other words, what is God calling one to do in one's time and place, in one's particular situation? It was in answer to this question that he decided to leave the safety of America and return to Germany as war was breaking out.

Bonhoeffer wrote in *Ethics*,

> *But when all this has been said it is still necessary really to examine what is the will of God, what is rightful in a given situation, what course is truly pleasing to God; for after all, there have to be concrete life and action. Intelligence, discernment, attentive observation of the given facts, all these now come into lively operation, all will be embraced and pervaded by prayer . . . Possibilities and consequences must be carefully assessed. In other words, the whole apparatus of human powers must be set in motion when it is a matter of proving what is the will of God.*[16]

For Bonhoeffer, there was no appeal to an absolute morality. Every situation must be assessed in light of the perceived will of God.

---

16. Bonhoeffer, *Ethics*, 40.

*The will of God may lie very deeply concealed beneath a great*
*number of available possibilities. The will of God is not a system*
*of rules which is established from the outset; it is something new*
*and different in each different situation in life, and for this reason*
*a [person] must ever new examine what the will of God may be.*[17]

Bonhoeffer believed that the Sermon on the Mount was the most important ethical guide in the Bible. But even more fundamental to ethics was
love. If one wishes to understand the will of God, one need look no further
than this: God is love.

> *God is love; that is to say not a human attitude, a conviction or a*
> *deed, but God Himself is love . . . No one knows God unless God*
> *reveals himself to him. And so no one knows what love is except*
> *in the self-revelation of God. Love, then, is the revelation of God.*
> *And the revelation of God is Jesus Christ . . . The New Testament*
> *answers the question "What is love?" quite unambiguously by*
> *pointing solely and entirely to Jesus Christ.*[18]

## nonviolent resistance

Aside from many personal ethical decisions, we are confronted by a world
of violence and evil. Violence surrounds us. Its presence is everywhere—in
the news, in our streets, in our homes, in our schools, in our workplaces, in
our sporting events, in our entertainment, and in our nation's international
affairs. In America, we live in a culture of violence which is aided and abetted by a deep and abiding love affair with guns.

Most people see only two ways of dealing with violence and oppressive power: fight or flight. Fight: war, violent rebellion, revenge, retaliation.
Flight: escape, emigration, quietism, passivity. Jesus rejects both these options. Neither passivity nor violence are the way of Jesus. He teaches a third
way, the way of nonviolent resistance to evil.

Rejection of violence does not mean acceptance of evil. Evil must
always be resisted. Jesus resisted evil at every step of his life. The *means*
of resistance is the issue. The model that Jesus provides us is nonviolent
resistance.

> *You have heard that it was said "An eye for an eye and a tooth for*
> *a tooth." But I say to you, do not [violently] resist an evildoer. But*
> *if anyone strikes you on the right cheek, turn the other also; and*

17. Ibid., 38.
18. Ibid., 50–51.

> *if anyone wants to sue you and take your coat, give your cloak as*
> *well; and if anyone forces you to go one mile, go the second mile.*[19]

I have enclosed the word *violently* in brackets in the previous quote. Typically, the text simply reads, "Do not resist an evildoer." But this gives the wrong impression of Jesus' meaning. The early church assumed this meant no use of arms, including self-defense. Some pacifists today believe that nonresistance means Christians must even reject nonviolent direct action and civil disobedience. That position seems strange since Jesus consistently resisted evil throughout his life, but he also refused violent means.

The Greek word translated as *resist* is *antistenai* (*an-tee'-steh-nay*) that means to stand (*stenai*) against (*anti*). It is a technical term involving the tactics of warfare. Two approaching armies march toward each other until they meet. They stand on the field of battle opposing one another. They then engage in a violent struggle. Therefore *antistenai* means to take a violent stand against the opponent.

Jesus was saying that his followers must not take a violent stance against evildoers—do not resist evil with violent means. Jesus is not recommending nonresistance to evil. He is recommending nonviolent resistance to evil. It is the process of resisting evil without doing evil.

Robert Rimbo (b. 1950), a bishop of the Evangelical Lutheran Church in America (ELCA) wrote to the congregations of his synod following the September 11, 2001 terrorist attacks. He reflected on Saint Paul's words in Romans 12:

> *Bless those who persecute you; bless and do not curse them . . . Do*
> *not repay anyone evil for evil, but take thought for what is noble*
> *in the sight of all.*

Reacting to his initial feelings that we Americans must strike back at those who committed this crime, the words of Romans 12 changed his response.

> *Because the moment you condemn them, the moment you curse*
> *them, you join them, and however good it may feel at the moment,*
> *it is still surrender. The only way to conquer evil is to absorb it,*
> *Paul says. Take it into yourself and disarm it. Neutralize its acids.*
> *Serve as a facemask for its smog. Put a straightjacket on it and*
> *turn it over to God. There is nothing sentimental or the least bit*
> *easy about this. There is not even a guarantee that it will work.*
> *But one thing is for sure: When we repay evil for evil, evil is all*
> *there is, in bigger and more toxic piles. The only way to reverse*

19. Matthew 5:38–41

*the process is to behave in totally unexpected ways, breaking the vicious cycle by refusing to participate in it. That is what love is. Not a warm feeling between like-minded friends but plain old imitation of Christ, who took all the meanness of the world and ran it through the filter of his own body, repaying evil with good, blame with pardon, death with life. It worked once and it can work again, whenever God can find people willing to give it a try.*

# CHAPTER 13

# agents of love

---

*Then he said to the crowd: "If any of you wants to be
my follower, you must turn from your selfish ways,
take up your cross daily, and follow me."*[1]

—Jesus of Nazareth

THE GOSPEL OF JOHN begins and ends with the call of Jesus, "Follow me."[2]
The disciples followed Jesus through the villages and towns of Galilee and
eventually to a cross outside the city of Jerusalem. It was a journey of challenge, excitement, wonder, and terror. The act of following Jesus no matter
where it leads is the essence of a life of discipleship. It is a journey that begins with a radical change in the direction of one's life. It takes the followers
of Jesus beyond familiar places toward situations far outside their comfort
zones. On the way, disciples discover that they have capabilities and talents that were previously unrealized. It is always a process of learning and
doing on the move.

Following Jesus is a response to his call to establish justice and peace in
the world. It makes one a troublemaker, a revolutionary, a seeker of change.
It calls on one to be an agent of transformation, or as Jesus said, to be like
a mustard seed in a tidy garden, a pinch of yeast in a large bowl of bread
dough, a dash of salt in a pot of soup, or a small lamp in a darkened room.
It is to add your light to the sum of lights so that little by little a violent,
hungry, and suffering world can be renewed for the sake of its children.

The way of Jesus is a path toward a vision of the way the world ought
to be, the way it is meant to be. It is a freely chosen path, but not without
risk. There is never any assurance of success; only a promise of continuing

1. Luke 9:23 (New Living Translation)
2. John 1:43 and John 21:19

218

challenge. It is matter of trying and failing, and sometimes succeeding, but always continuing. Guided by the vision, the journey itself is the most important thing. To the peasants of Galilee, Jesus said it was like plowing a straight furrow in a field—keep your eyes straight ahead and don't look back.[3]

The way of Jesus is a conspiracy of love, compassion, justice, and peace. In the first century, Jesus led his small movement in a concerted action to subvert the normality of civilization and the prevailing domination systems of his society. He called for economic justice, he shared meals with those who were considered outcasts and rabble, he taught creative nonviolent responses to domination, and he publically demonstrated at the seat of political and religious power. He was executed for daring to challenge the status quo that benefitted the top 1 percent of his society.

The way of Jesus led to the cross. That is where Jesus calls us to follow today. This is not some inward spiritual journey. This is a confrontation with the real world of power, violence, poverty, disease, suffering, and death. But we are not alone. There are many others walking beside us. The spirit of Jesus leads the way. And he bids us to come and join him in the journey to a better world.

## following Jesus

To follow Jesus means listening to his teaching; digging into his words and learning their meaning in the context of empire and domination—and like his disciples, sometimes understanding it, sometimes not quite getting it. However, discipleship is based upon the fundamental concept that lessons are to be put into practice as they are learned. The learning and the doing are a lifelong process.[4]

To follow Jesus is to embark on a lifelong journey of transformation—moving from a life of self-centered concern to a commitment to the common good of all; moving from cultural captivity to a life of counter-cultural opposition to all forms of domination, oppression, injustice, and violence.

To follow Jesus means living a life of radical love: extending oneself to help one's neighbors. And it means loving our enemies and praying for their transformation. It involves working toward reconciliation with good and bad alike.

3. Luke 9:62. "Jesus said to him, 'No one who puts a hand to the plough and looks back is fit for the kingdom of God.'"

4. In *Meeting Jesus Again for the First Time*, Marcus Borg describes discipleship as journeying with Jesus. The following thoughts are an elaboration of his work.

To follow Jesus means being compassionate. Empathy with the situation of those who suffer and compassion toward their plight means opening our eyes to the needs around us and being moved to the point of action—caring for the stranger at the side of the road, the least, the lost, and the lonely.

To follow Jesus means welcoming and accepting others. It is the practice of extreme hospitality—breaking down the barriers that divide us and accepting others without judgment. It means mixing with the unloved and undesirable.

To follow Jesus means sharing with others. It calls us to a seemingly limitless generosity—graciously sharing our lives and resources. It means giving freely without thought of return.

To follow Jesus means becoming a servant. It means engaging in personal service to people in need—meeting fundamental human needs of food, clothing, and shelter.

To follow Jesus means making the reign of love—societies governed with compassion, equality, and justice—a priority in our lives.

To follow Jesus means seeking justice. It means becoming an agent of change for a world in which everyone gets a fair share of resources and opportunities—working toward an overflowing justice that provides everyone with enough to meet their fundamental needs. It means speaking out on behalf of those who have no voice. It means challenging the politics of selfishness and pursuing a politics of compassion

To follow Jesus means working for change from the bottom of society, not the top; from the margins, and not the center.

To follow Jesus means using creative nonviolence in situations of conflict. It means seeking change without resort to violence and absorbing hostility with nonviolent defiant action.

To follow Jesus means becoming a peacemaker. It involves breaking the cycle of violence and reciprocation. It means working toward reconciliation between people.

To follow Jesus means forgiving each other. It is a life of extravagant forgiveness—reconciling with those we have hurt and those who have hurt us, forgiving again and again and again.

To follow Jesus means living in a sense of mutual community with others. It is a journey in the company of other disciples. We need community to sustain us.

To follow Jesus means living like an itinerant or sojourner. It means living simply and not being bound by possessions. It means living lightly on the earth.

To follow Jesus means to live faithfully in spite of the consequences. It means a willingness to be ridiculed and mocked, to suffer unjustly and, if necessary, to die for the sake of the reign of love.

To follow Jesus means finding meaning and purpose in a compassionate love that binds us to the welfare of all.

## bearing the vision

We cannot do everything to end poverty, violence, and injustice in the world. But we can do some things. We can engage in personal acts of compassion. We can speak out on behalf of the voiceless and stand in solidarity with them. We can form or participate in movements of resistance and liberation. These are the things Jesus did.

Here are five aspects of living out the transformative vision of Jesus in our specific time and place.

- Be a bearer of the vision of the reign of love. Hold up a vision of how things ought to be.

- Be a conscience for the world. Critically assess how things are today. Point out the distance between the reality and the vision.

- Be a prophetic voice and an advocate. Identify those who are being hurt by the politics of selfishness and domination. Speak out for those who have no voice. Be a moral compass for elected officials.

- Be a change agent. Be a co-conspirator in the conspiracy of love where you are.

- Be a peacemaker. Be an agent of change without recourse to violence. Ultimately, become an agent of reconciliation, forgiveness, and peace.

So, it's time to begin, if you haven't already. Here are three tiny steps to get you on your way to the transformation of yourself, of your society, and of the world.

- First, observe. Look around to see what the needs are. Identify where people are hurting and suffering. Ask yourself where your heart is drawn.

- Second, reflect. Pray, read, think, talk, journal. Do you have a sense of call or mission? Can you visualize what your heart is calling you to do?

- Finally, act. Start small, but do something!

Edward Everett Hale (1822–1909), a Unitarian minister and author, put it very clearly.

> *I am only one, but still I am one. I cannot do everything, but still I can do something; and because I cannot do everything, I will not refuse to do something I can do.*[5]

## the task ahead

Kenneth Untener (1937–2004), a Roman Catholic Bishop of Saginaw, Michigan, once reflected on the task that lies before us.

> *It helps, now and then, to step back and take the long view. The Kingdom is not only beyond our efforts: it is beyond our vision. We accomplish in our lifetime only a tiny fraction of the magnificent enterprise that is the Lord's work. Nothing we do is complete, which is another way of saying that the Kingdom always lies beyond us. No sermon says all that should be said. No prayer fully expresses our faith. No confession brings perfection. No pastoral visit brings wholeness. No program accomplishes the Church's mission. No set of goals and objectives includes everything. That is what we are about. We plant the seeds that one day will grow. We water seeds already planted knowing they hold future promise. We lay foundations that will need further development. We provide yeast that affects far beyond our capabilities. We cannot do everything and there is a sense of liberation in realizing that. This enables us to do something, and to do it very, very well. It may be incomplete, but it is a beginning, a step along the way, an opportunity for the Lord's grace to enter and do the rest. We may never see the end results, but that is the difference between the Master Builder and the worker. We are workers, not master builders; ministers, not messiahs. We are prophets of a future that is not our own.*[6]

Dorothy Day (1897–1980) addressed the hopelessness and cynicism that can overtake each of us as we look at what needs to be done in the world.

---

5. Greenough, *A Year of Beautiful Thoughts*, 172.

6. Kenneth Untener, "A Step Along the Way." This prayer composed by Untener in 1979 was later attributed to Óscar Romero when Untener included it in a reflection book after the archbishop's assassination in 1980. Online: http://www.usccb.org/prayer-and-worship/prayers-and-devotions/prayers/archbishop_romero_prayer.cfm

*Young people say, "What good can one person do? What is the
sense of our small effort?" They cannot see that we must lay one
brick at a time, take one step at a time; we can be responsible
only for the action of the present moment but we can beg for an
increase of love in our hearts that will vitalize and transform all
our individual actions, and know that God will take them and
multiply them, as Jesus multiplied the loaves and fishes.[7]*

She said that when she was confronted by the seeming futility of issues
like war and poverty and human suffering, she became more confirmed in
her faith in the "little way" of Saint Thérèse (1873–1897). Thérèse of Li-
seaux was a Carmelite nun who died at the tender age of twenty-four. She
saw her vocation as reaching far beyond the convent walls helping those in
need throughout the world. The "little way" involves finding the spiritual in
the little things of ordinary life, through a commitment to the tasks before
us and to the people we meet daily. Dorothy Day said that those who are
striving for change must simply do the things that come to hand, say their
prayers, and beg for an increase of faith.

When you become discouraged by the seeming immensity of the
task—and you will—remember this story shared by Grahame Russell, a
Canadian human rights lawyer who works in Central America. This little
fable involves a conversation between two birds—a dove and a coal-mouse,
which is a small bird like a chickadee or titmouse.

*"Tell me the weight of a snowflake," a coal-mouse asked a wild
dove. "Nothing more than nothing," was the answer. "In that case,
I must tell you a marvelous story," the coal-mouse said.*

*"I sat on the branch of a fir tree, close to its trunk, when it
began to snow, not heavily, not in a raging blizzard, no, just like in
a dream, without any violence. Since I didn't have anything else to
do, I counted the snowflakes settling on the twigs and branch. Their
number was exactly 3,741,952. When the next snowflake dropped
onto the branch—nothing more than nothing, as you say—the
branch broke off." Having said that, the coal-mouse flew away.*

*The dove, since Noah's time an authority on the matter,
thought about the story for a while, and finally said to herself:
"Perhaps there is only one person's voice lacking for peace and
justice to come about in the world."[8]*

---

7. Day. *Loaves and Fishes*, 176.

8. Russell, *The Never Ending*, original source unknown.

# bibliography

Ayers, Danielle and Lydia Bean. "Reimagining the Bible Belt." *Sojourners* (July 2015) 18–21.

Bergoglio, Jorge Mario (Pope Francis). *Evangelii Gaudium* (2013). No pages. Online: http://www.vatican.va/holy_father/francesco/apost_exhortations/ documents/papa-francesco_esortazione-ap_20131124_evangelii-gaudium_ en.html#I.%E2%80%82Some_challenges_of_today%E2%80%99s_world

Bonhoeffer, Dietrich. *The Cost of Discipleship*. New York: Macmillan, 1959.

———. *Ethics*. New York: Macmillan, 1965.

———. *Letters and Papers from Prison*. New York: Macmillan, 1972.

———. *No Rusty Swords*. New York: Harper & Row, 1965.

———. *Sanctorum Communio*. London: Forgotten Books, Reprint 2013. (This was Bonhoeffer's 1927 doctoral dissertation first published in 1930. Harper & Row published it in English as *The Communion of Saints* in 1963.)

Booker, Cory. "Conspiracy of Love." (Commencement address, Stanford University, June 17, 2012). No pages. Online: http://news.stanford.edu/news/2012/june/ transcript-cory-booker-061912.html.

Borg, Marcus. "Beyond Belief, a Conversation with Marcus Borg," *The Lutheran* (July 1994) 12–13.

———. *The Heart of Christianity*. San Francisco: HarperSanFrancisco, 2003.

———. *Jesus, a New Vision: Spirit, Culture and the Life of Discipleship*. New York: HarperCollins, 1987.

———. *Meeting Jesus Again for the First Time*. San Francisco: HarperSanFrancisco, 1994.

Caputo, John D. *What Would Jesus Deconstruct?* Grand Rapids: Baker Academic, 2007.

Chunovic, Louis C., editor. *Chris-In-The-Morning: Love, Life, and the Whole Karmic Enchilada*. Chicago: Contemporary Books, 1993.

Coffin, William Sloane. *Credo*. Louisville: Westminster John Knox, 2004.

Cox, Harvey. *The Future of Faith*. New York: HarperOne, 2009.

Crossan, John Dominic. *The Birth of Christianity: Discovering What Happened in the Years Immediately After the Execution of Jesus*. New York: HarperCollins, 1998.

————. *The Greatest Prayer: Rediscovering the Revolutionary Message of the Lord's Prayer*. New York: HarperCollins, 2010.

Day, Dorothy. *Loaves and Fishes*. Maryknoll, NY: Orbis, 1997.

Dozier, Verna J. *The Dream of God: A Call to Return*. Boston: Cowley, 1991.

Eisenstein, Charles. *The More Beautiful World Our Hearts Know is Possible*. Berkeley: North Atlantic, 2013.

Ellul, Jacques. *The Meaning of the City*. Grand Rapids: Eerdmans, 1970.

Fosdick, Harry Emerson. "Shall the Fundamentalists Win?" *Christian Work* 102 (June 10, 1922) 716-722.

Fowler, James W. *Stages of Faith: The Psychology of Human Development and the Quest for Meaning*. San Francisco: Harper & Row, 1981.

Fox, Matthew. *On Becoming a Musical Mystical Bear*. New York: Paulist, 1972.

Fuller, Robert C. *Spiritual, but Not Religious: Understanding Unchurched America*. Oxford and New York: Oxford University Press, 2001.

Galbraith, John Kenneth. "Let us Begin: An Invitation to Action on Poverty." *Harpers* (March 1964).

Gallup, George H. Jr. and Robert Bezilla. *The Religious Life of Young Americans: A Compendium of Surveys on the Spiritual Beliefs and Practices of Teen-Agers and Young Adults*. Princeton, NJ: Gallup International Institute, 1992.

Greenough, Jeanie Ashley Bates. *A Year of Beautiful Thoughts⊠*. New York: T.Y. Crowell, 1902.

Howard, Alice and Waldon Howard. *Exploring the Road Less Traveled: a Study Guide for Small Groups*. New York: Simon & Schuster, 1985.

James, William. *The Varieties of Religious Experience*. New York: Mentor, 1953.

Jeremias, Joachim. *Jerusalem in the Time of Jesus*. Philadelphia: Fortress, 1969.

Jones, Robert P., Daniel Cox, Juhem Navarro Rivera, E. J. Dione, Jr., William A. Galston. "Do Americans Believe Capitalism and Government Are Working?: Religious Left, Religious Right and the Future of the Economic Debate." Public Religion Research Institute and the Brookings Institution, 2013. Online: http://publicreligion.org/site/wp-content/uploads/2013/07/2013-Economic-Values-Report-Final-.pdf

Jordan, Clarence and Dallas Lee, editor. *The Substance of Faith and Other Cotton Patch Sermons*. New York: Association, 1972.

Keen, Sam. *Hymns to an Unknown God*. New York: Bantam, 1994.

Kierkegaard, Søren and Charles E. Moore, editor. *Provocations: Spiritual Writings of Kierkegaard*. Maryknoll, NY: Orbis, 2003.

King, Martin Luther Jr. "Beyond Vietnam: A Time to Break Silence," (Speech, Riverside Church in New York City, April 4, 1967). No pages. Online: http://www.hartford-hwp.com/archives/45a/058.html.

————. *Where Do We Go from Here: Chaos of Community?* Boston: Beacon, 2010.

Kraybill, Donald B. *The Upside-Down Kingdom*. Scottsdale, PA: Herald, 1978.

Mack, Burton. *Who Wrote the New Testament?* New York: HarperCollins, 1995.

Massey, Morris. *What You Are Is Where You Were When*, (DVD). Cambridge, MA: Enterprise Media, 1986.

McLaren, Brian. *The Secret Message of Jesus: Uncovering the Truth That Could Change Everything*. Nashville: W Publishing Group, 2006.

Menchú, Rigoberta. *I, Rigoberta Menchú: An Indian Woman in Guatemala*. London: Verso, 2009.

Moyers, Bill. Foreword to *Faith Works: How Faith-based Organizations are Changing Lives, Neighborhoods, and America*, by Jim Wallis, xv–xix. Berkeley, CA: PageMill, 2001.

Nanus, Burton. *Visionary Leadership: Creating a Compelling Sense of Direction for Your Organization.* 1992.

Nin, Anaïs. *The Diary of Anaïs Nin, Volume 1: 1931–1934.* New York: Swallow, 1967.

Nolan, Albert. *Jesus Before Christianity.* Maryknoll, NY: Orbis, 1976.

Ortberg, John. *The Me I Want to Be: Becoming God's Best Version of You.* Grand Rapids: Zondervan, 2010.

Peck, M. Scott. *The Different Drum: Community Making and Peace.* New York: Simon & Schuster, 1987.

———. *Further Along the Road Less Traveled: the Unending Journey toward Spiritual Growth.* New York: Simon & Schuster, 1993.

Polak, Frederik Lodewijk. *The Image of the Future.* New York: Oceana, 1961.

Rainer, Thom S. and Jess W. Rainer. *The Millennials: Connecting to America's Largest Generation.* Nashville: B&H, 2011.

Rauschenbusch, Walter. *A Theology for the Social Gospel.* Louisville: Westminster John Knox, 1997.

Robinson, John A. T. *Honest to God.* Philadelphia: Westminster, 1963.

Rocha, Zildo. *Helder, O Dom: uma vida que marcou os rumos da Igreja no Brasil (Helder, the Gift: A Life that Marked the Course of the Church in Brazil).* Petrópolis: Editora Vozes, 1999.

Roof, Wade Clark. *A Generation of Seekers: The Spiritual Journeys of the Baby Boom Generation.* San Francisco: HarperSanFrancisco, 1993.

Russell, Grahame. *The Never Ending.* San Jose, Costa Rica: G. Russell, 1992.

Smith, Emily Esfahani and Jennifer L. Aaker. "Millennial Searchers," *The New York Times* (November 30, 2013).

Spinner, Chuck. *A Book of Prayers: To the Heavens from the Stars.* Bloomington, IN: AuthorHouse, 2008.

Taylor, Barbara Brown. *An Altar in the World: A Geography of Faith.* New York: HarperCollins, 2009.

Tillich, Paul. *Dynamics of Faith.* New York: Harper, 1958.

———. *Systematic Theology / Volume 1.* Chicago: University of Chicago Press, 1951.

Turner, Frederick Jackson. *The Frontier in American History.* New York: Holt, 1921.

Vanier, Jean. *Becoming Human.* New York: Paulist, 2008

Wallis, Jim. *Agenda for a Biblical People.* New York: Harper & Row, 1976.

———. *On God's Side: What Religion Forgets and Politics Hasn't Learned About Serving the Common Good.* Grand Rapids: Brazos, 2013.

Westerhoff, John. *Will Our Children Have Faith?* New York: Seabury, 1976.

Wink, Walter. *The Human Being: Jesus and the Enigma of the Son of the Man.* Minneapolis: Fortress, 2002.

———. *The Powers That Be: Theology for a New Millennium.* New York: Doubleday, 1998.

Winner, Lauren. "Gen X Revisited." *The Christian Century* (November 8, 2000).

Wuthnow, Robert. *The Restructuring of American Religion: Society and Faith Since World War II.* Princeton, NJ: Princeton University Press, 1988.

Yergin, Daniel and Joseph Stanislaw. *The Commanding Heights: The Battle for the World Economy.* New York: Simon & Schuster, 2002. (See also the PBS Frontline

television series "Commanding Heights: The Battle for the World Economy" based
   on the book. Online: http://www.pbs.org/wgbh/commandingheights/hi/story/.)
Zinn, Howard. "The Power and the Glory: Myths of American Exceptionalism." *Boston
   Review* (Summer 2005). No pages. Online: http://bostonreview.net/BR30.3/zinn.
   php.
———. *You Can't Be Neutral on a Moving Train: A Personal History of Our Times.*
   Boston: Beacon, 1994.

Milton Keynes UK
Ingram Content Group UK Ltd.
UKHW051331301223
435229UK00018B/565